IVAN GOGIN

Graphics by Alexa...

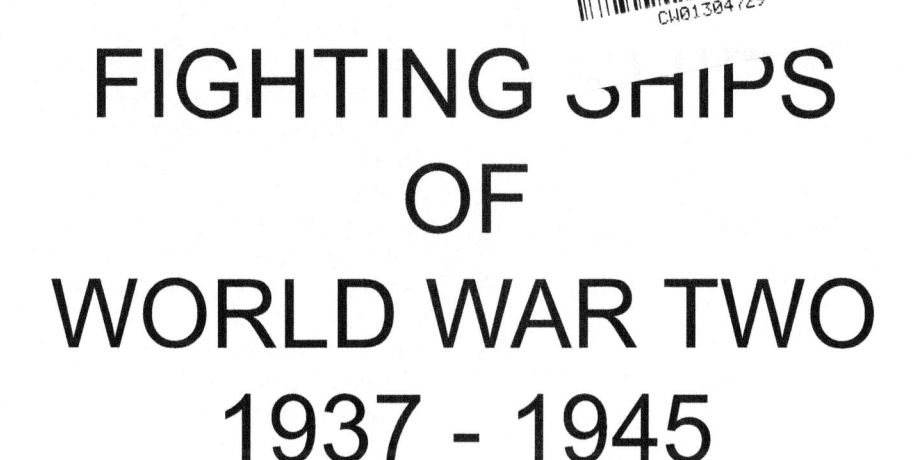

FIGHTING SHIPS OF WORLD WAR TWO 1937 - 1945

Volume VI

Italy

Gatchina
2023

Contents

Foreword	2
1937	3
Abbreviations	4
Organization of the Italian Navy during the World War Two	6
Order of battle of the Italian Navy on June 10th, 1940	7
Battleships	11
Aircraft carriers and seaplane tender	16
Cruisers	19
Destroyers and torpedo boats	36
Submarines	61
Escort and patrol ships	80
Coastal forces	87
Mine warfare ships	94
Amphibious warfare ships	102
Auxiliary vessels intended for combat support	105
Customs	106
Ship-based aircraft	107
Naval weapons	108

Foreword

We are pleased to present you the sixth volume of 'Fighting ships of World War Two', dedicated to the Regia Marina, the Italian Navy. The first volume contains information about the Royal Navy and Commonwealth navies: Canadian, Australian, New Zealand, Indian, South African and Burmese Government ships. The US Navy is described in the second volume. The third volume is dedicated to the Imperial Japanese Navy. The fourth volume of the 'Fighting ships of World War Two' series describes the Kriegsmarine, the German Navy. The fifth volume describes the Marine Nationale (French Navy).

The reference contains the maximum possible number of side views, reduced from the point of view of common sense and space limitation, in uniform 1:1250 scale. The format of the publication, is forced to limit us to information on merchant and fishing vessels with less with a capacity of less than 500 grt, performing patrol, minesweeping and other combat duties, and purpose-built craft with the displacement of less than 10 t.

Ship data blocks contain the name of the ship (Builder, laid down, launched, completed or commissioned -reason and date of deletion from the fleet list). If only two dates are present in the group "laid down - launched - commissioned", then they mean the dates of launching and commissioning. If there is only one date, then it indicates the date of commissioning.

Tables containing data on civilian ships converted into combat ones contain the following columns: Name (previous names); date of launching / commissioning by the Navy; capacity in grt (if the number is indicated in *Italic*, then the displacement is in t); length x width x draft, m; maximum speed, knots; armament; fate.

Technical data blocks include the standard / full load displacement in tons (usually long tons) or surface / submerged displacement for submarines, length overall (oa) (if the length between the perpendiculars is indicated, it is written pp, if the length by the waterline is wl) x breadth x mean draught in meters (or maximal draught (max)), composition of the machinery (if necessary, number of shafts in brackets), maximum power of the main engines in horsepower, maximum speed in knots, maximum fuel capacity in tons, maximum cruising range in nautical miles at cruising speed in knots (in brackets), complement, maximum operating depth for submarines in meters. Armor protection is described briefly, the reader can find a detailed description of the protection arrangement in the text below. Armament is described according to the following system: Artillery - number of mounts x number of guns in the mount - caliber of guns in millimeters/barrel length in calibers and the mark or common name of the gun. If the ship had gun mounts

ITALY

with a different gun number, then these mounts are marked with «+» sign. For example, (2 x 4 + 1 x 2) — 356/45 BL Mk I means that the ship was armed with two quadruple and one twin mount with 356/45 Mk I breech-loading guns. Machine guns with a caliber of less than 20 mm are marked without barrel length and gun mark. Torpedoes: number of torpedo banks x number of tubes in the bank - torpedo caliber for rotating turntable mounts or number of tubes - torpedo caliber for fixed tubes (for example, on submarines, MTBs or old ships). The numbers in brackets after the number of DCTs and DCRs are the total number of depth charges carried.

The aircraft data should be read as follows:

Hellcat Mk II: 13.08 x 10.17 x 4.11 m, 31.0 m², 4155 / 6400 kg, 1 Pratt & Whitney R-2800-10W, 2200 hp, 611 km/h, 2600 (270) km, 15.1 m/s, 11500 m, 1 seat; 6 x 12.7 MG or (2 x 20 guns + 4 x 12.7 MG), 6 x 127-mm rockets or 908-kg bombs (2 x 454-kg).
Means: Hellcat Mk II model data: wingspan 13.08m, length 10.17m, height 4.11m, wing area 31.0m², empty weight 4155 kg / maximum takeoff weight 6400 kg, 1 Pratt & Whitney R-2800-10W engine with 2200-hp power, maximal speed 611 km/h, flying range 2600 km at a speed of 270 km/h, maximum rate of climb 15.1 m/s, service ceiling 11500 m, 1 seat; armament consisted of 6 12.7-mm MGs or 2 20-mm guns and 4 12.7-mm MGs, 6 127-mm rockets or 908 kg of bombs.

Hellcat Mk II (fighter-bomber, 854 transferred spring 1944- 1945 (including FR Mk II and PR Mk II), serv. spring 1944-8.1946, USN F6F-5, Pratt & Whitney R-2800-10W (2200hp), strengthened armor, 6 x 12.7 MG or 2 x 20 guns and 4 x 12.7 MG, 6 x 127mm rockets or 908 kg bombs (2 x 454-kg));
Means: Hellcat Mk II modification, fighter-bomber assignment, 865 served in the RN, entered the Navy in the spring 1944-1945 and served in the spring 1944 - August 1946. Further, the differences from the previous modification are briefly described.

Preamble. Why 1937?

The first echoes of the thunderstorm, which subsequently swept the whole world and remained in the memory of mankind as the most destructive and deadly war, were heard on October 25, 1936, when Germany and Japan signed the Agreement against the Communists International, which provided for the destruction of communism in general and the Soviet Union in particular. 11/6/1937 Italy joins the pact. An Axis was formed, with the goal of creating a new order. The order in which German Nazis, Japanese militarists and Italian fascists were to be given the right to decide which of the peoples inhabiting the planet would live.

The Axis initially faced little resistance to aggression. In 1935-1936, Italy invaded Ethiopia. In 1936, German troops occupied the Rhine demilitarized zone. Germany annexed Austria in March 1938, the Sudetenland in October, and Czechoslovakia in March 1939. But the war broke out at the other end of Eurasia.

Back in 1931-1932, Japanese troops captured Chinese Manchuria, creating a puppet state on its territory. The League of Nations did not react in any way to the aggression. Creeping aggression associated with constant armed clashes and the seizure of new territories continued for another five years, but in 1937 Japan switched to full-scale military operations. Armies of millions clashed in a vast theater of operations that engulfed the entire eastern China. On July 7, 1937, World War II began.

Based on the fact that in July 1937 the first large-scale conflict began, which was undoubtedly part of the Second World War and lasted until September 1945, we propose to consider the incident on the Marco Polo bridge on July 7, 1937 as its actual beginning. And so, our series is an overview of all warships in the world from July 1937 to September 1945.

Abbreviations

AA - anti-aircraft
AEW - airborne early warning
AP - armor-piercing
ASW - anti-submarine warfare
ASWRL - anti-submarine warfare rocket launcher
aw - above water
BDE - British destroyer escort
bhp - brake horsepower
BL - breech-loading
brt - British registered tons
BU - broken up
CIC - combat information center
CMB - coastal motor boat
Compl. - complement
CT - conning tower
CTL - constructive total loss
cwt - hundredweight
cyl - cylinder
DC - depth charge
DC - reciprocating engine, diagonal, compound
DCR - depth charge rack
DCT - depth charge thrower
DE - destroyer escort
DP - dual-purpose
DSE - reciprocating engine, diagonal, single expansion
DTE - reciprocating engine, diagonal, triple expansion
DYd - dockyard
ECM - electronic countermeasures
FNFL - Forces Navales Françaises Libres (Free French Naval Forces)
FY - Fiscal Year
GM - metacentric height
grt - gross registered tons

HA - high angle
HDML - harbour defence motor launch
HMS - His/Her Majesty's Ship
hp - horse power(s)
HP - high pressure
HQ – headquarters
HC - reciprocating engine, horizontal, compound
HSE - reciprocating engine, horizontal, single expansion
HTE - reciprocating engine, horizontal, triple expansion
ihp - indicated horsepower
IJA - Imperial Japanese Army
IJN - Imperial Japanese Navy
JMSDF - Japan Maritime Self-Defense Force
kt(s) - knot(s)
LA - low angle
lb - pound(s)
LCA - Landing Craft, Assault
LCF - Landing Craft, Flak
LCG - Landing Craft, Gun
LCG(L) - Landing Craft, Gun (Large)
LCG(M) - Landing Craft, Gun (Medium)
LCI(G) - Landing Craft, Infantry (Gun)
LCI(L) - Landing Craft, Infantry (Large)
LCI(S) - Landing Craft, Infantry (Small)
LCM - Landing Craft, Mechanical
LCP - Landing Craft, Personnel
LCP(R) - Landing Craft, Personnel (Rocket)
LCS - Landing Craft, Support
LCS(L) - Landing Craft, Support (Large)
LCS(M) - Landing Craft, Support (Medium)
LCS(S) - Landing Craft, Support (Small)

LCT - Landing Craft, Tank
LCT(R) - Landing Craft, Tank (Rocket)
LCV - Landing Craft, Vehicle
LCV(P) - Landing Craft, Vehicle (Personnel)
LP - low pressure
LSC - Landing Ship, Carrier
LSD - Landing Ship, Dock
LSF - Landing Ship, Fighter Direction
LSG - Landing Ship, Gantry
LSH(L) - Landing Ship, Headquarters (Large)
LSI - Landing Ship, Infantry
LSI(H) - Landing Ship, Infantry (Hand)
LSI(L) - Landing Ship, Infantry (Large)
LSI(M) - Landing Ship, Infantry (Medium)
LSI(S) - Landing Ship, Infantry (Small)
LSS - Landing Ship, Stern Chute
LST - Landing Ship, Tank
MA/SB - Motor anti-submarine boat
max - maximum
MG - machine gun
MGB - motor gunboat
Mk - Mark
ML - motor launch
MMS - motor minesweeper
Mod - model
MTB - motor torpedo boat
nm - nautical mile(s)
No(s) - number(s)
N Yd - Navy Yard
oa - overall
pdr - pounder(s)
pp - between perpendiculars

QF - quick-firing
RAN - Royal Australian Navy
RCMP - Royal Canadian Mounted Police
RCN - Royal Canadian Navy
RIM - Royal Indian Marine
RIN - Royal Indian Navy
RN - Royal Navy
RNVR - Royal Naval Volunteer Reserve
RNZN - Royal New Zealand Navy
RSAN - Royal South African Navy
RSI - 'Repubblica Sociale Italiana'
SAN - South African Navy
SAP - semi-armor piercing
SB - Shipbuilding
SE - single-ended
shp - shaft horsepower
std - standard
sub - submerged
t — ton(s)
TC - torpedo cradle
TNT - trinitrotoluene
TS - training ship
TT - torpedo tube(s)
US - United States
USCG - United States Coast Guard
USN - United States Navy
VC – reciprocating engine, vertical, compound.
VQE - reciprocating engine, vertical, quadruple expansion
VQuE - reciprocating engine, vertical, quintuple expansion
VTE - reciprocating engine, vertical, triple expansion
Wks - Works

Organization of the Italian Navy during the World War Two

In the 1930s, Italy pursued an aggressive foreign policy. On October 3, 1935, Italian troops invaded Ethiopia and by May 1936 captured the country. In 1936, the Italian Empire was proclaimed. The Mediterranean Sea was named "Our Sea" (*Mare Nostrum*). The act of unjustified aggression provoked discontent among the Western powers and the League of Nations. The deterioration of relations with the Western powers pushed Italy towards a rapprochement with Germany. On November 25, 1936, Germany and Japan concluded the Anti-Comintern Pact, Italy joined the pact on November 6, 1937.

Italy entered World War II on June 10, 1940, and immediately the Italian Navy began active hostilities against the Royal Navy in the Mediterranean. The heavy losses suffered by the Italians in the very first year of hostilities forced them to devote most of their efforts to the operations of small and sabotage craft.

The Second World War for the Regia Marina ended on September 8, 1943, when the Kingdom of Italy surrendered to the United States and Great Britain. The Italian Navy was ordered to pass to Malta for capitulation. However, the war continued in the country. On September 23, in the territories of northern Italy occupied by Germany, the Italian Social Republic (RSI) was proclaimed, which ceased to exist on April 29, 1945, when the remnants of German troops in Italy surrendered. Not all the ships of the Regia Marina surrendered to the Allies: some ships did not surrender and continued to fight under the RSI flag, some were captured by the Germans.

On October 13, 1943, the Kingdom of Italy declared war on Germany. On April 29, 1945, the war in Italy ended.

When Italy entered the war, the main forces of the navy were based at Taranto (1st Fleet) and La Spezia (2nd Fleet), submarines were dispersed between La Spezia, Napoli, Messina, Taranto, and Cagliari. The coastal defense forces were divided into Sea Departments: Upper Tyrrhenian (La Spezia), Lower Tyrrhenian (Naples) with the subordinate commands of Sicily (Messina) and Sardinia (La Maddalena), Upper Adriatic (Venice) and Ionian / Lower Adriatic (Taranto). The Aegean (Rhodes), Albanian (Durrazzo (now *Durres*)), Libyan (Benghazi), East African (Massawa) and Far East (Tiensin, China) naval commands included forces overseas.

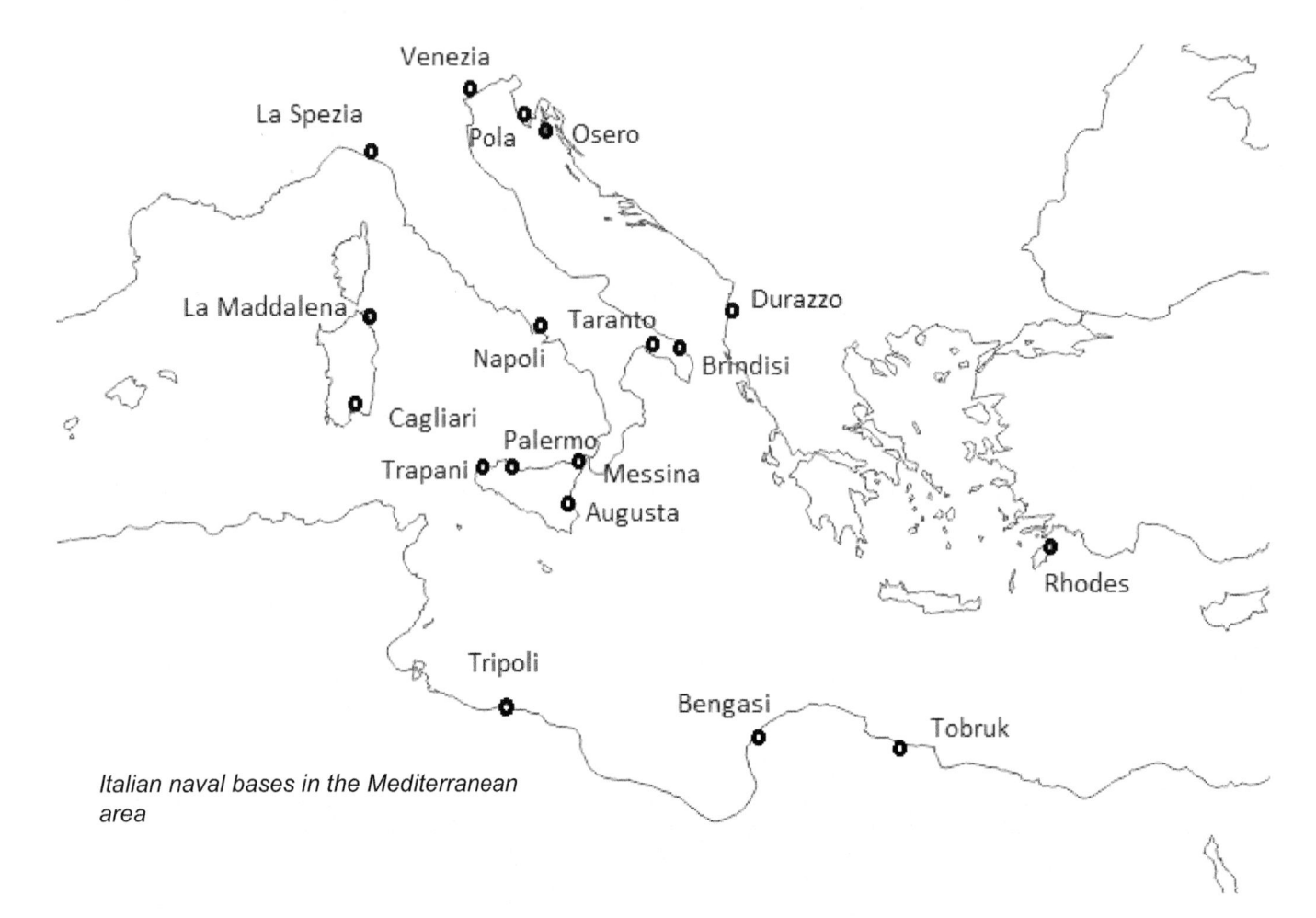

Italian naval bases in the Mediterranean area

ITALY

Italian naval bases overseas

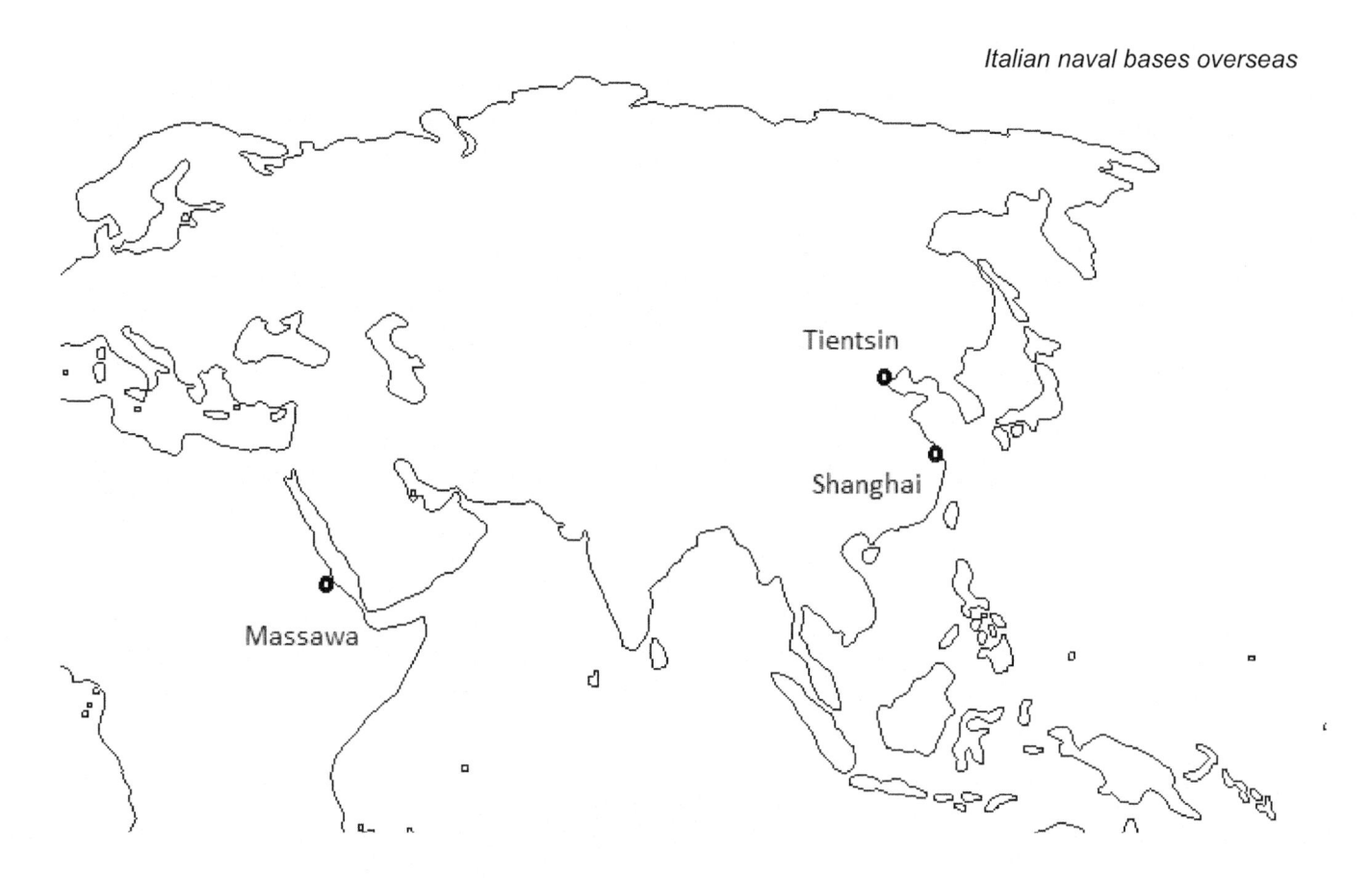

Separately, it should be noted that the Italian Navy had practically no aviation - it was assumed that the Air Force planes would be allocated for operational control of the Navy as needed, which sharply reduced the combat capabilities of the Navy.

In 1941-1943, several dozen Italian submarines operated in the Atlantic, based at Bordeaux and La Pallice, sinking a total of 109 ships.

In April 1941, Italians lost Massawa, however, the forces of the Red Sea Flotilla left the base in February. On June 11, 1941, the fighting in the Red Sea ended - British captured Assab, the last Italian port in the area.

In May 1942, at the request of the German command, several boats and midget submarines were transferred to the Black Sea, entering the 4th MAS flotilla. The unit was based at Constanta, Sevastopol and Yalta, in September 1943 it was captured by the Germans, some of the boats were transferred to Romania, but in August 1944 everything was captured by the Red Army during the capture of Constanta.

Perhaps the most exotic formation of Regia Marina in the Second World War was the 12th MAS squadron, operating against the Soviet Union on Lake Ladoga, based at Lahdenpohja in May - October 1942.

Order of battle of the Italian Navy on June 10th, 1940

1st Fleet (Taranto)

1st Squadron (Taranto) – heavy cruisers Zara (F) (2 Ro.43), Gorizia (2 Ro.43), Fiume (2 Ro.43)

Destroyer Division 9 – destroyers Vittorio Afieri (F), Alfredo Oriani, Giosue Carducci, Vincenzo Gioberti

4th Squadron (Taranto) – light cruisers Alberico da Barbiano (F) (2 Ro.43), Luigi Cadorna (2 Ro.43), Alberto di Giussano (2 Ro.43), Armando Diaz (2 Ro.43), destroyer Lanciere

5th Squadron (Taranto) – battleships Conte de Cavour (FF), Giulio Cesare (F), Caio Duilio, Andrea Doria

Destroyer Division 7 – destroyers Freccia (F), Dardo, Saetta, Strale

Destroyer Division 8 – destroyers Folgore (F), Baleno, Fulmine, Lampo

8th Squadron (Taranto) – light cruisers Emmanuele Filiberto Duca degli Abruzzi (F) (4 Ro.43), Giuseppe Garibaldi (4 Ro.43)

Destroyer Division 16 – destroyers

Nicoloso Da Recco (F), Emanuele Pessagno, Luca Tarigo, Antonio Usodimare

9th Squadron (Taranto) – battleships Littorio (F) (3 Ro.43), Vittorio Veneto (3 Ro.43)

Destroyer Division 14 – destroyers Ugolino Vivaldi (F), Antonio da Noli, Lanzerotto Malocello, Leone Pancaldo

Destroyer Division 15 – destroyers Antonio Pigafetta (F), Alviso da Mosto, Giovanni da Verazzano, Nicolo Zeno

Seaplane tender Giuseppe Miraglia, water tanker - amphibious transports Isonzo, Po, Garda, tug Atlante, Lipari

2nd Fleet (La Spezia)

2nd Squadron (La Spezia) – light cruisers Giovanni delle Bande Nere (F) (2 Ro.43), Bartolomeo Colleoni (2 Ro.43)

Destroyer Division 10 – destroyers Maestrale (F), Libeccio, Grecale, Scirocco

3rd Squadron (La Spezia) – heavy cruisers Trento (F) (3 Ro.43), Bolzano (3 Ro.43), Trieste (3 Ro.43)

Destroyer Division 11 – destroyers Artigliere, Aviere, Camicia Nera, Geniere

6th Squadron (La Spezia) – heavy cruiser Pola (FF) (F)

Destroyer Division 12 – destroyers Carabiniere (F), Ascari, Corazziere, Lanciere

7th Squadron (La Spezia) – light cruisers Eugenio di Savoia (F) (2 Ro.43), Emanuele Filiberto Duca d'Aosta (2 Ro.43), Muzio Attendolo (2 Ro.43), Raimondo Montecuccoli (2 Ro.43)

Destroyer Division 13 – destroyers Alpino, Bersagliere, Fuciliere, Granatiere

Repair ship Quarnaro, oiler Cocito, water tanker – amphibious transports Volturno, Istria, Flegettone, Mincio, tugs Mare Ercole, Portoferraio

Submarine Fleet (La Spezia)

– submarine tenders Pacinotti, Volta, submarine rescue ship Anteo

1st Submarine Squadron (La Spezia)

Submarine Division 11 (La Spezia) – submarines Pietro Calvi, Giuseppe Finzi, Enrico Tazzoli, Ettore Fieramosca

Submarine Division 12 (La Spezia) – submarines Comandante Cappellini, Comandante Faa di Bruno, Lazzaro Mocenigo, Sebastiano Veniero, Glauco, Otaria

Submarine Division 13 (La Spezia) – submarines Berillo, Onice, Gemma

Submarine Division 14 (La Spezia) – submarines Iride, Argo, Velella

Submarine Division 15 (La Spezia) – submarines Gondar, Neghelli, Ascianghi, Scire

Submarine Division 16 (La Spezia) – submarines Pietro Micca, Foca

Submarine Division 17 (La Spezia) – submarines H1, H2, H4, H6, H8

2nd Submarine Squadron (Napoli)

Submarine Division 21 (Napoli) – submarines Marcello, Dandolo, Provana

Submarine Division 22 (Napoli) – submarines Barbarigo, Emo, Morosini, Guiglielmo Marconi, Leonardo da Vicni

3rd Submarine Squadron (Messina)

Submarine Division 31 (Messina) – submarines Vettor Pisani, Marcantonio Colonna, Giovanni Bausan, Des Geneys

Submarine Division 33 (Trapani) – submarines Fratelli Bandiera, Luciano Manara, Ciro Menotti, Santore Santarosa

Submarine Division 34 (Augusta) – submarines Goffredo Mameli, Pier Capponi, Tito Speri, Giovanni da Procida

Submarine Division 35 (Messina) – submarines Durbo, Tembien, Beilul

Submarine Division 37 (Augusta) – submarines Marcantonio Bragadin, X2, X3

4th Submarine Squadron (Taranto)

Submarine Division 40 (Brindisi) – submarines Balilla, Antonio Sciesa, Enrico Toti, Domenico Millelire

Submarine Division 41 (Taranto) – submarines Generale Liuzzi, Antonio Bagnolini, Reginaldo Giuliani, Capitano Tarantini

Submarine Division 42 (Brindisi) – submarine Benedetto Brin

Submarine Division 43 (Taranto) – submarine Luigi Settembrini

Submarine Division 44 (Brindisi) – submarine Anfitrite

Submarine Division 45 (Taranto) - submarines Salpa, Serpente

Submarine Division 46 (Taranto) – submarines Dessie, Dagabur, Uarsciek, Uebi Scebeli

Submarine Division 47 (Taranto) – submarines Malachite, Rubino, Ambra

Submarine Division 48 (Brindisi) – submarine Ondina

Submarine Division 49 (Taranto) – submarines Atropo, Zoea, Filippo Corridoni

7th Submarine Squadron (Cagliari)

Submarine Division 71 (Cagliari) – submarines Alagi, Adua, Axum, Aradam

Submarine Division 72 (Cagliari) – submarines Diaspro, Corallo, Turchese, Medusa

ITALY

Upper Tyrrhenian Sea Department (La Spezia)
(11 Z.501)

1st MAS Squadron (La Spezia)
MAS Division 1 – MAS438 – 441
MAS Division 5 – MAS505, 507, 510, 525
MAS Division 12 – MAS526 – 529
MAS Division 13 – MAS534, 535, 538, 539
MAS Division 14 – MAS530 – 533
Torpedo Boat Division 10 (La Spezia) – torpedo boats Vega, Sagittario, Perseo, Sirio
Torpedo Boat Division 16 (La Spezia) – torpedo boats Mozambano, Curtatone, Castelfidardo, Calatafimi
Gunboat Rimini, minelayers Crotone, Fasana, Orlando, Gasperi, personnel transport Matteuci, water tanker Dalmazia

Lower Tyrrhenian Sea Department (Napoli)
(4 Z.501)

Torpedo Boat Division 3 (Napoli) – torpedo boats Generale Marcello Prestinari, Generale Antonio Cantore, Giacinto Carini, Antonio La Masa
Torpedo boat Division 4 (Napoli) – torpedo boats Procione, Orione, Orsa, Pegaso
Minesweeper D1, minelayer Partenope, ammunition transport Buffoluto, water tankers Arno, Metauro, store carriers Pacinotti, Alessandro Volta

Sicily Naval Command (Messina)
(33 Z.501, 10 Z.506/B)

1st Torpedo Boat Squadron (Messina)
Torpedo Boat Division 13 (Messina) – torpedo boats Circe, Clio, Calliope, Calipso
Torpedo Boat Division 14 (Messina) – torpedo boats Partenope, Polluce, Pleiadi, Pallade
2nd Torpedo Boat Squadron (Messina)
Torpedo Boat Division 1 (Messina) – torpedo boats Airone, Ariel, Aretusa, Alcione
Torpedo Boat Division 12 (Messina) – torpedo boats Altair, Antares, Aldebaran, Andromeda
2nd MAS Squadron (Messina)
MAS Division 2 – MAS424, 509, 543, 544
MAS Division 9 – MAS512 – 515
MAS Division 10 – MAS516 – 510
MAS Division 15 – MAS547 – 550
Torpedo Boat Division 5 (Messina) – torpedo boats Simone Schiaffino, Giuseppe Dezza, Giuseppe La Farina, Giuseppe Cesare Abba
Minesweeper Division 2 (Messina) – 10 minesweepers
Minesweeper Division 3 (Palermo) – 9 minesweepers
Minesweeper Division 4 (Augusta) – 9 minesweepers
Submarine chaser Albatros, minelayers Buccari, Brioni, Adriatico, oiler Prometeo, water tankers Verde, Bormida, Brenta, lighthouse tender Scilla

Sardinia Naval Command (La Maddalena)
(25 Z.501, 7 Z.506)

Torpedo Boat Division 2 (La Maddalena) – torpedo boats Generale Achille Papa, Generale Carlo Montanari, Generale Antonio Cascino, Generale Antonio Chinotto
Torpedo Boat Division 9 (La Maddalena) – torpedo boats Canopo, Cassiopea, Fratelli Cairoli, Antonio Mosto
MAS Division 4 (La Maddalena) – MAS501 – 504
Minelayers Durazzo, Pelagosa, Caralis, Deffenu, Mazara

Upper Adriatic Sea Department (Venezia)

Torpedo Boat Division 15 (Venezia) – torpedo boats Cofienza, Solferino, San Martino, Palestro
Minelayers Albona, Laurana, Rovigno, lighthouse tender Lido, training vessels Cristoforo Colombo, Amerigo Vespucci

Pola Naval Command (Pola)
(4 Z.501)

MAS Division 6 – MAS423, 426, 432, 437
Torpedo boat Ernesto Giovannini, minelayers Azio, San Giusto, oiler Lete, water tankers Scrivia, Verbano

Quarnaro Naval Command (Osero, Lussino)

Ionian and Lower Adriatic Sea Department (Taranto)
(10 Z.501)

Cruiser Group (Taranto) – light cruisers Bari, Taranto
Destroyer Division 2 (Taranto) – destroyers Espero, Borea, Zeffiro, Ostro
Torpedo Boat Division 6 (Taranto) – torpedo boats Rosolino Pilo, Francesco Stocco, Giuseppe Missori, Giuseppe Sirtori, Giacinto Carini, Antonio La Masa
Minesweeper Division 1 (Taranto) – 10 minesweepers
Gunboats Otranto, Gallipoli, minelayers Vieste, Barletta, personnel transports Cherso, Materiali Lussino, water tankers Sesia, Garigliano, Tirso

Brindisi Naval Command (Brindisi)

Destroyer group (Brindisi) – destroyers Augusto Riboti, Carlo Mirabello
Torpedo Boat Division 7 (Brindisi) – torpedo boats Angelo Bassini, Enrico Cosenz, Giacomo Medici, Nicolo Fabrizzi
MAS Division 3 (Brindisi) – MAS540, 541
Gunboat Cirene, oiler Adige

Aegean Sea Naval Command (Rhodes)
(12 Z.501, 2 Z.506/B)

Destroyer Division 4 (Rhodes) – destroyers Francesco Crispi, Quintino Sella
Torpedo Boat Division 8 (Rhodes) – torpedo boats Lupo, Lince, Lira, Libra
5th Submarine Squadron (Rhodes) – submarine tender Caboto
Submarine Division 51 (Rhodes) – submarines Narvalo, Squalo, Tricheco, Delfino
Submarine Division 52 (Rhodes) – submarines Jalea, Jantina, Ametista, Zaffiro
3rd MAS Saquadron (Rhodes)
MAS Division 7 – MAS430, 431, 433, 434
MAS Division 11 – MAS520 – 523
MAS Division 16 – MAS536, 537, 542
MAS Division 22 – MAS545, 546, 551
Gunboat Senzini, minelayers Legnano, Lero, oiler Cerere

Albania Naval Command (Durazzo)
(1 Z.501)

Minesweepers Vigilante, Vedetta, water tanker Pagano

Libya Naval Command (Bengasi)

Destroyer Division 1 (Tobruk) – destroyers Espero, Borea, Zeffiro, Ostro
Torpedo Boat Division 11 (Tripoli) – torpedo boats Cigno, Castore, Climente, Centauro
6th Submarine Squadron (Tobruk)
Submarine Division 61 (Tobruk) – submarines Sirena, Argonauta, Fisalia, Smeraldo, Naiade
Submarine Division 62 (Tobruk) – submarines Diamante, Topazio, Nereide, Galatea, Lafolle
Armored cruiser San Giorgio, minelayer Monte Gargano, gunboats Palmaiola, De Lutti, Grazioli Lante, Giovanni Berta, Valoroso, Alula, water tankers Lima Campanella, Ticino, Polifemo

Italian East Africa Naval Command (Massawa, Eritrea)

Destroyer Division 3 (Massawa, Eritrea) – destroyers Francesco Nullo, Nazario Sauro, Cesare Battisti, Daniele Manin
Destroyer Division 5 (Massawa, Eritrea) – destroyers Pantera, Tigre, Leone
Torpedo Boat Detachment (Massawa, Eritrea) – torpedo boats Giovanni Acerbi, Vincenzo Orsini
8th Submarine Squadron (Massawa, Eritrea)
Submarine Division 81 (Massawa, Eritrea) – submarines Gugliemotti, Galileo Ferraris, Luigi Galvani, Galileo Galilei
Submarine Division 82 (Massawa, Eritrea) – submarines Perla, Macalle, Archimede, Evangelista Torricelli
MAS Division 21 (Massawa, Eritrea) – MAS204, 206, 210, 213, 216
Gunboats Eritrea, Porto Corsini, Biglieri, Posamine, Ostia, water tankers Niobe, Sile, Sebeto, Bacchiglione, submarine rescue ship Ciclope, tugs Ausonia, Portovenere

Far East Naval Command (Tientsin, China)

Gunboats Lepanto (Shanghai, China), Ermano Carlotto (Tientsin, China)

Navy Fleet Train

ITALY

Ammunition transports Panigaglia, Vallelunga, store ship Asmara, oilers Brennero, Bronte, Give, Nettuno, Tarvisio, Urano, petrol tankers Stige, Marte, personnel transports Enrichetta, Tripoli, tugs Ciclope, Egadi, Favignana, Gagliardo, Luni, Maittino, Marsigli, Montecristo, Nereo, Porto Empedocle, Robusto, Tenace, Titano, Teseo, Vigoroso, cable vessels Citta di Milano, Giasone, survey vessels Ammiraglio Magnaghi, Cariddi, Marsigli, hospital vessels Aquileia, California, Po, target vessel San Marco, destroyer (target control ship) Audace, yachts Aurora, Illiria, Savoia

BATTLESHIPS

GIULIO CESARE class battleships

Conte di Cavour	R. Arsenale di La Spezia	10.8.1910	10.8.1911	1.4.1915	sunk 12.11.1940
Giulio Cesare	Ansaldo, Genoa	24.6.1910	15.10.1911	14.5.1914	to the USSR 2.1949 (Novorossiysk)

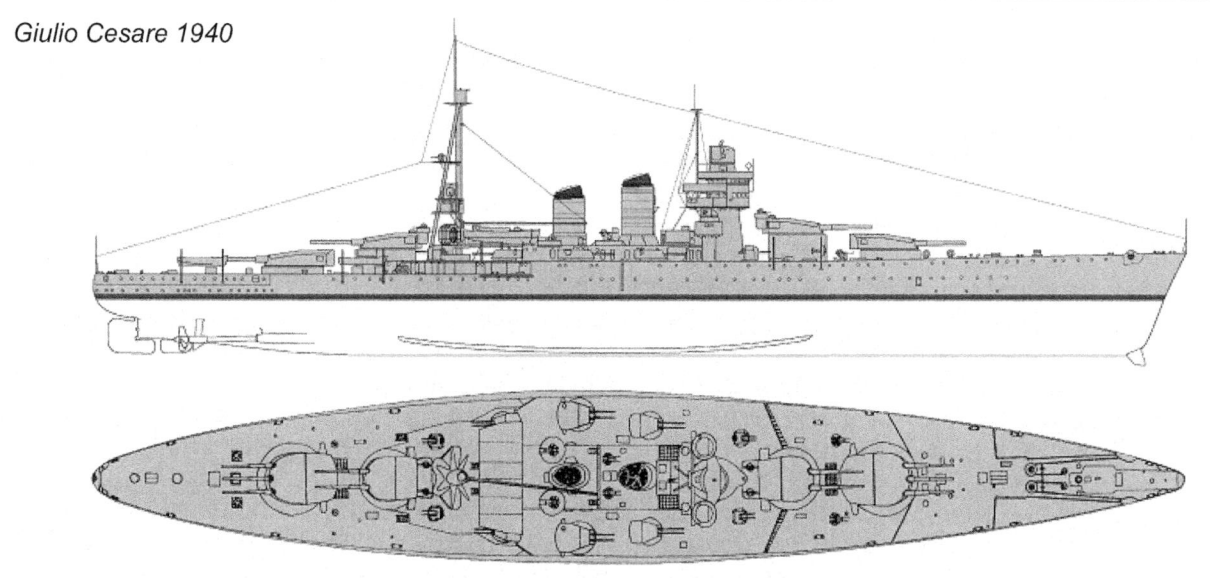

Giulio Cesare 1940

Before the reconstruction: 22922 / 24250 (*Conte di Cavour*) or 23183 / 24801 (*Giulio Cesare*) t, 176.1 x 28.0 x 8.7 m, 4 sets Parsons geared steam turbines, 20 Blechynden (*Conte di Cavour*) or 12 Blechynden + 12 Babcock & Wilcox (*Giulio Cesare*) boilers, 31278 (*Conte di Cavour*) or 30700 (*Giulio Cesare*) hp, 22.2 (*Conte di Cavour*) or 21.6 (*Giulio Cesare*) kts, 1450 t coal + 850 t oil, 4800 nm (10 kts), complement 1235; belt 250-80, decks 24+30+30+44, turrets 280, CT 280; (3 x 3 + 2 x 2) – 305/46 Vickers 1909 (*Conte di Cavour*) or Ansaldo 1909 (*Giulio Cesare*), 18 x 1 – 120/50 Vickers 1909 (*Conte di Cavour*) or Ansaldo 1909 (*Giulio Cesare*), 13 x 1 – 76/50 Vickers 1909 (*Conte di Cavour*) or Ansaldo 1909 (*Giulio Cesare*), 6 x 1 – 76/40 Ansaldo 1917, 3 – 450 TT (1 bow, 2 beam), 1 catapult, 1 seaplane.

After the reconstruction: 26400 / 29032 (*Conte di Cavour*) or 29100 (*Giulio Cesare*) t, 186.4 x 28.6 x 9.2 m, 2 sets Beluzzo geared steam turbines, 8 Yarrow boilers, 75000 hp (93000 forced), 27 kts (28 forced), 2472 t oil, 6400 nm (13 kts), complement 1236; belt 250-220, decks 100-80 + 44, turrets 280, CT 260; (2 x 3 + 2 x 2) – 320/44 M1934, 6 x 2 – 120/50 OTO 1933, 4 x 2 – 100/47 OTO 1928, 6 x 2 – 37/54 Breda 1932, 6 x 2 – 13.2 MG, 2 catapults (*Giulio Cesare*), 2 seaplanes (Ro.43) (*Giulio Cesare*)

The *Giulio Cesare* class battleships were the mainstay of the Regia Marina during the First World War, although they were not very successful. The protection of ships by the beginning of the war no longer met modern requirements, underwater protection was practically absent, and even speed, the traditional trump card of Italian shipbuilders, was inferior to the latest

Giulio Cesare 1938

dreadnoughts of other countries.

By the early 1930s, the two surviving ships of this class had completely lost their combat value, and since France, the main enemy of Italy in the Mediterranean, had the same obsolete battleships, no work was carried out to modernize the ships of the *Conte di Cavour* class. The situation changed after it became known about the construction in France of the fast battleship *Dunkerque*. Italy's response came quickly enough, but was unusual. For a number of reasons, both economic and political, instead of building a new ship, Italy took the path of radical modernization of the existing ones.

Work on *Cavour* and *Cesare* began in 1933. The ships lost all artillery and superstructures, most of the hull above the armored deck was dismantled. The hull, in order to improve streamlining, was lengthened fwd by 10 m, and a new yacht stem was formed. Due to the elimination of the medium gun casemate, the forecastle was lengthened to about 60% of the hull length. The old 4-shaft machinery was dismantled and replaced by much more powerful twin-shaft one. Progress in the field of ship power plants over the 20 years that have passed since the completion of the ships has allowed at three times more powerful machinery to reduce its weight by a third. The machinery compartments were arranged in a 'staggered' order: the port side turbine set was positioned aft of the boiler room, and the starboard side turbine set was fwd of the boiler room. The midship triple turret between the funnels was eliminated, and the number of main guns was decreased to ten 320-mms, and these were old 305-mm barrels drilled for a new caliber and mounted on a new carriage, providing a greater, 27° elevation angle. The secondary artillery after modernization was presented by 120-mm/50 guns in six twin turrets, placed on the same level amidships. The weight savings resulting from the use of lighter machinery and the reduction in the number of main gun turrets from 5 to 4 were aimed at strengthening the protection: more than 3000 t of additional armor was installed, mostly horizontal, although the protection of barbettes and the CT was also increased. The underwater protection of the Pugliese design, consisting of two concentric tubes one inside the other (the inner one was "breakable" or "soft"), also had 25-mm protection. Work on both ships came to end in 1937: *Conte di Cavour* returned to service in June,

Giulio Cesare in October. At the time Italy's accession to WWII, they were the unique fully combat-ready Italian battleships.

During repairs in 1943, it was planned to rearm *Cavour* with more modern artillery: 6 twin 135-mm/45, 12 single 65-mm/64 and 5 twin and 3 single 20-mm/65.

After the reconstruction the main belt had a depth of 2.8 m and protected the entire length of the ship. Its thickness was 250 mm between the end barbettes, tapering to 170 mm from the middle part to the lower edge, decreasing to 80 and 130 mm at the fore and aft ends, respectively. The upper 220-mm belt between the end barbettes had a depth of 2.3 m. An additional 130-mm belt between the stem and barbette No 4 had a length of 138 m. New 70-mm sides of the citadel inside the hull protected the machinery and barbettes between the main and middle decks.

The main deck had a thickness of 50 mm in the flat part (the central part near the centerline was absent) and was connected to the lower edge of the main belt by 40-mm slopes. The middle deck between barbettes No 1 and 4 laid on the level of the upper edge of the upper 220-mm belt and was 80-mm over the machinery, 100-mm over the magazines and 30-mm over the other parts of the hull. The upper deck between the stem and the casemate was 30-mm, there was a 44-mm forecastle deck above the former casemate.

The turrets had 240-mm faces, sides and rears and 85-mm crowns. The barbettes had 280-mm protection with additional 50-mm plates mounted around them with a small gap. The CT had 260-mm sides, 120-mm roof and 100-mm deck. The fore superstructure had 32-48-mm splinter protection.

The new anti-torpedo protection of the Pugliese design with an inner tube with a diameter of 3.4 m had a depth of 7 m and could withstand an explosion of 350 kg of TNT. The longitudinal torpedo bulkhead had a thickness of 40 mm and was connected to the 70-mm side of the inner citadel at the level of the main deck.

Late 1937, *Giulio Cesare*: - 2 catapults with seaplanes.
Late 1940, both: - 6 x 2 - 13.2 MG; + 6 x 2 - 20/65 Breda 1935.
1941, *Giulio Cesare*: + 2 x 2 - 37/54 Breda 1932, 2 x 2 - 20/65 Breda 1935.

Conte di Cavour was sunk by a single air torpedo from British Swordfish of the *Illustrious* air group at Taranto 12.11.1940 in shallow water and abandoned. Raised 1.7.1941 and towed to Trieste. Until September 1943, the repair was not completed - the ship was in semi-annual readiness. 10.9.1943 scuttled by crew. Salvaged by the Germans in 1943-1944 and sunk by US aircraft 15.2.1945.

Giulio Cesare in the battle of Punto Stilo 9.7.1940 was hit by a 381-mm shell and was under repair for two months.

ITALY

CAIO DUILIO class battleships

| **Andrea Doria** | R. Arsenale di La Spezia | 24.3.1912 | 30.3.1913 | 13.3.1916 | stricken 11.1956 |
| **Caio Duilio** | R. Cantiere di Castellamare di Stabia | 24.2.1912 | 24.4.1913 | 10.5.1915 | stricken 9.1956 |

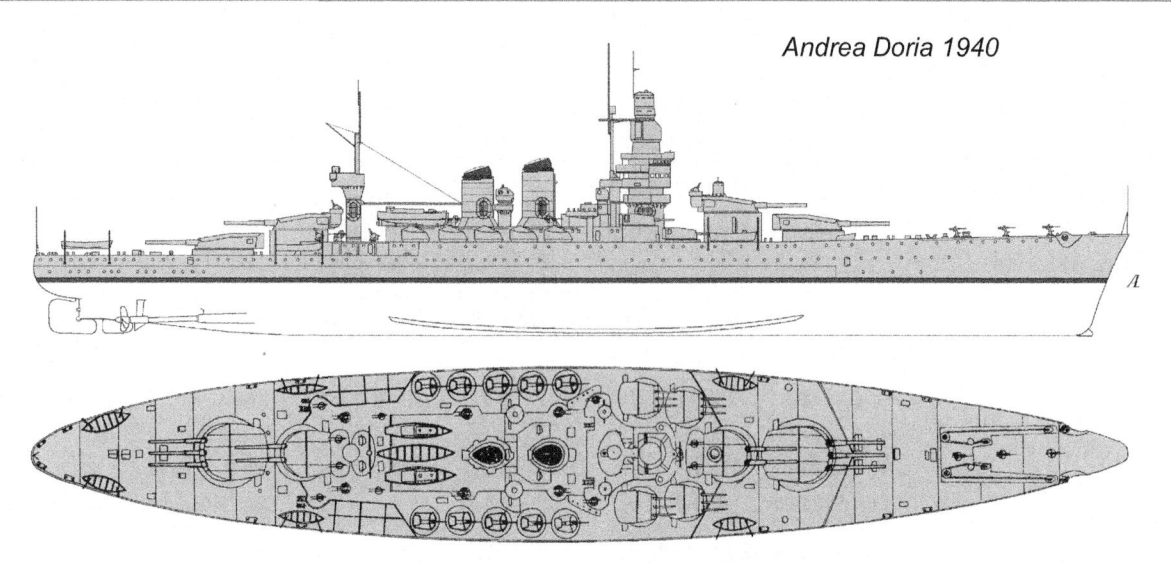

Andrea Doria 1940

Before the reconstruction: 22956 / 24729 (*Andrea Doria*) or 22994 / 24715 (*Caio Duilio*) t, 176.1 x 28.0 x 8.9 m, 4 sets Parsons geared steam turbines, 20 Yarrow boilers, 30000 (*Andrea Doria*) or 31009 (*Caio Duilio*) hp, 21 (*Andrea Doria*) or 21.3 (*Caio Duilio*) kts, 1488 t coal + 886 t oil, 4800 nm (10 kts), complement 1233; belt 250-80, decks 24+30+44+44, turrets: 280, CT: 280; (3 x 3 + 2 x 2) – 305/46 Vickers 1909 (*Andrea Doria*) or Ansaldo 1909 (*Caio Duilio*), 16 x 1 – 152/45 Ansaldo 1911, 19 x 1 – 76/50 Vickers 1909 (*Andrea Doria*) or Ansaldo 1909 (*Caio Duilio*), 3 – 450 TT (1 bow, 2 beam).

After the reconstruction: 23887 / 28882 (*Andrea Doria*) or 29391 (*Caio Duilio*) t, 186.9 x 28.6 x 9.1 m, 2 sets Beluzzo geared steam turbines, 8 Yarrow boilers, 75000 hp (87000 forced), 26 kts (28 forced), 2214 t oil, 4250 nm (12 kts), complement 1485; belt 250-220, decks 100-80 + 44, turrets 280, CT 260; (2 x 3 + 2 x 2) – 320/44 M1936, 4 x 3 – 135/45 OTO 1937, 10 x 1 – 90/50 Ansaldo 1938, 6 x 2 – 37/54 Breda 1932, 3 x 1 – 37/54 Breda 1939, 8 x 2 – 20/65 Breda 1935.

Andrea Doria class battleships were built as a development of the *Conte di Cavour* class and had a slightly smaller breadth, thicker barbette armor and differed from their predecessors in the lower arrangement of the midship triple main gun turret and the structure of the secondary artillery.

After the modernization in 1937 of two ships of the *Conte di Cavour* class, in April 1937 the modernization of *Doria* in Trieste and *Duilio* in Genoa was started. The scope of work was practically the same as on the previous class: the hull was lengthened, the armament and machinery were replaced, the protection was strengthened, although there were also differences. So, *Doria* and *Duilio* received slightly less powerful machinery. Secondary artillery significantly differed: instead of 120-mm guns, there were 135-mm/45 guns in four triple turrets grouped around the fore superstructure. The outdated 100-mm/47 AA guns on *Doria* and *Duilio* were replaced by the latest 90-mm guns, as was the case on the *Vittorio Veneto* class.

By the beginning of the war in the Mediterranean, the *Doria* class ships were late and were only recommissioned in July (*Duilio*) and October 1940 (*Doria*).

The main belt had a depth of 2.8 m and protected the entire length of the ship. Its thickness was 250 mm between the end barbettes, tapering to 170 mm from the middle part to the lower edge, decreasing to 80 and 130 mm at the fore and aft ends, respectively. The upper 220-mm belt between the end barbettes had a depth of 2.3 m. An additional 130-mm belt between the stem and barbette No 4 had a length of 138 m. New 70-mm sides of the citadel inside the hull protected the machinery and barbettes between the main and middle decks.

The main deck had a thickness of 50 mm in the flat part (the central part near the centerline was absent) and was connected to the lower edge of the main belt by 40-mm slopes. The middle deck between barbettes No 1 and 4 laid on the level of the upper edge of the upper 220-mm belt and was 80-mm over the machinery, 100-mm over the magazines and 30-mm over the other parts of the hull. The upper deck between the stem and the casemate was 44-30-mm, there was a 44-mm forecastle deck above the former casemate.

The turrets had 280-mm faces, 240-mm sides and rears and 85-mm crowns. The barbettes had 280-mm protection with additional 50-mm plates mounted around them with a small gap. The CT had 260-mm sides, 120-

Andrea Doria 1943

The new anti-torpedo protection of the Pugliese design with an inner tube with a diameter of 3.4 m had a depth of 7 m and could withstand an explosion of 350 kg of TNT. The longitudinal torpedo bulkhead had a thickness of 40 mm and was connected to the 70-mm side of the inner citadel at the level of the main deck.
Spring 1942, both: + 2 x 2 - 37/54 Breda 1932.
1944, both: - 3 x 1 - 37/54, 2 x 2 - 20/65.
During a British carrier-based air raid on Taranto 12.11.1940, *Duilio* was hit by one torpedo and was under repair until May 1941. Both ships sailed for Malta in September 1943. After the end of the war, they remained under the Italian flag as training ships.

mm roof and 100-mm deck. The fore superstructure had 32-48-mm splinter protection.

VITTORIO VENETO class battleships

Vittorio Veneto	CRDA, Trieste	28.10.1934	22.7.1937	28.4.1940	stricken 1.1948
Littorio, 7.1943- **Italia**	Ansaldo, Genoa	28.10.1934	22.8.1937	6.5.1940	stricken 6.1948
Roma	CRDA, Trieste	18.9.1938	9.6.1940	14.6.1942	sunk 9.9.1943
Impero	Ansaldo, Genoa	14.5.1938	15.11.1939	-	captured incomplete 10.9.1943

40517 / 45029 (*Vittorio Veneto*) or 40724 / 45236 (*Littorio*) or 40992 / 45485 (*Roma*) t, 237.8 or 240.7 (*Roma*) x 32.8 x 9.6 m, 4 sets Parsons geared steam turbines, 8 Yarrow boilers, 128200 hp, 30 kts, 4140 t oil, 4700 nm (14 kts), complement 1830-1950; belt 280 + 70, decks 162-90 + 45, turrets 350-280, CT 260; 3 x 3 – 381/50 Ansaldo 1934, 4 x 3 – 152/55 OTO 1936 (*Vittorio Veneto, Roma*) or 4 x 3 – 152/55 Ansaldo 1934 (*Littorio*), 4 x 1 – 120/40 Armstrong 1891, 12 x 1 – 90/50 OTO 1939, 8 x 2 – 37/54 Breda 1938, 4 x 1 – 37/54 Breda 1939, 8 (*Vittorio Veneto, Littorio*) or 14 (*Roma*) x 2 – 20/65 Breda 1935, 1 catapult, 3 seaplanes (2 Ro.43, 1 Ro.44, 1943- 2 Re.2000)

The design of Vittorio Veneto class battleships began in Italy in the early 1930s, almost simultaneously with the modernization of *Andrea Doria* and *Conte di Cavour* classes under the leadership of General Pugliese, the chief designer of the Navy. The first two ships, *Littorio* and *Vittorio Veneto*, were built under the 1934 Programme. Although at the time of laying the standard displacement of battleships, according to the restrictions of the Washington Treaty, should not exceed 35000 t, for Italian battleships this value was immediately increased by 5000 t, because, even at the design stage, it turned out that creating a balanced ship with the Treaty restrictions was unrealistic.

Based on the capabilities of the domestic industry, not the maximum allowed 406-mm guns were chosen as the main caliber, but the designers settled on 381-mm guns. The Italians tried to compensate for the smaller caliber with a higher muzzle velocity, but they had to pay with the rapid wear of the barrel and, as a result, a decrease in the accuracy of fire. An interesting feature of the ships was the unusually high location of the aft turret in attempt to protect the catapult located on the quarterdeck from the effects of powder gases when firing astern.

The protection, traditionally considered the weak point of Italian ships, was extremely strong on *Vittorio Veneto*. With sufficiently strong protection, the ships of the *Vittorio Veneto* class proved to be among the fastest battleships in the world, clearly second only to the latest USN ships. On trials, both first ships exceeded the contract speed by more than 1 knot, and during the daily service their speed exceeded 28 kts.

The next pair, *Roma* and *Impero*, was built according to the 1938 Programme. To improve seaworthiness, the forecastle deck received a slight rise fwd, which slightly increased the overall length. The outfitting of the second ship was not completed: in September 1943, her hull was captured by German troops and 20.2.1945 was sunk by Allied aircraft at Trieste.

The main belt between the end barbettes had a depth of 3.8 m and was inclined outwards at an angle of 11°. It consisted of an outer layer of 70 mm and an inner layer of 280 mm with a gap of 250 mm between them. The 36-mm main splinter longitudinal bulkhead was placed in 1.4 m from the main belt inside the hull. The second 25-mm splinter longitudinal bulkhead was inclined at 27° inward. This belt was closed by 200-mm fore and 280-mm aft bulkheads, which were reduced to 70 mm below

Vittorio Veneto

ITALY

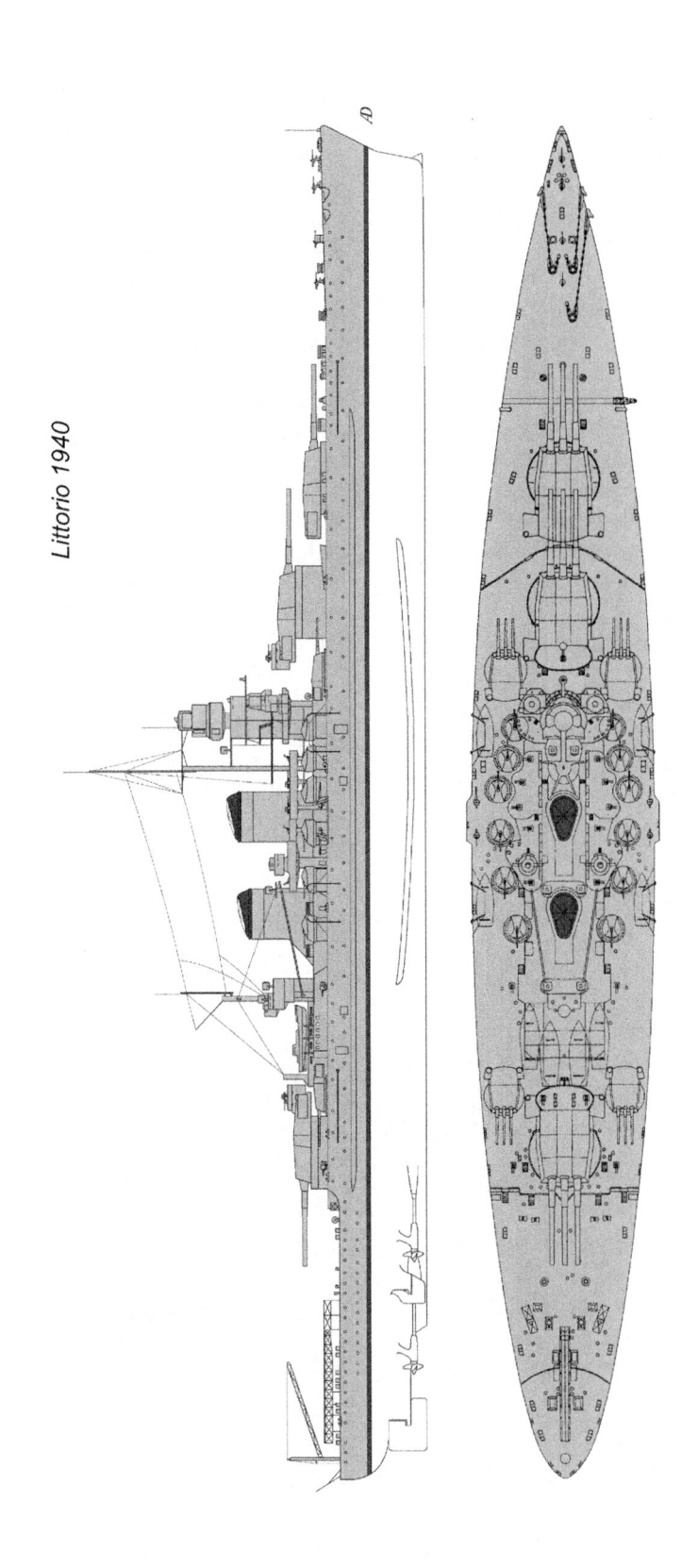

Littorio 1940

Roma

the main deck. The thickness of the main deck outside the end barbettes was 70-mm in the fore and 130-100-mm in the aft. The ship's side above the main belt was protected by 70-mm armor between the end barbettes and 45-mm armor between the barbette No 1 and stem. The flat main deck was connected to the upper edge of the main belt and consisted of 100-mm (90-mm closer to the side) armor on 12-mm plating, increasing to 150-mm armor on 12-mm plating over the magazines. The lower 100-mm armored deck with 100-mm slopes protected the aft ship's end between the aft armored bulkhead and the stern. The forecastle deck consisted of 36-mm armor on 9-mm plating.

The barbettes of the main gun turrets had 350-mm protection above and 280-mm below the forecastle deck. The turrets had 350-mm faces and 200-mm sides, rears and crowns. The secondary turrets had 280-mm faces, 130-80-mm sides and rears and 150-mm (fore pair) or 100-mm (aft pair) roofs. Their barbettes had 150-mm armor above the forecastle deck and 100-mm below.

The fore superstructure had 60-mm protection and the CT had 260-210-mm armor.

The underwater protection of the Pugliese design included a 40-mm curved lower deck leading into a vertical 40-mm longitudinal bulkhead connected to a double bottom. The inner tube with a diameter of 3.8 m had 6-mm sides. Underwater protection was 7.6-m deep and could withstand an explosion of 350 kg of TNT.

9.1941, *Littorio*: + EC-3/bis radar.
Spring 1942, *Vittorio Veneto*: + 8 x 2 - 20/65 Breda 1935.
Spring 1942, *Littorio*: - EC-3/bis radar; + 6 x 2 - 20/65 Breda 1935, EC-3/ter radar.
6.1943, *Vittorio Veneto*; 8.1943, *Roma*; 9.1943, *Littorio*: + EC-3/ter radar.

Littorio was badly damaged during a British carrier air raid 11.11.1940 on Taranto, receiving three torpedo hits and was under repair until April 1941. *Vittorio Veneto* was damaged by an air torpedo in the battle of Matapan and was under repair until August 1941. In December 1941 damaged by a torpedo from British submarine *Urge* and was under repair until March 1942. 30.7.1943 *Littorio* was renamed *Italia*. During the transition of the Italian fleet to Malta, *Roma* received 2 hits of SD-1400X guided bombs launched from a German Do 217 bomber. The hits caused a fire and an explosion of ammunition; the battleship sank W of the Strait of Bonifaccio. On the same campaign, *Italia* was hit by a similar bomb.

AIRCRAFT CARRIERS AND SEAPLANE TENDER

AQUILA aircraft carrier

Aquila (ex-Roma)	Ansaldo, Genoa	30.11.1924	26.2.1926	(9.1926)	conversion incomplete

23130 / 28350 t, 232.5 x 30.1 x 7.2 m, 4 sets Beluzzo geared steam turbines, 8 Thornycroft boilers, 151000 hp, 29.5 kts, 3600 t oil, 5500 nm (18 kts), complement 1408; belt 600 concrete; 8 x 1 – 135/45 Ansaldo 1938, 12 x 1 – 65/64 Ansaldo-Terni 1939, 22 x 6 – 20/65 Breda 1941, 2 catapults, 51 aircraft (Re.2001); EC-3/ter radar.

Year	fighters
1943 (planned)	51 Re.2001 or 66 Re.2001G

Flight deck: 216.2 x 25.3 m. Hangar: 160.0 x 18.0 m. Two elevators, (each 15.2 x 14.3 m, 6.5 t). Two catapults of K-252 type. Aircraft fuel stowage: 327000 l.

Former passenger liner *Roma* (32583grt). Back in the mid-1930s, this ship was planned to be converted to seaplane carrier capable of launching, in addition to seaplanes, also wheeled planes landing on coastal airfields. For some reason, the project remained unrealized, and the idea of creating an aircraft carrier was returned only after an air raid on Taranto 11.11.1940. In January 1941, the development of an aircraft carrier design based on the liner's hull began.

ITALY

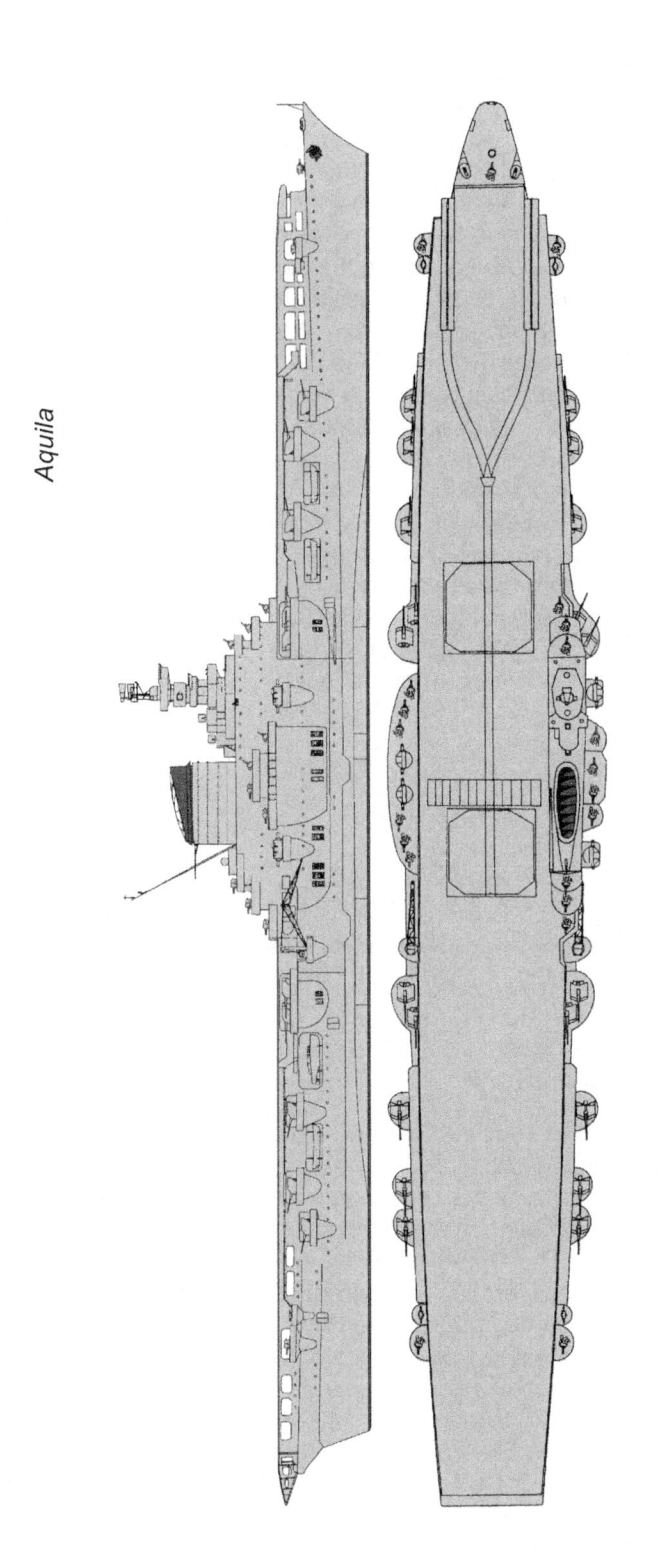

Aquila

Sparviero

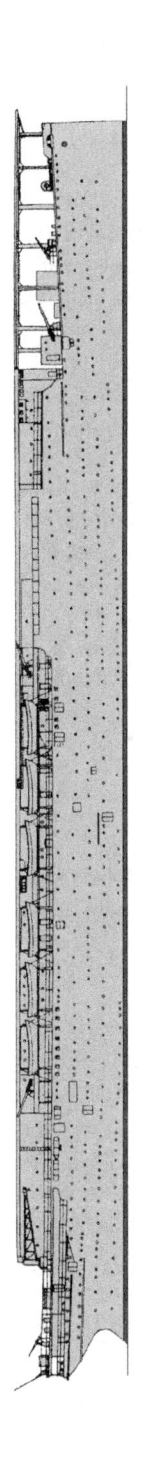

The conversion of *Roma,* renamed *Aquila* in February 1942, was of a cardinal nature. The hull of the ship was lengthened, equipped with bulges and a clipper bow. To increase stability and underwater protection, the inner part of the bulges adjacent to the hull was filled by concrete. Inside, the hull was thoroughly redesigned, having received several additional longitudinal bulkheads. The machinery was completely redesigned, borrowing turbines and boilers from the incomplete light cruisers *Cornelio Silla* and *Paolo Emilio*. To increase resistance to damage, the 'pseudo-staggered' machinery arrangement was used: in each compartment, on one side of the centre line, one turbine unit was mounted, and on the other, two boilers.

Above the upper deck, the former liner was completely rebuilt. A new long superstructure, in which the 160 x 18-m hangar was located, formed the basis for the 216.2 x 25.3-m flight deck. The airplanes could be handled by two elevators. All special aviation equipment (catapults, arresters, elevators) was of German origin.

Aquila, in the plans of the Italian command, was to play the role of an "air defense umbrella" of battle forces on the high seas, so fighters were to become her main armament. Since at the time of the drafting of the design, Italy did not have carrier-based aircraft, as a temporary measure, it was envisaged to base Re.2001 fighter-bombers with a non-folding wing. Only 26 aircraft could fit in the hangar, another 15 were supposed to be carried there, hanging below the ceiling. Another 10 fighters were planned to be carried directly on the flight deck. In the event that the developing Re.2001G version with a folding wing was adopted, the air group was to be increased to 66 aircraft, and all of them could be placed in the hangar.

The artillery consisted of 135-mm single-purpose guns taken from the incomplete cruisers of the *Capitani Romani* class.

Conversion work began in June 1941. By September 1943, the ship was 80% ready. She was captured by German troops at Genoa. *Aquila* was damaged by Allied aircraft 16.6.1944, again seriously damaged by Italian-crewed *Chariot* human torpedoes 19.4.1945 and scuttled by the Germans.

The internal compartments of the new bulges were filled with 600-mm layer of concrete. The magazines and the steering gear had box-shaped protection: magazines had 80-60-mm armor; the steering gear had 30-mm protection.

SPARVIERO aircraft carrier

Sparviero (ex-Falco, ex-Augustus)	Ansaldo, Genoa	1924	13.12.1926	(10.1927)	conversion incomplete

23000 (std) t, 202.4 (wl) x 30.0 x 9.2 m, 4 MAN diesels, 28000 hp, 18 kts; belt 90+30; 6 x 1 – 152/45 Ansaldo 1911, 4 x 1 – 102/35 Schneider-Armstrong 1914-15, some small AA guns, 25 – 30 aircraft (Re.2001)

Year	fighters
1944 (planned)	25 Re.2001 or 30 Re.2001G

Flight deck: 150.0 x 25.0 m. Two elevators, m. b. 2 catapults of the K-252 type.

Former 30418-grt passenger liner *Augustus*. She was similar to the liner *Roma*, but unlike the latter, she had diesel machinery. The project for the conversion of *Augustus* to an aircraft carrier was ready in 1936, but for some reason the conversion was cancelled. They returned to the idea of conversion in 1942. At one time, they wanted to carry out a conversion similar to *Aquila*, but very soon the design was converted into a pre-war project, only slightly modified. She was named *Falco* and soon *Sparviero*.

The scope of work on *Sparviero* was planned to be much smaller than on *Aquila*. The hull below the upper deck did not undergo any noticeable changes, except for the installation of bulges abreast machinery, designed to also ensure stability. The machinery remained unchanged.

On the upper deck there was a single-level hangar, in the formation of which old superstructures were partially used. The flight deck was connected to the hangar by two elevators. The launch of the aircraft was supposed to be carried out, apparently, with the help of a catapult, but there is no exact data on this.

The conversion was started by Ansaldo in September 1942. By September 1943, little progress had been made on the conversion. *Sparviero* was captured at Genoa 9.9.1943 by German troops. She was scuttled by the Germans 5.10.1944 at the same place as a breakwater.

There could be a 90-mm main belt, the bulges should have a 30-mm outer plating.

ITALY

GIUSEPPE MIRAGLIA seaplane carrier

| **Giuseppe Miraglia** (ex-Città di Messina) | Furness SB, Haverton Hill, UK / Arsenale di La Spezia | 5.3.1921 | 20.12.1923 | 1927 | submarine depot ship 9.1943 |

Giuseppe Miraglia 1940

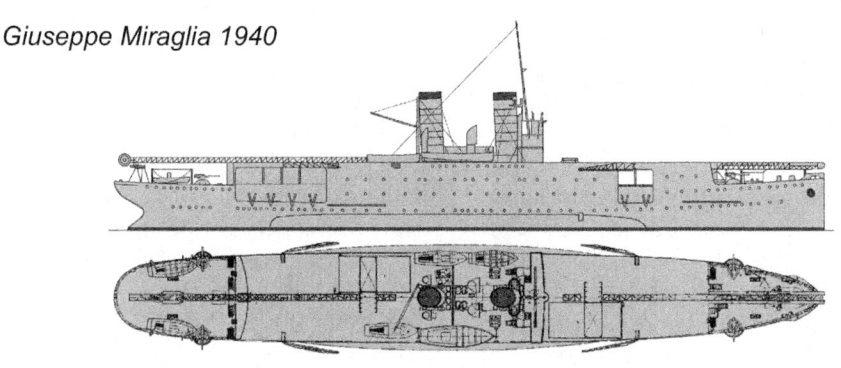

4880 / 5913 t, 121.2 x 15.0 x 5.2 m, 2 sets Parsons geared steam turbines, 8 Yarrow boilers, 12000 hp, 21 kts, 430 t oil, complement 196; 4 x 1 – 102/35 Schneider-Armstrong 1914-15, 2 catapults, 20 aircraft (17 CANT.25, 1937- 17 Ro.43).

Laid down as a passenger steamer *Città di Messina*, bought incomplete by the Italian Government to be converted to a seaplane tender. Refurbishment work began 24.1.1925. A large hangar was fitted amidships. Above the hangar on the centre line were superstructures and two funnels. Fwd and aft of them, the hangar roof formed a kind of flight deck, which served for pre-launch maintenance of aircraft. The launch was carried out by two catapults, one in the bow and the second in the stern. Handling of landed seaplanes was carried out by cranes through the side doors in the walls of the hangar.

At the beginning of the war, *Giuseppe Miraglia* was used as a training vessel, and after September 1943 as a depot ship for Italian submarines in Malta.

Giuseppe Miraglia 1932

CRUISERS

SAN GIORGIO armored cruiser

| **San Giorgio** | R. Cantiere di Castellamare di Stabia | 4.7.1905 | 27.7.1908 | 1.7.1910 | scuttled 22.1.1941 |

San Giorgio 1940

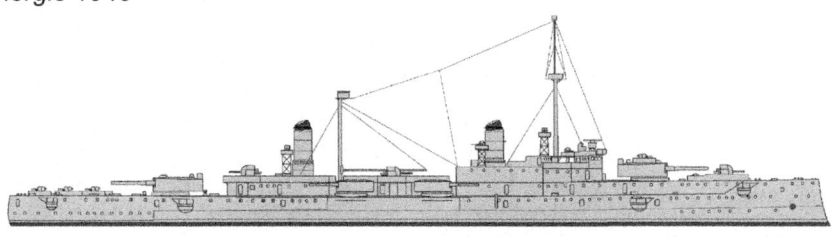

10167 / 11300 t, 140.8 x 21.0 x 7.3 m, 2 VTE, 14 Blechynden boilers, 19500 hp, 23.2 kts, 1560 t coal + oil, 6270 nm (10 kts), complement 705; belt 200, deck 50, main gun turrets 200, secondary gun turrets 160, CT 250; 2 x 2 – 254/45 Armstrong 1907, 4 x 2 – 190/45 Armstrong 1908, 10 x 1 – 76/50 Vickers 1908, 6 x 1 –

San Giorgio 1940

76/40 Armstrong 1917, 3 – 450 TT (sub, 1 fwd, 2 beam). *San Giorgio* and *San Marco* (in 1931 converted to wireless-controlled target) became the largest and strongest armored cruisers of the Italian Navy. They were ordered shortly after the *Amalfi* class and had similar armament but better protection, improved seaworthiness and habitability. *San Marco* was distinguished by the machinery: she became the first Italian ship with steam turbines. In 1937-1938, *San Giorgio* was converted to coast defense ship at La Spezia and returned to service in June 1938. In the early 1940, she was converted to AA floating battery and passed to Tobruk.

The main armor belt on the entire ship's length tapered to 80 mm at the lower edge, the medium belt between the stem and the aft main gun turret, and the upper belt between the 190-mm gun turrets reaching the upper deck had 200-mm thickness, the main and upper belts were closed by 150-mm bulkheads abreast the 254-mm gun and 190-mm gun barbettes respectively. The thickness of the main belt in short sections at the ends of the ship was 100 mm. The main deck was connected to the lower edge of the main belt by slopes.

6.1938: the number of boilers was reduced to 8, the boilers were converted to pure oil combustion (18200 hp, 18.6 kts, 1300 t oil), two funnels were removed; - 10 x 1 - 76/50, 6 x 1 - 76/40, 3 - 450 TT; + 4 x 2 - 100/47 OTO 1928, 2 x 2 - 13.2 MG; displacement was 9470 / 11500 t.

Early 1940: + 1 x 2 - 100/47 OTO 1928, 6 x 2 - 20/65 Breda 1935, 5 x 2 - 13.2 MG.

San Giorgio was badly damaged at Tobruk 22.1.1941 by the air group of British carrier *Eagle* and scuttled by her own crew in shallow water.

TRENTO class heavy cruisers

| Trento | OTO, Livorno | 8.2.1925 | 4.10.1927 | 3.4.1929 | sunk 15.6.1942 |
| Trieste | STT, Trieste | 22.6.1925 | 24.10.1926 | 21.12.1928 | sunk 10.4.1943 |

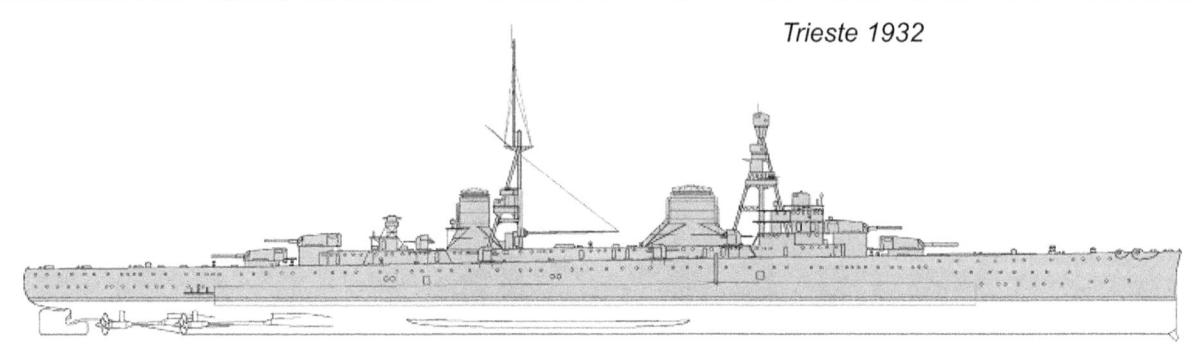

Trieste 1932

Trieste 1930s

10344 / 13334 (*Trento*) or 10339 / 13326 (*Trieste*) t, 197.0 x 20.6 x 6.8 m, 4 sets Parsons geared steam turbines, 12 Yarrow boilers, 120000 hp (150000 forced), 34 kts (36 forced), 2214 t oil, 4160 nm (16 kts), complement 723-781; belt 70, decks 50-20, turrets 80, CT 100-40; 4 x 2 – 203/50 Ansaldo 1924, 8 x 2 – 100/47 OTO 1924, 4 x 1 – 40/39 Vickers-Terni 1917, 4 x 1 – 12.7 MG, 8 – 533 TT (beam, 12), 1 catapult, 3 seaplanes (M.41 or CANT.25, 1938- Ro.43)

The first Italian 'Washington' cruisers. They were built according to the 1924-1925 Programme. When they were created, the main thrust was made at high speed. To achieve the speed of 34 kts laid down in the technical design, they had to give more than a third of the length of the hull to a 4-shaft 120000-hp machinery. The use of such powerful and heavy machinery, weighing more than 2300 t, placed *en echelon*, left not too much displacement for armament and protection. In order to stay within the allowed 10000 tons, the Italians went to the maximum lightening of the hull structure, but still both ships turned out to be more than 300 t heavier than the established limit.

The protection, as on all the first 'Washington' cruisers, did not match the armament, although, unlike the British and French shipbuilders, the Italians

ITALY

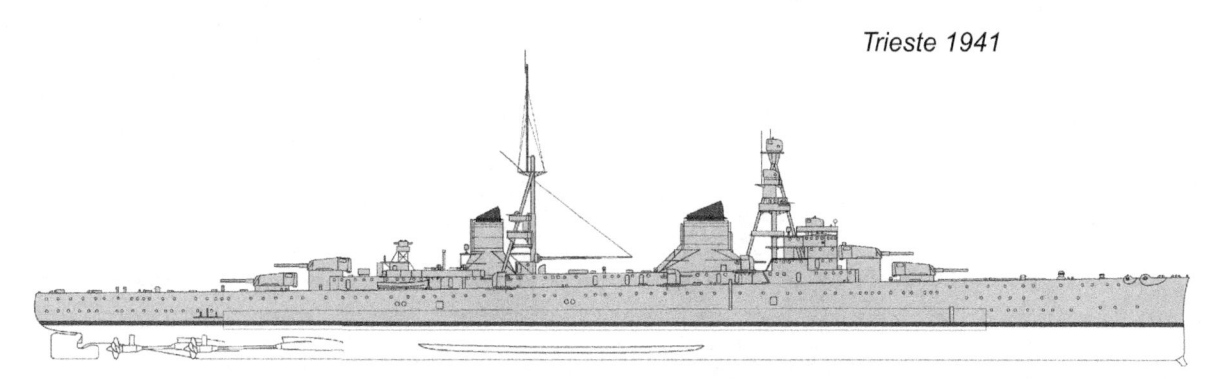

Trieste 1941

could install a 70-mm armored belt between the end barbettes. Alas, the belt could only withstand 203-mm shells at considerable distances, at which the 50-mm armored deck could no longer stop shells falling at a high angle. For 203-mm shells, *Trento* and *Trieste* turned out to be the same "cardboard", as all the other 'Washington' cruisers. 203-mm/50 main guns in four turrets had a maximum elevation of 45°. The design of the turrets was unsuccessful, and the design rate of fire of 3 rounds per minute could not always be achieved. All the turrets were very cramped. *Trento* and *Trieste* became the first Italian ships, which even at the design stage provided for aviation armament, and a forecastle was chosen as a place for the catapult under deck of which, forward of the No1 turret, there was a hangar for two seaplanes: they were delivered to the catapult by an elevator.

On 8-hrs trials, both ships came close to the contractual 36 kts, reaching 35.6-35.7 kts, however, *Trento* and *Trieste* showed this outstanding speed with a displacement only slightly higher than the standard one. During the trials, a strong vibration of the tripod foremast and the fire control system on it was revealed. During daily service, the speed on the high seas reached about 31 kts.

They were originally classified as light cruisers, but were soon rerated as heavy cruisers.

The 70-mm main belt expanded between the end barbettes (8 m fwd of the "A" and 5 m aft of the "Y") and was closed with a 60-mm upper and 50-mm fore or 40-mm aft lower bulkheads. 50-mm thick flat main deck was connected to the upper edge of the main belt. The aft end outside the citadel was protected by a 20-mm lower deck with 30-mm slopes. The barbettes and communication tube were protected by 70-mm armor above and 60-mm armor below the upper deck. The turrets had 80-mm protection. The CT had 100-mm sides, 40-mm deck and 50-mm roof. The director had 80-mm sides and 60-mm roof.

1937-1938, both: - 2 x 2 - 100/47, 4 x 1 - 40/39, 4 x 1 - 12.7 MG; + 4 x 2 - 37/54 Breda 1932, 4 x 2 - 13.2 MG.

1942, *Trento*: - 4 x 2 - 13.2 MG; + 4 x 1 - 20/65 Breda 1940.

1943, *Trieste*: - 4 x 2 - 13.2 MG; + 8 x 1 - 20/65 Breda 1940.

Trento 15.6.1942 was damaged by a torpedo from British Beaufort torpedo bomber taking off from Malta, and 4 hours later sunk by two torpedoes from British submarine *Umbra*. *Trieste* was badly damaged 21.11.1941 by a torpedo from British submarine *Utmost*; 10.4.1943 sunk at La Maddalena by US B-24 bombers.

ZARA class heavy cruisers

Fiume	STT, Trieste	29.4.1929	27.4.1930	23.11.1931	sunk 29.3.1941
Gorizia	OTO, Livorno	17.3.1930	28.12.1930	23.12.1932	damaged 10.4.1943, repair incomplete
Pola	OTO, Livorno	17.3.1931	5.12.1931	21.12.1932	sunk 29.3.1941
Zara	OTO, Muggiano	4.7.1929	27.4.1930	20.10.1931	sunk 29.3.1941

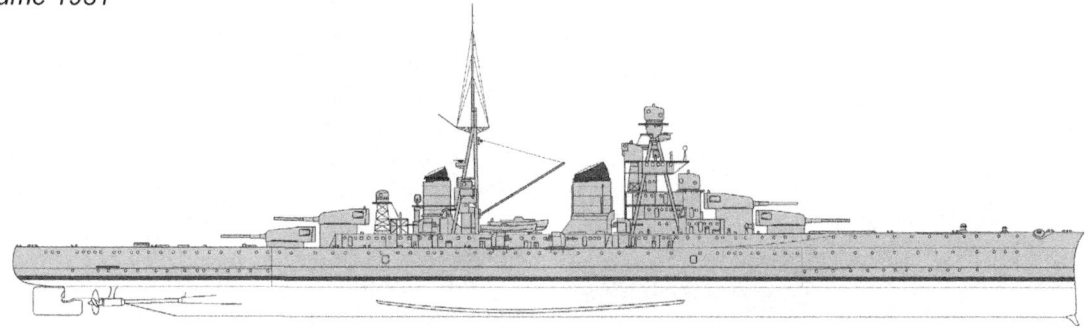

Fiume 1931

Pola 1939

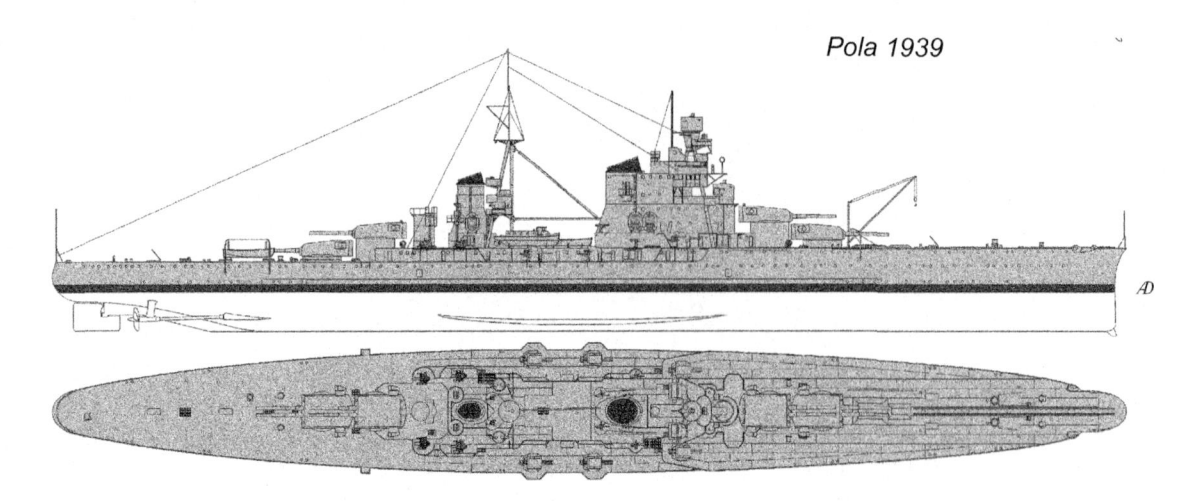

11326 / 13944 (*Fiume*) or 11712 / 14330 (*Gorizia*) or 11545 / 14133 (*Pola*) or 11680 / 14300 (*Zara*) t, 182.8 x 20.6 x 7.2 m, 2 sets Parsons geared steam turbines, 8 Yarrow (*Fiume*) or Thornycroft boilers, 95000 hp, 32 kts, 2362 t oil, 5230 nm (16 kts), complement 841; belt 150-100, decks 70-20, turrets 150-120, CT 150-70; 4 x 2 – 203/53 Ansaldo 1927, 8 x 2 – 100/47 OTO 1928, 4 x 1 – 40/39 Vickers-Terni 1917, 4 x 1 – 12.7 MG, 1 catapult, 3 seaplanes (M.41 or CANT.25, 1938- Ro.43)

One of the most successful 'Washington' cruisers. The starting point for the design was the *Trento* class, which was significantly redesigned in an effort to get a more balanced ship with protection adequate to the caliber of the main guns. Initially, it was supposed to increase the thickness of the belt to 200 mm, however, even with a decrease in the designed speed to 32 kts, the "Treaty's" 10000 t turned out to be exceeded by almost 4000 t. They began to scale down the design: a high free-board flush-decked hull was abandoned in favor of a lower free board, with a rather short forecastle, which gave a gain of several hundred tons, although it had negative effect on seaworthiness. The thickness of the belt was reduced to 150 mm, the TTs originally included in the design were cancelled.

Significant savings were achieved due to lighter machinery previously designed for the 1st and 2nd classes of *Condottieri* scouts. Although the listed measures made it possible to significantly reduce the standard displacement, it continued to exceed the Treaty limits by about 1500 t.

Gorizia 1938

Without advertising the design overload, the Italians officially announced the 10000-t displacement of the new cruisers of the 1928-1929 Programme (*Zara* and *Fiume*), followed by *Gorizia* of 1929-1930 Programme and *Pola* of 1930-1931 Programme. The last ship was intended to be used as a flagship and differed slightly from the others in having an enlarged fore superstructure integrated with the fore funnel.

The *Zara* class cruisers turned out to be one of the most protected 'Washington' cruisers. The mass of armor was 2700 t, three times more than on *Trento*.

As already mentioned, the machinery repeated the structure adopted on the 1st and 2nd classes of *Condottieri* scouts, only the number of boilers was increased from 6 to 8, but differed in an arrangement: for the first time in the Italian Navy, the staggered arrangement was used on *Zara*. From bow to stern followed: No1 boiler room (2 boilers); No1 engine room (starboard shaft turbine set) and No2 boiler room (1 boiler) on the starboard and port sides respectively; No3 and No4 boiler rooms (2 boilers each); No5 boiler room (1 boiler) and No2 engine room (port shaft turbine set). Although the normal long-term machinery power was 76000 hp, with the possibility of forcing up to 95000 hp, during trials the power reached 120000 hp, and the speed was 33-35.2 kts; during the service the cruisers reached about 29-30 kts.

In terms of armament, the *Zara* class ships differed from their predecessors with new 203-mm M1929 guns, using a heavier 125-kg projectile versus 113-kg on *Trento*.

Paradoxically, these ships were originally ranked according to the Italian classification as light cruisers. The absurdity of such an attribution was obvious, and they were very quickly reclassified first into the category of armored, to distinguish from the comparable, but the much less protected *Trento* class, and then heavy cruisers.

The 150-mm main belt, tapering to 100 mm at the lower edge, ran from the fore side of the "A" to the aft side of the "Y" barbettes and was closed by 120-mm

ITALY

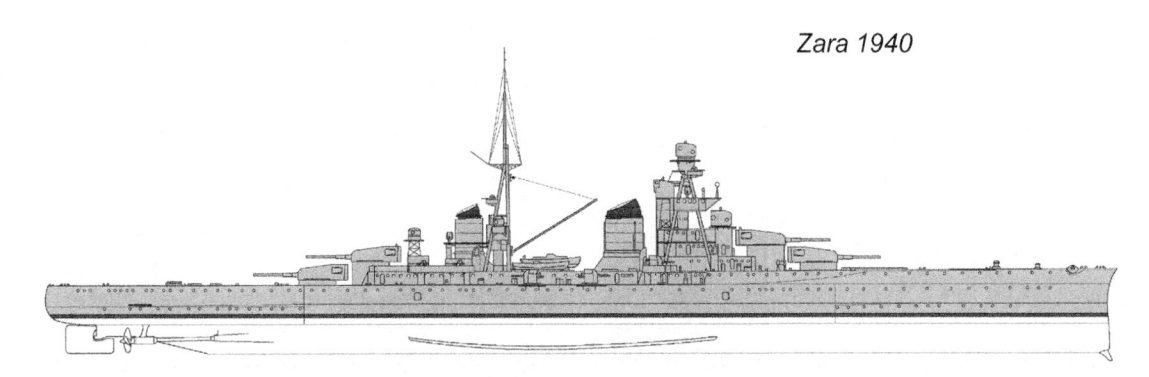

Zara 1940

bulkheads (90-mm below the waterline), it was covered by a 70-mm main deck. The entire freeboard above the main belt had 30-mm thickness, the upper deck was 20-mm. The turrets had 150-mm faces, 75-mm sides and 70-mm crowns. Barbettes had 150-mm protection above the upper deck, 140-mm between the upper and main decks and 120-mm below the main deck. The CT had 150-mm sides, 80-mm roof and 70-mm deck. The director had 120-mm vertical and 95-mm horizontal protection. The steering gear was protected by a 20-mm lower deck with 30-mm slopes.

1937, all: - 2 x 2 - 100/47, 4 x 1 - 40/39, 4 x 1 - 12.7 MG; + 4 x 2 - 37/54 Breda 1932, 4 x 2 - 13.2 MG.

Summer 1940, all: + 2 x 1 - 120/15 OTO 1934.

1942, *Gorizia*: - 2 x 1 - 120/15; + 2 x 2 - 37/54 Breda 1938.

Pola 15.12.1940 was damaged by British air bombs at Naples and was under repair until early March 1941.

Three ships of this class were lost in the Battle of Matapan 28-29.3.1941. By the evening of the 28.9.1941, *Pola* was damaged by a torpedo from British Albacore torpedo bomber from the aircraft carrier *Formidable* and lost speed. On the night 29.9.1941 she was sunk by a torpedo from British destroyer *Jervis*. *Zara* and *Fiume*, which arrived to her aid late in the evening of 28.9, were badly damaged by gunfire from British battleships *Barham*, *Warspite* and *Valiant*. *Fiume* was sunk immediately, *Zara* 29.3.1941 was finished off by a torpedo from British destroyer *Jervis*.

Gorizia was badly damaged 10.4.1943 by three bombs from US B-24 bombers, and by September 1943 was still under repair at Spezia. Scuttled by crew 8.9.1943, later salvaged by the Germans. Sunk again in the same place 26.6.1944 by Italian-manned British *'Chariot'* human torpedoes, launched from MTB *MS74*.

BOLZANO heavy cruiser

| **Bolzano** | Ansaldo, Genoa | 11.6.1930 | 31.8.1932 | 19.8.1933 | damaged 13.8.1942, repair incomplete |

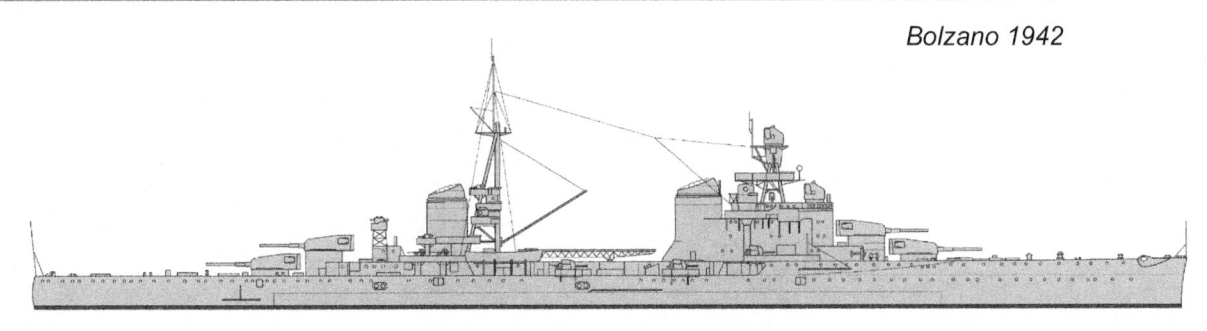

Bolzano 1942

10890 / 13665 t, 196.9 x 20.6 x 6.8 m, 4 sets Parsons geared steam turbines, 10 Yarrow-Ansaldo boilers, 150000 hp, 36 kts, 2224 t oil, 4430 nm (16 kts), complement 725; belt 70, decks 50-20, turrets 80, CT 100-40; 4 x 2 – 203/53 Ansaldo 1929, 8 x 2 – 100/47 OTO 1928, 2 x 1 – 40/39 Vickers-Terni 1917, 4 x 2 – 13.2 MG, 8 – 533 TT (aw, beam, 12), 1 catapult, 3 seaplanes (CANT.25 or M.41, 1938- Ro.43).

Bolzano was built according to the 1929-1930 Programme and was a development of the *Trento* class cruisers with increased speed. The main differences were a hull with a lengthened forecastle as on *Zara* instead of flush-deck ones, an improved machinery, forced to 150000 hp, a new fore superstructure, as on *Pola*, new M1929 guns instead of M1924 on *Trento*.

Although the machinery power was increased, the number of boilers was reduced from 12 to 10 due to the greater steam capacity of each boiler. The general layout of the machinery basically repeated *en echelon* scheme, adopted on *Trento*, but now the fore group included not 8, but 6 boilers. The second, aft group included, as before, 4 boilers in two rooms, but the internal arrangement was different from the predecessors. This was due to the need to place funnels at a greater distance to move

Bolzano prewar

the catapult from the forecastle, where it was exposed to waves on *Trento* class, to the midships. Protection practically did not differ from that adopted on *Trento*.

Bolzano became the fastest Italian 'Washington' cruiser: on trials she reached 36.81 kts with a power of 173772 hp. During the daily service, the speed also turned out to be quite high, reaching about 33 kts.

Bolzano 13.8.1942 was damaged by a torpedo from British submarine *Unbroken*. They decided to combine the repair of battle damages with the conversion to a semi-aircraft carrier intended to carry and launch 12 Re.2000 fighters. Landing aircraft on the deck was not provided, after completing the task, they had to fly to the nearest coastal airfield. To launch aircraft, two catapults were provided on the forecastle. It was planned to store the fighters openly on the deck, while all the superstructures forward of the fore funnel had to be dismantled, and the fore funnel was divided into two, moved to the sides. All old armament was to be removed and replaced with 10 single 90-mm/50 guns and 20 twin 20-mm/65 MGs. The displacement after conversion should be reduced to 9000 / 11800 t. The conversion did not start.

The 70-mm main belt was located between the fore side of the "A" and the aft side of the "Y" barbettes and was closed by 60-mm upper and 50-mm fore or 40-mm aft lower bulkheads. A flat main deck 50-mm thick was connected to the upper edge of the main belt. The ends of the ship outside the citadel were protected by a 20-mm lower deck with 30-mm slopes. The barbettes and communication tube had 70-mm protection above and 60-mm below the upper deck. The turrets had 80-mm protection. The CT had 100-mm sides, 40-mm deck and 50-mm roof. The director had 80-mm sides and 60-mm roof.

1937: - 2 x 2 - 100/47, 2 x 1 - 40/39; + 4 x 2 - 37/54 Breda 1932.
1942: - 4 x 2 - 13.2 MG; + 4 x 1 - 20/65 Breda 1940.

25.8.1941, *Bolzano* was torpedoed by British submarine *Triumph* and was under repair for 3 months. 13.8.1942 she was again damaged by a torpedo from British submarine *Unbroken* and ran aground. She was salvaged a month later and towed to La Spezia, but repairs and a planned conversion to a semi-aircraft carrier were never completed. 9.9.1943 *Bolzano* was captured at La Spezia by the Germans. She was sunk on 22 June 1944 at La Spezia by a British 'Chariot Mk I' human torpedo launched from Italian destroyer *Grecale*.

QUARTO scout cruiser

| **Quarto** | R. Arsenale di Venezia | 14.11.1909 | 19.8.1911 | 31.3.1913 | stricken 1.1939 |

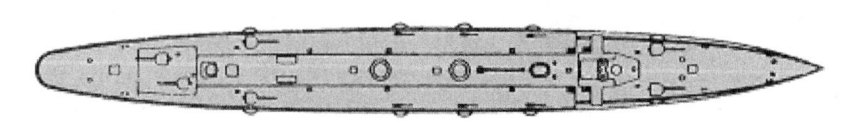

Quarto 1914

3271 / 3442 t, 131.6 x 12.8 x 4.1 m, 4 Parsons steam turbines, 10 Blechynden boilers, 25000 hp, 28 kts, 2300 nm (15 kts), complement 247; deck 40, CT 100; 6 x 1 – 120/50 Armstrong 1909, 3 x 1 – 76/50 Vickers 1909, 3 x 2 – 13.2 MG, 2 – 450 TT (sub, beam), 200 mines, 1 seaplane (CANT.25 or M.41).

The best protected cruiser of the Italian Navy during the First World War. *Quarto* was commissioned as a scout and reclassified as a cruiser in September 1938. 8 boilers operated on liquid fuel and 2 on mixed fuel.

The main protection consisted of a 40-mm deck with slopes.

ITALY

Ex-German TARANTO light cruiser

Taranto (ex-Strassburg)	KMW Wilhelmshaven, Germany	4.1910	24.8.1911	(9.10.1912) / 20.7.1920	scuttled 9.9.1943

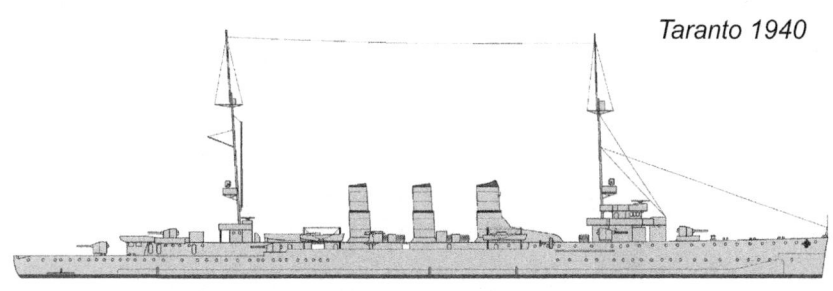

Taranto 1940

4564 / 5281 t, 138.7 x 13.5 x 5.1 m, 2 Marine steam turbines, 14 Marine boilers, 13000 hp, 21 kts, 1330 t coal + 130 t oil, 5820 nm (12 kts), complement 486; belt 60-18, deck 60-20, shields 50, CT 100; 7 x 1 – 149/43 SK C/09, 2 x 1 – 76/40 Ansaldo 1917, 2 x 2 – 13.2 MG, 120 mines.

The German *Strassburg* of the *Magdeburg* class, received for reparations 20.7.1920 but commissioned by the Italian Navy only 2.6.1925. In 1936-1937, during the modernization, the power of the machinery was reduced from 27000 to 13000 hp and the maximum speed from 27.5 to 21 kts.

The 60-mm belt protected the machinery and magazines for about 80 % of the ship's length, its thickness was reduced to 18 mm in the boa, there was a 40-mm transverse bulkhead between the 60-mm and 18-mm parts of the belt, the aft part of the waterline was not protected. The 40-20-mm armored deck was connected to the lower edge of the belt with 60-40-mm slopes. The guns were protected by 50-mm shields, ammunition tubes had 20-mm armor. The CT had 100-mm sides and 20-mm roof.

1940-1941: + 4 x 2 - 20/65 Breda 1935, 3 x 2 - 13.2 MG. In 1942, *Taranto* was laid up into reserve. 9.9.1943 she was scuttled by her own crew at La Spezia to avoid capture, salvaged by the Germans and sunk again 23.10.1943 by Allied aircraft. Salvaged again by the Germans, but 23.9.1944 again sunk by Allied aircraft.

Ex-German BARI protected cruiser

Bari (ex-Pillau, ex-Muravyov-Amurskiy)	Schichau, Danzig, Germany	1913	11.4.1914	(14.12.1914) / 20.7.1920	damaged 28.6.1943, never repaired

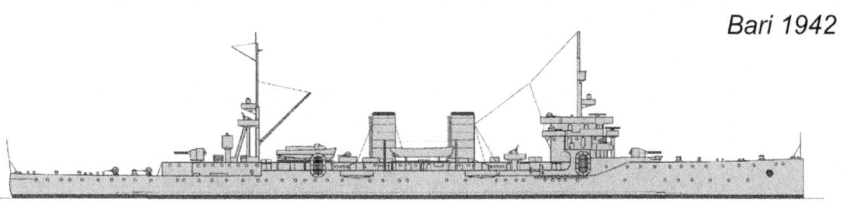

Bari 1942

4248 / 5220 t, 135.3 x 13.6 x 6.0 m, 2 Marine steam turbines, 4 Yarrow boilers, 21000 hp, 24.5 kts, 1500 t oil, 4000 nm (14 kts), complement 440; deck 80-20, shields 50, CT 75; 8 x 1 – 149/43 SK C/09, 3 x 1 – 76/40 Ansaldo 1917, 3 x 2 – 20/65 Breda 1935, 3 x 2 – 13.2 MG, 120 mines.

Ordered by Russia in Germany as *Muravyov-Amurskiy*, confiscated by Germany after the outbreak of World War I and renamed *Pillau*. She was transferred to Italy 20.7.1920 for reparations and commissioned in 1924 as a TS. In 1934-1935, Bari was converted to 'colonial' cruiser at La Spezia. By the spring of 1943, the conversion of *Bari* to AA ship began; she was supposed to carry 8 single 90-mm/50, 8 37-mm/54 and 8 20-mm/70 guns.

The main deck was 80-mm thick amidships and 20-mm thick at the ends and had 40-mm slopes. The CT had 75-mm sides and 50-mm roof. The guns were protected by 50-mm shields.

1940-1941: + 6 x 1 - 20/65 Breda 1940.

Bari in wartime

Bari was heavily damaged by US aircraft 28.6.1943 at Livorno and sank in shallow water two days later. Salvage work was halted after September 1943. The wreck was again damaged 8.9.1943 by the Italians to avoid capture, and partly scrapped by the Germans in 1944.

CONDOTTIERI A (1st) group (ALBERTO DI GIUSSANO class) light cruisers

Alberico da Barbiano	Ansaldo, Genoa	16.4.1928	23.8.1930	9.6.1931	sunk 13.12.1941
Alberto di Giussano	Ansaldo, Genoa	29.3.1928	27.4.1930	5.2.1931	sunk 13.12.1941
Bartolomeo Colleoni	Ansaldo, Genoa	21.6.1928	21.12.1930	10.2.1932	sunk 19.7.1940
Giovanni delle Bande Nere	R Cantieri di Castellamare di Stabia	31.10.1928	27.4.1930	4.1931	sunk 1.4.1942

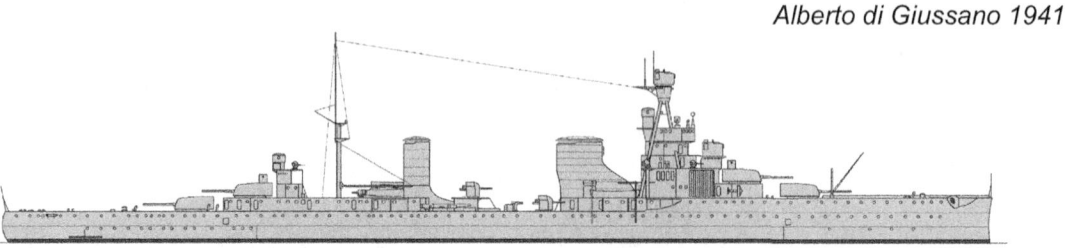

Alberto di Giussano 1941

5155 (*Alberico da Barbiano*) or 5110 (*Alberto di Giussano*) or 5170 (*Bartolomeo Colleoni*) or 5130 (*Giiovanni delle Bande Nere*) / 6844 t, 169.3 x 15.5 x 5.3 m, 2 sets Beluzzo geared steam turbines, 6 Yarrow boilers, 95000 hp, 36.5 kts, 1230 t oil, 3800 nm (18 kts), complement 520; belt 24+18, decks 20, turrets 23, CT 40-25; 4 x 2 – 152/53 Ansaldo 1926, 3 x 2 – 100/47 OTO 1928, 4 x 2 – 13.2 MG, 2 x 2 – 533 TT, 1 catapult, 2 seaplanes (CANT.25 or M.41, 1937-1939- Ro.43), 84 – 138 mines (except *Alberto di Giussano*).

The first Italian cruisers built after the First World War. They were created in response to the emergence of new French leaders of *Jaguar*, *Lion* and *Aigle* classes. The command of the Italian Navy believed that in order to act against them, it was necessary to create large scout cruisers in addition to the '*Navigatori*' class destroyers. It was assumed that such ships with not less speed than their 37-kt French opponents, due to stronger armament would have unconditional superiority. The project of scouts, which had as its starting point the greatly enlarged hull of '*Navigatori*' class destroyer, was transformed into the *Giovanni delle Bande Nere* class light cruiser, also known as the 1st series of the '*Condottieri*' class.

To achieve a speed of 37 kts, the designers made a number of changes, often unjustified. Thus, the streamlines were closer to that of a destroyer, than a cruiser, with an L/B ratio of more than 10, and were combined with a fairly light hull structure. As a result, during the service, problems with the longitudinal strength of the hull repeatedly arose. The machinery of extremely high unit power (at the time of construction the highest power in the Italian Navy) also had a light 'destroyer' construction. From the '*Navigatori*' class, the design of the scout inherited the *'en echelon'* layout of the machinery, all boilers were installed on the center line.

When designing the protection scheme for new cruisers, separate armor arrangement was used: in addition to the 24-mm belt between the end turrets, an 18-mm longitudinal armored bulkhead was located at some distance inside the hull.

The main combat power of these ships was 8 152-mm M1926 guns in four twin turrets with a maximal elevation angle of 45°. To save weight, both guns were mounted in a common slide, which predetermined a significant spread of shells.

To adjust the fire of the 152-mm guns, the cruisers were equipped with seaplanes, placed, as on heavy cruisers of the *Trento* class, in the bow. Since there was no place for a deck hangar forward of the No1 turret, it was arranged in the fore superstructure, from where the seaplane moved along special railway bypassing the turrets on a trolley to the catapult on the forecastle.

Alberto di Giussano prewar

ITALY

Four ships were ordered according to the 1927-1928 Programme. On trials, all of them significantly exceeded the contract speed and the power of the machinery, and one of them, *Alberico da Barbiano* kept 39.6 kts with a power of 112760 hp in 8 hours, and developed 42.05 kts in 32 minutes with a power of 123479 hp, becoming the fastest cruiser in the world. These results, outstanding at first glance, fade somewhat against the background of real speed during the daily service, not exceeding 30 kts. The ships of the 1st series of the '*Condottieri*' class were not so successful, with predictably insufficiently seaworthiness, with a small supply of fuel and poor habitability due to the dense layout. Too weak protection and turned out to be moderate speed deprived them of the opportunity to act on equal terms against the cruisers of the main enemy in the Mediterranean, Great Britain. A clear confirmation of this is the sinking of *Bartolomeo Colleoni* by Australian light cruiser *Sydney* with only 32-kt contract speed. The second Italian cruiser, *Giovanni delle Bande Nere*, saved in this battle only that the Australian ship had used up all her ammunition.

At the end of the 1930s, all 4 ships underwent strengthening of the hull structure after damages in stormy weather.

The main 24-mm belt extended to the main deck between the aft side of the "A" barbette and the fore side of the "X" barbette, the parts of belt between the fore and aft sides of the "A" barbette and the fore side of the "X" barbette and the aft side of the "Y" barbette extended only up to the lower deck and had 20-mm thickness. Inside the hull, 2 m from the side, 18-mm longitudinal splinter bulkhead was placed. The belt was closed with 20-mm bulkheads. A flat 20-mm main deck was connected to the upper edge of the main belt. The directors had 25-mm protection. The turrets had 23-mm armor. The CT had 40-25-mm sides and 30-mm protection of the communication tube.

1938-1939, all: + 4 x 2 - 20/65 Breda 1935, 2 DCT (40 DC).

Bartolomeo Colleoni was sunk NW of Crete by Australian cruiser *Sydney* and British destroyers *Havock, Hyperion, Hasty, Hero, Hereward,* and *Ilex* 19.7.1940. Received a 152-mm projectile hit in the engine room, lost speed and was finished off by destroyer torpedoes. *Alberico da Barbiano* and *Alberto di Giussano* were sunk by torpedoes from British destroyers *Legion, Maori, Sikh,* and Dutch destroyer *Isaac Sweers* while transporting petrol to Libya 13.12.1941 at Cape Bon. The first received three torpedo hits from *Sikh*, the second received one torpedo hit from *Legion*. *Giovanni delle Bande Nere* was sunk 1.4.1942 off Stromboli by British submarine *Urge*. She received two torpedo hits and broke in half.

CONDOTTIERI B (2nd) group (LUIGI CADORNA class) light cruisers

Luigi Cadorna	CRDA, Trieste	19.9.1930	30.9.1931	11.8.1933	stricken 5.1951
Armando Diaz	OTO, Muggiano	28.7.1930	10.7.1932	29.4.1933	sunk 25.2.1941

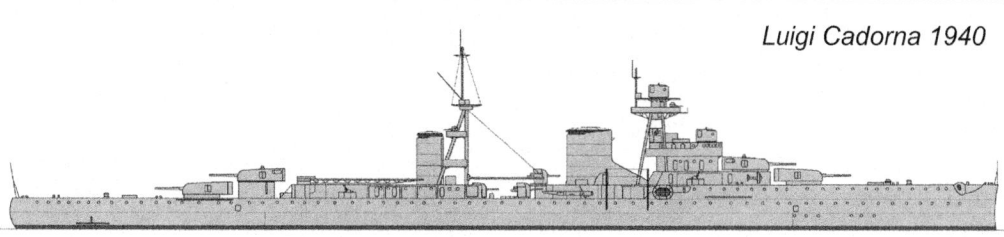

Luigi Cadorna 1940

5232 / 7001 (*Luigi Cadorna*) or 5321 / 7080 (*Armando Diaz*) t, 169.3 x 15.5 x 5.5 m, 2 sets Parsons geared steam turbines, 6 Yarrow boilers, 95000 hp, 36.5 kts, 1211 t oil, 2930 (*Luigi Cadorna*) or 3088 (*Armando Diaz*) nm (16 kts), complement 544; belt 24+18, decks 20, turrets 40, CT 70-25; 4 x 2 – 152/53 OTO 1929, 3 x 2 – 100/47 OTO 1928, 2 x 1 – 40/39 Vickers-Terni 1917, 4 x 2 – 13.2 MG, 2 x 2 – 533 TT, 1 catapult, 2 seaplanes (CANT.25 or M.41, 1938-1939- Ro.43)

Two ships of the 1929-1930 Programme were built according to a modified design of the 1st "*Condottieri*" series. Measures were taken to reduce the top weight, which had a positive effect on stability, and the strength of the hull was increased. The height of the fore superstructure was reduced due to the abandonment of the seaplane hangar. The fixed catapult was transferred from the forecastle deck to the aft superstructure between the aft funnel and the No3 turret, setting it at an angle of 30° to the center line. There was no hangar, the seaplanes were stored openly in a special area next to the catapult. The composition and arrangement of armament was not changed, with the exception of 152-mm/53 guns of the new model M1929 in more spacious turrets.

Both cruisers of the *Luigi Cadorna* class exceeded the contract speed on trials, however, like the ships of the 1st '*Condottieri*' series, by the beginning of the war their speed did not exceed 31-32 kts.

Cruisers of the 1929-1930 Programme turned out to be somewhat more successful than their predecessors, but during their construction it turned out that they were inferior to the new light cruisers of other countries in everything except speed, so the further development of the scouts in the Italian Navy was abandoned in favor of

Armando Diaz 1934

creating larger and well-protected cruisers.

The main 24-mm belt extended to the main deck between the aft side of the "A" barbette and the fore side of the "X" barbette, the parts of belt between the fore and aft sides of the "A" barbette and the fore side of the "X" barbette and the aft side of the "Y" barbette extended only up to the lower deck and had 20-mm thickness. Inside the hull, 2 m from the side, 18-mm longitudinal splinter bulkhead was placed. The belt was closed with 20-mm bulkheads. A flat 20-mm main deck was connected to the upper edge of the main belt. The directors had 25-mm protection. The turrets had 40-mm armor. The CT had 70-mm sides and 25-mm roof; the communication tube had 30-mm protection.

1938, both: - 2 x 1 - 40/39; + 4 x 2 - 20/65 Breda 1935, 2 DCT (40 DC).

Late 1943, *Luigi Cadorna*: - 4 x 2 - 13.2 MG, catapult with seaplanes; + 4 x 1 - 20/70 Oerlikon.

1944, *Luigi Cadorna*: - 2 x 2 - 533 TT.

Armando Diaz was sunk 25.2.1941 off Sfax by British submarine *Upright*.

CONDOTTIERI C (3rd) group (RAIMONDO MONTECUCCOLI class) light cruisers

Raimondo Montecuccoli	Ansaldo, Genoa	1.10.1931	2.8.1934	30.6.1935	stricken 6.1964
Muzio Attendolo	CRDA, Trieste	10.4.1931	9.9.1934	7.8.1935	damaged 13.8.1942, repair incomplete

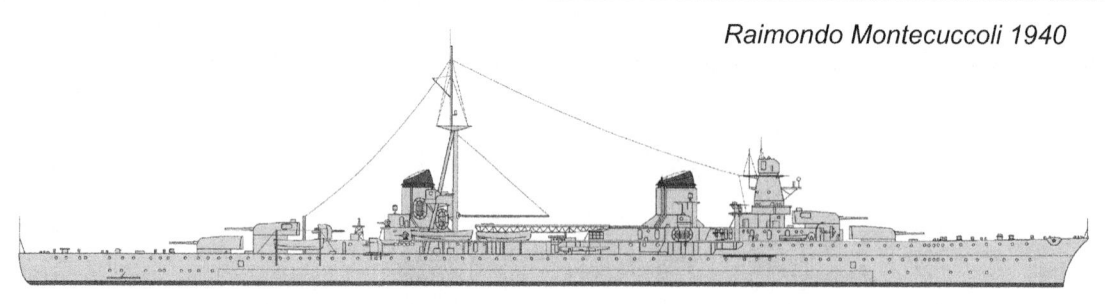

Raimondo Montecuccoli 1940

7405 / 8853 (*Raimondo Montecuccoli*) or 8848 (*Muzio Attendolo*) t, 182.2 x 16.6 x 6.0 m, 2 sets Beluzzo (*Raimondo Montecuccoli*) or Parsons geared steam turbines, 6 Yarrow boilers, 106000 hp, 37 kts, 1297 (*Raimondo Montecuccoli*) or 1275 (*Muzio Attendolo*) t oil, 4120 nm (18 kts), complement 588-650; belt 60+25, decks 30-20, turrets 70, CT 100-40; 4 x 2 – 152/53 OTO 1929, 3 x 2 – 100/47 OTO 1928, 4 x 2 – 37/54 Breda 1932, 4 x 2 – 13.2 MG, 2 x 2 – 533 TT, 1 catapult, 2 seaplanes (CANT.25 or M.41, 1938-1939- Ro.43), 2 DCT (12), 112 – 146 mines.

Built according to the 1930-1931 Programme. An attempt to create a more balanced ship than the "*Condottieri*" of the first two series. Due to the increased more than by 2000 t displacement, it was possible to significantly improve seaworthiness and protection. The mass of armor compared to the predecessors was increased by more than 2.5 times: from 575 to 1350 t.

The armor scheme basically repeated that adopted on the '*Condottieri*' of the 1st and 2nd series, but with a significant increase in the thickness of its elements: the external armor belt to 60 mm, the longitudinal bulkhead between the end barbettes to 25 mm and 30 mm abreast the magazines. In addition, the plating above the armor belt over the entire height of the freeboard had a thickness of 20 mm. Unfortunately, the increase in vertical protection was not complemented by any adequate increase in horizontal protection. As a result, the cruiser did not have an invulnerability zone from 203-mm guns and a very narrow zone between 69 and 81 cables from 152-mm guns.

The armament structure remained practically unchanged, only the catapult was moved to a new place between the funnels. It was partially rotatable and could rotate at an angle up to 30° from the center line.

The *En echelon* layout of the machinery was not changed, however, its power was slightly increased to compensate for the increase in displacement. To increase the damage resistance of the stretched machinery space, all boilers were placed in separate rooms, except for boiler room No1 with two boilers. On trials, *Montecuccoli* exceeded the contractual 37 kts and reached 38.7 kts, however, her displacement was less than the standard one, and the power of the machinery exceeded the design one by 18%. During service, they easily kept a speed of 34 kts.

The ships of the 3rd "*Condottieri*" series turned out to be appeared much more successful than their

ITALY

predecessors and became the first full-fledged light cruisers of the Italian Navy.

The main 60-mm belt reached the main deck between the center of the "A" barbette and the fore side of the "X" barbette, a 25-mm (30-mm abreast the magazines) longitudinal splinter bulkhead was located inside the hull 2 m from the side. The belt was closed with 40-mm upper and 20-mm lower bulkheads. The entire freeboard above the main belt and the platform between the lower edge of the belt and the longitudinal splinter bulkhead had 20-mm thickness. A flat 30-mm main deck was connected to the upper edge of the main belt, the main deck outside the citadel had a thickness of 20 mm. The barbettes had 50-mm protection above the weather decks, 45-mm between the weather and main decks and 30-mm below the main deck. The CT had 100-mm sides, 30-mm roof and 25-mm deck, rest of the fore superstructure had 50-40-mm protection. The turrets had 70-mm armor.

7.1943, *Raimondo Montecuccoli*: + EC.3/ter radar. Late 1943, *Raimondo Montecuccoli*: - 4 x 2 - 13.2 MG; + 10 x 1 - 20/70 Oerlikon.

Raimondo Montecuccoli 1938

1944, *Raimondo Montecuccoli*: - 2 x 2 - 533 TT; + 2 x 1 - 20/70 Oerlikon, Type 291 radar.
Early 1945, *Raimondo Montecuccoli*: - catapult with seaplanes.
Raimondo Montecuccoli was badly damaged by US air bombs 4.12.1942 at Naples and was under repair until mid-1943. *Muzio Attendolo* 13.8.1942 was damaged by a torpedo from British submarine *Unbroken*, the bow was torn off by an explosion. During repairs at Naples 4.12.1942 she was sunk by US air bombs.

CONDOTTIERI D (4th) group (EMANUELE FILIBERTO DUCA D'AOSTA class) light cruisers

Emanuele Filiberto Duca d'Aosta	OTO, Livorno	29.10.1932	22.4.1934	13.7.1935	to the USSR 3.1949 (Kerch)
Eugenio di Savoia	Ansaldo, Genoa	6.7.1933	16.3.1935	16.1.1936	to Greece 7.1951 (Elli)

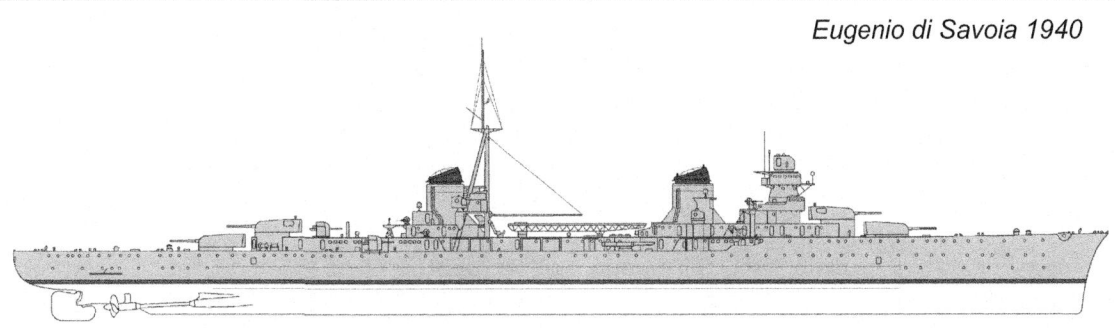

Eugenio di Savoia 1940

8317 / 10374 (*Emanuele Filiberto Duca d'Aosta*) or 8610 / 10672 (*Eugenio di Savia*) t, 186.9 x 17.5 x 6.5 m, 2 sets Parsons or Beluzzo (*Eugenio di Savoia*) geared steam turbines, 6 Thornycroft or Yarrow (*Eugenio di Savoia*) boilers, 110000 hp, 36.5 kts, 1653 t oil, 3900 nm (14 kts), complement 578-694; belt 70+35, decks 35-30, turrets 90, CT 100-25; 4 x 2 - 152/53 OTO 1929, 3 x 2 - 100/47 OTO 1928, 4 x 2 - 37/54 Breda 1932, 6 x 2 - 13.2 MG, 2 x 3 - 533 TT, 1 catapult, 2 seaplanes (CANT.25 or M.41, 1938-1939- Ro.43), 2 DCT (12), 112 - 146 mines.

The ships of the 1931-1933 Programme were built according to the *Montecuccoli* design modified in the direction of further strengthening the protection. The mass of armor increased to 1700 t was used to thicken the belt to 70 mm and the internal armored bulkhead up to 35 mm, but the thickness of horizontal protection increased only by 5 mm. As a result, the new ships were characterized by the same drawback as their predecessors, a too narrow immunity zone from the fire of 152-mm guns and the absence of such a zone

Eugenio di Savoia

Emanuele Filiberto Duca d'Aosta 1942

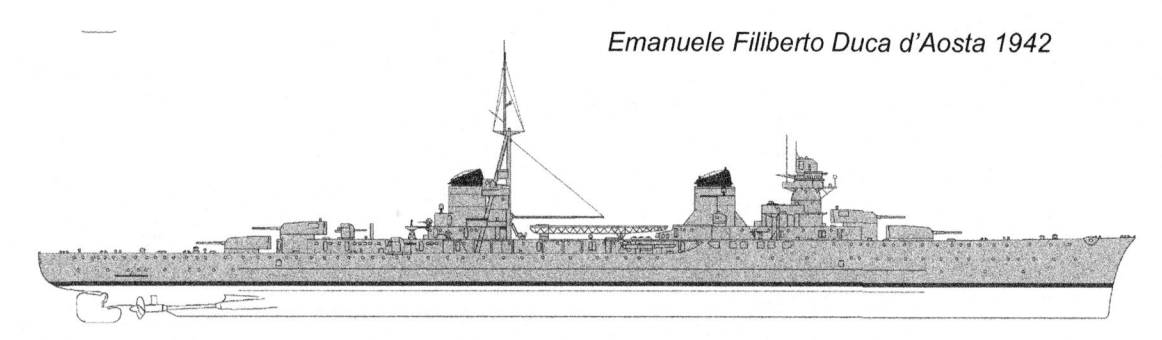

under the fire of 203-mm guns. The increase in the mass of armor led to an increase in displacement by about 1000 t. To maintain speed at the level of 36-37 kts, the power of the machinery was increased to 110000 hp. As a result, some changes took place in its layout: on the previous "*Condottieri*" of the first three series, two thirds of the boilers were placed in the fore group, and one third in the aft; accordingly, the fore funnel, which contained the smoke ducts of four boilers, was noticeably wider, than the aft one. On the 4th "*Condottieri*" class the boilers were placed more evenly: three for each funnel of the same size. Each boiler was located in a separate compartment.

Both cruisers exceeded the contracted trial speed, but like their predecessors, with a displacement close to the standard one, and the forced power of the machinery; the actual sea speed was about 34 kts.

The main 70-mm belt reached the main deck between the center of the "A" barbette and the fore side of the "X" barbette, a 30-mm longitudinal splinter bulkhead (35-mm abreast the magazines) was located inside the hull 2 m from the side. The belt was closed with 50-mm upper and 30-mm lower bulkheads. The entire freeboard above the main belt and the platform between the lower edge of the belt and the longitudinal splinter bulkhead had 20-mm thickness. A flat 35-mm main deck was connected to the upper edge of the main belt, the main deck outside the citadel had 30-mm thickness. The barbettes had 70-mm protection above the weather decks, 60-mm between the weather and main decks and 50-mm below the main deck. The CT had 100-mm sides, 30-mm roof and 25-mm deck and a communication tube with 30-20-mm protection. The rest of the fore superstructure had 50-40-mm protection. The turrets had 90-mm armor.

Mid-1943, *Emanuele Filiberto Duca d'Aosta*: + FuMo 39 radar. 8.1943, *Eugenio di Savoia*: + EC.3/ter radar. Autumn 1943, both: - 6 x 2 - 13.2 MG; + 10 x 1 - 20/70 Oerlikon.

1944, both: - 2 x 3 - 533 TT, catapult with seaplanes; + 2 x 1 - 20/70 Oerlikon. Summer 1944, *Emanuele Filiberto Duca d'Aosta*: - FuMo39 radar; + Type 286 radar.

Early 1945, *Emanuele Filiberto Duca d'Aosta*: - Type 286 radar.

Eugenio di Savoia 4.12.1942 was damaged at Naples by US air bombs and was under repair until the spring of 1943.

CONDOTTIERI E (5th) group (LOUIGI DI SAVOIA DUCA DEGLI ABRUZZI class) light cruisers

Luigi di Savoia Duca degli Abruzzi	OTO, Muggiano	28.12.1933	21.4.1936	1.12.1937	stricken 4.1961
Giuseppe Garibaldi	CRDA, Trieste	12.1933	21.4.1936	20.12.1937	stricken 11.1976

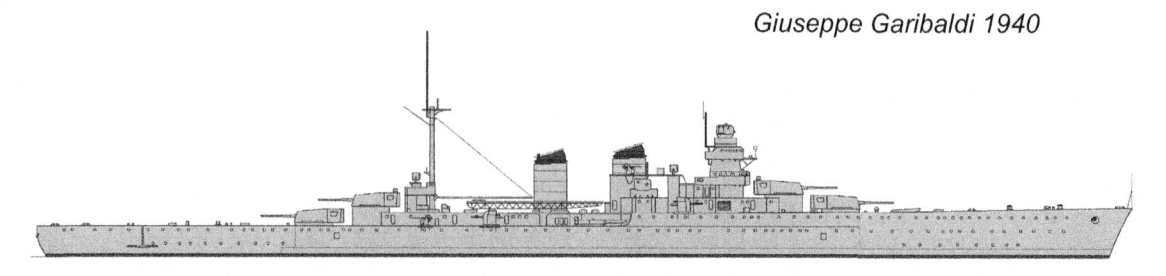

Giuseppe Garibaldi 1940

9440 / 11575 (*Luigi di Savoia Duca degli Abruzzi*) or 9050 / 11117 (*Giuseppe Garibaldi*) t, 187.0 x 18.9 x 6.8 m, 2 sets Parsons geared steam turbines, 8 Yarrow boilers, 100000 hp, 34 kts, 1700 t oil, 4125 nm (17 kts), complement 640-692; belt 100 + 30, decks 40 + 15-10, turrets 135, CT 140-30; (2 x 3 + 2 x 2) – 152/55 Ansaldo 1934, 4 x 2 – 100/47 OTO 1928, 4 x 2 – 37/54 Breda 1932, 4 x 2 – 13.2 MG, 2 x 3 – 533 TT, 2 catapults, 2 – 4 seaplanes (Ro.43, Ro.44), 2 DCT (12), 120 mines.

In the design of the cruisers of the 1932-1933 Programme, the emerging trend to increase the of armor protection of Italian light cruisers was further developed, and the designers for the first time reduced the design speed. Due to the increase in displacement by 1000

ITALY

t compared to the 4th class of the *"Condottieri"* and a decrease in the design speed by 2.5 kts they turned out, perhaps, the most successful of the pre-war Italian cruisers, which was not much inferior, and in some ways even surpassed foreign analogues.

On the new cruisers, the mass of armor reached 2131 t. The protection scheme as a whole repeated that used earlier, but *Garibaldi* had several fundamental differences. So, the side armor was traditionally made separate, but this time the outer belt had a thickness of only 30 mm, and the inner one, inclined at an angle of 12°, was much thicker being 100-mm. It was connected to the upper edge of the outer belt, and falling below the waterline, was bended, and adjoined to its lower edge. The transverse bulkheads were also made separate, but had a simpler design, consisting of parallel sheets, but in this case, the outer sheet was thinner than the inner one. Above the belt, the freeboard plating had a thickness of 20 mm, and the upper deck, for the first time on Italian cruisers, was made of 15-mm steel near the side and 10-mm closer to the centerline. The hull beam was increased by almost 1.5 m, which made it possible to place the boilers not on the centerline, but two abreast. On *Garibaldi,* the length of the machinery spaces turned out to be one and a half time less than on her predecessors, and this despite the fact that the arrangement scheme was *en echelon*. The reduction in the machinery length, in turn, allowed to more rationally place armament and reduce the length of the belt: the main gun turrets were shifted further from the ship's ends and the ends became noticeably lighter. The number of main guns was increased to 10 and, importantly, the new turrets finally managed to get rid of the vicious practice of placing guns in a common gun slide. The M1936 guns were new.

Due to re-planning of the machinery, there were no places left for an aviation catapult on the centerline amidships, so two had to be installed along the sides abreast the aft funnel. As well as on the 3rd and 4th *"Condottieri"* classes, they had limited turning angle. The hangar was not provided.

According to the 1939-1940 Programme, it was planned to build two cruisers close to the 5th *"Condottieri"* class cruisers (*Constanzo Ciano* and *Venezia*), but in June 1940 they were excluded from the Programme. The

Giuseppe Garibaldi 1938

main difference between these cruisers was to be higher machinery power and the transition to new 90-mm AA guns, the superstructure was to be almost unchanged.

The outer 30-mm belt reached the main deck between the center of the "A" barbette and the fore side of the "X" barbette, the 100-mm inner belt was inclined at an angle of 12° outside and was connected with its top to the upper side of the outer belt, bending below the waterline and connecting with its lower edge to the lower edge of the outer belt. The belt was closed with 30-mm outer and 100-mm inner bulkheads. The entire freeboard above the main belt was 20-mm thick. A flat 40-mm main deck was connected to the upper edge of the main belts, the upper deck was 15 mm, reducing to 10 mm near the centerline. The barbettes had 100-mm protection above the weather decks, 90-mm between the weather and main decks and 50-30-mm below the main deck. The CT had 140-mm sides, 70-mm roof, 25-mm deck and 30-mm protection of the communication tube, the rest of the fore superstructure had 50-40-mm protection. The turrets had 135-mm armor. The funnel uptakes had 50-20-mm protection.

1943, both: - 4 x 2 - 13.2 MG; + 4 x 2 - 20/65 Breda 1935, 2 x 1 - 20/65 Breda 1940. Summer 1943, *Luigi di Savoia Duca degli Abruzzi*: + FuMo 39G radar.

1944, both: - 2 x 3 - 533 TT, catapults, seaplanes; + 2 x 1 - 100/47 OTO 1937. 1944 - 1945, *Giuseppe Garibaldi*: + Type 286 radar. 1944 - 1945, *Luigi di Savoia Duca degli Abruzzi*: - FuMo 39G radar; + Type 286, Type 281 radars.

Giuseppe Garibaldi 27.7.1941 was hit by a torpedo from British submarine *Upholder*, was damaged and was under repair for 4 months.

CAPITANI ROMANI (ATTILIO REGOLO) class light cruisers

Attilio Regolo	OTO, Livorno	28.9.1939	28.8.1940	14.5.1942	to France 8.1948 (Châteaurenault)
Caio Mario	OTO, Livorno	28.9.1939	17.8.1941	-	completed as a hulk 1.1943
Claudio Druso	CT, Riva Trigoso	27.9.1939	-	-	cancelled 6.1940
Claudio Tiberio	OTO, Livorno	28.9.1939	-	-	cancelled 6.1940

Cornelio Silla	Ansaldo, Genoa	12.10.1939	28.6.1941	-	captured incomplete by Germany 9.1943
San Marco *(ex-Giulio Germanico)*	Cantieri di Castellamare di Stabia	3.4.1939	26.7.1941	19.1.1956	discarded 1971
Ottaviano Augusto	CNR, Ancona	23.9.1939	28.4.1941	-	captured incomplete by Germany 9.1943
Paolo Emilio	Ansaldo, Genoa	12.10.1939	-	-	cancelled 6.1940
Pompeo Magno	CNR, Ancona	23.9.1939	24.8.1941	4.6.1943	discarded 1980
Scipione Africano	OTO, Livorno	28.9.1939	12.1.1941	23.4.1943	to France 8.1948 (Guichen)
Ulpio Traiano	CNR, Palermo	28.9.1939	30.11.1942	-	sunk incomplete 3.1.1943
Vipsanio Agrippa	CT, Riva Trigoso	10.1939	-	-	cancelled 6.1940

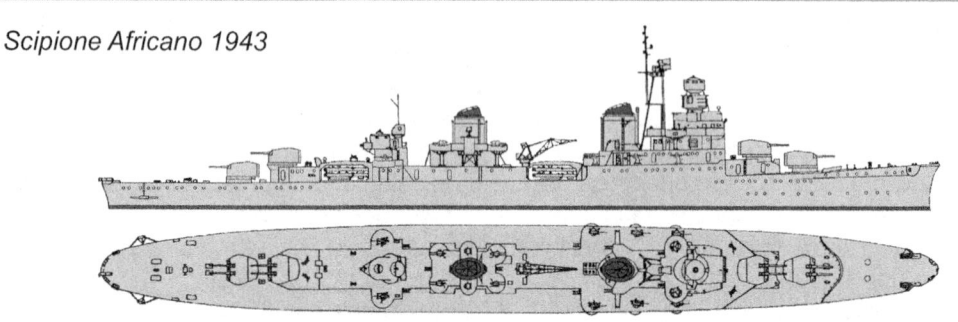

Scipione Africano 1943

3686 / 5334 t, 142.9 x 14.4 x 4.9 m, 2 sets Beluzzo or Parsons (*Ottaviano Augusto, Pompeo Magno*) geared steam turbines, 4 Thornycroft boilers, 110000 hp, 40 kts, 1387 t oil, 3000 nm (25 kts), complement 418; turrets 20, bridge 15; 4 x 2 – 135/45 OTO/Ansaldo 1938, 8 x 1 – 37/54 Breda 1939, 4 x 2 – 20/65 Breda 1935 (*completed ships*) or 4 x 2 – 20/70 Scotti-OM 1941 (*incomplete ships*), 2 x 4 – 533 TT (12), 2 DCT, 2 DCR (24), 114 – 136 mines.

San Marco as completed: 3987 / 5600 t, 142.2 x 14.4 x 6.4 m, 2 sets Beluzzo geared steam turbines, 4 Thornycroft boilers, 110000 hp, 38.5 kts, 1400 t oil, 3000 nm (25 kts), complement 494; 3 x 2 – 127/38 Mk 12, (3 x 4 + 4 x 2) – 40/56 Bofors, 1 x 3 – 305 Menon ASWRL, 4 DCT, 1 DCR; SPS-6, SG-6B, Mk 12/22 radars, SQS-11 sonar.

Light cruisers of the *Capitani Romani* class became the response to the new French destroyer leaders of the *Fantasque* and *Mogador* classes, and in their design, there was a return to the ideas of the "super-destroyer" embodied in the first series of the "Condottieri" classes scouts, with a high speed and strong armament but the minimal protection. Design work on the new "ocean scout" began in 1937. At the beginning of 1939, the design was ready. In the final form, the ships were supposed to have a displacement of 3400 t, eight 135-mm guns in four turrets, six of the latest 65-mm AA guns and 2 quadruple TTs. The latter had a rather original "two-level" design: two tubes in the lower tier and two in the upper one. The seaplane originally planned during the design was abandoned. The machinery was placed *en echelon*. The estimated speed was 40 kts, exceeding that of the French leaders. Curiously, when announcing the construction of new ships in 1939, the Italians announced a speed of 44 kt: a propaganda move aimed at demoralizing the enemy.

At the early design stages, a hull with a pronounced forecastle was envisaged, but later it was abandoned in favor of a flush-decked hull, with a noticeable deck sheer, which provided some weight savings without loss of seaworthiness. Although weight reduction measures were included in the construction, including the wide use of light aluminum alloys and electric welding, the building overload was about 300 t. Due to the lack of the 65-mm AA guns, they had to be replaced with the usual twin 37-mm guns.

The 1937 Programme provided for the construction of 12 ships. The laying of the keel was in 1939-1940, but in June 1940, work on four ships, *Claudio Druso, Claudio Tiberio, Paolo Emilio* and *Vipsanio Agrippa*, was stopped, and the hulls were in 1941-1942 scrapped on the stocks. The building of the remaining ships was stopped with the outbreak of war, and until September

Scipione Africano 1943

ITALY

1943 only three entered service. One more, *Ulpio Traiano*, was sunk at Palermo 3.1.1943 being fitted afloat by British 'Chariot' human torpedoes. The completion of *Caio Mario* as a cruiser was abandoned in 1942, being completed in January 1943 as an oil hulk. *Caio Mario* and incomplete *Cornelio Silla* (84% availability), *Ottaviano Augusto* (over 90% availability) and *Giulio Germanico* (94% availability) were captured by German forces in September 1943. *Caio Mario* was scuttled by the Germans at La Spezia in 1944, and in April 1945 they blew up the wreck. *Ottaviano Augusto* was sunk by Allied aircraft at Ancona 1.11.1943. *Cornelio Silla* was sunk by Allied aircraft at Genoa in July 1944. *Giulio Germanico* was scuttled by the Germans at Castellamare di Stabia 28.9.1943. *Ulpio Traiano* was sunk by British 'Chariot' human torpedoes. *Giulio Germanico* was captured by the Germans 11.9.1943 and scuttled by them 28.9.1943.

The turrets had 20-mm faces, 6-mm sides and rears. The bridge had 15-mm protection.

Summer 1943, *Attilio Regolo*, *Scipione Africano*: + EC.3 radar.

Attilio Regolo 2 months after commissioning was damaged by a torpedo from British submarine *Unruffled*. The bow forward of the first 135-mm gun mount was broken off. The repair lasted until the mid-1943.

Ex-Thai ETNA class light cruisers

Etna (ex-Taksin)	CRDA, Trieste	23.9.1939	28.5.1942	-	captured incomplete by Germany 10.9.1943
Vesuvio (ex-Naresuan)	CRDA, Trieste	26.8.1939	6.8.1941	-	captured incomplete by Germany 10.9.1943

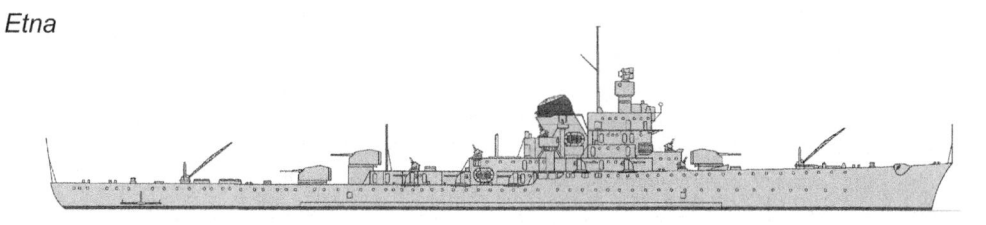

Etna

5900 / 6533 t, 153.8 x 14.5 x 6.0 m, 2 sets Parsons geared steam turbines, 3 Yarrow boilers, 40000 hp, 28 kts, complement 580; belt 60, deck 35-20, turrets 20, CT 60; 3 x 2 – 135/45 OTO/Ansaldo 1938, 10 x 1 – 65/64 Ansaldo-Terni 1939, 10 x 2 – 20/65 Breda 1935; troops, 600 m³ cargo; FuMO 39 radar.

Small cruisers named *Taksin* and *Naresuan* were ordered by Thailand from Italy in 1938. According to the original design, they were supposed to have a standard displacement of 5500 t, s speed of 30 kts and an armament consisted of 3 twin 152-mm gun mounts, 6 single 76-mm AA guns, 4 twin 13.2-mm MGs, 2 triple 533-mm TT banks and a catapult for seaplanes. An interesting feature of these ships was that, despite only one funnel, the machinery was located *en echelon*: from the bow to the stern there were No1 and 2 boiler rooms, No1 engine room, No3 boiler room and No2 engine room.

The laying of the cruisers took place at the end of 1939, and in December 1941, work was suspended, 6.8.1942, the Italian Government confiscated both ships. *Taksin* and *Naresuan* were renamed *Etna* and *Vesuvio* respectively. The design was modified to an AA cruiser. All armament was replaced with new one, while the catapult and TTs were removed. In addition to providing air defense for escorts, it was supposed to assign additional functions of fast cargo vessels. For this, holds with a capacity of 400 m³ were provided.

By September 1943, the readiness of the ships was 60-65%. 10.9.1943 they were captured by the Germans at Trieste, and in 1944 scuttled in shallow water, salvaged the following year but BU in 1948.

The main deck had a thickness of 35 mm between the internal longitudinal splinter bulkheads and 20 mm between these bulkheads and the belt. The belt had a thickness of 60 mm. The turrets had 20-mm protection; the CT had 60-mm sides.

Ex-French FR11 class light cruisers

FR11 (ex-Jean de Vienne)	Arsenal de Brest, France	20.12.1931	31.7.1935	(10.2.1937)	captured incomplete by Germany 9.1943
FR12 (ex-La Galissonnière)	Arsenal de Lorient, France	15.12.1931	18.11.1933	(1.4.1936)	captured incomplete by Germany 9.1943

French sister-ship Georges Leygues 1939

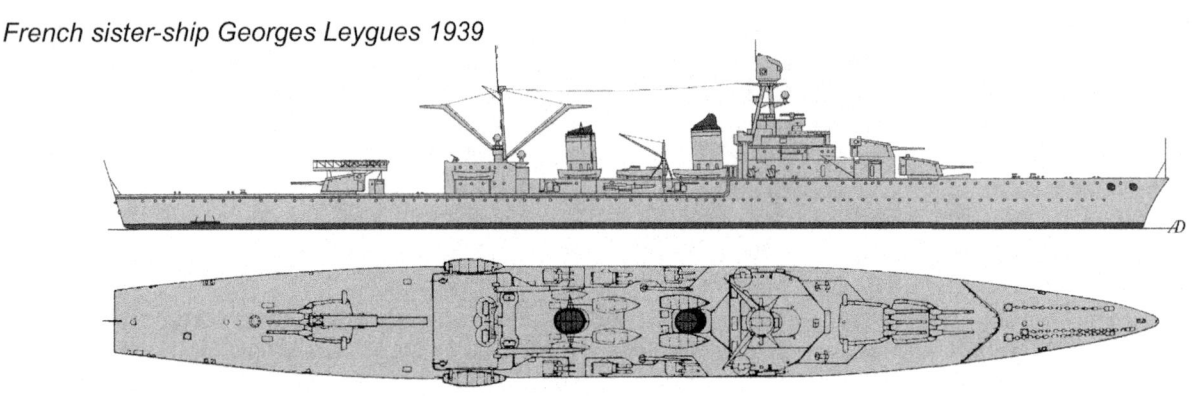

7600 / 9100 t, 179.5 x 17.5 x 5.4 m, 2 sets Rateau-Bretagne (*FR11*) or Parsons geared steam turbines, 4 Indret boilers, 84000 hp, 31 kts, 1569 t oil, 6800 nm (14 kts), complement 540; belt 105, deck 38, turrets 100-50, CT 95-50; 3 x 3 – 152/55 M1930, 4 x 2 – 90/50 M1930, 1 x 2 – 37/50 M1933, 1 x 2 – 25/60 M1938, 6 x 2 – 13.2 MG, 2 x 2 – 550 TT, 1 catapult, 3 (*FR11*) or 4 (*FR12*) seaplanes (Loire 130).

After he suicide of the French fleet at Toulon in November 1942, the Italians managed to salvage two cruisers of the *La Galissonière* class in 1943: *Jean de Vienne* and *La Galissonière*, which received new numbers *FR11* and *FR12*. The ships were towed to Italy and managed to start refurbishment, but after September 1943, work was stopped. Ex-*La Galissonnière* was captured by the Germans in September 1943 and 18.8.1944 sunk by US B-25 bombers. Ex-*Jean de Vienne* ran aground 24.11.1943 after an Allied air raid and was scrapped after the war.

A 20-mm anti-torpedo bulkhead protected the hull between the end barbettes. The main 105-mm belt protected the machinery and the command center under the main deck, it was about 2 m narrower abreast the magazines. The transverse bulkheads were 60-mm thick between the main deck and the upper platform and 20-mm thick between the upper platform and the double bottom. They were placed forward of the barbette No1, between the command center and barbette No2, between the machinery spaces and barbette No3 and aft of the barbette No3. The belt was closed by the 38-mm main deck. The steering gear compartment had 38-mm crown, 26-mm sides and 20-mm transverse bulkheads. The turrets had 100-mm faces, 50-mm sides and crowns and 40-mm rears. The barbettes had 95-mm protection avbove the upper deck and 70-mm between the main and upper decks. The CT had 95-mm sides and 50-mm roof and had a communication tube with 45-mm thick armor.

Armed merchant cruisers

More than 1000 grt capacity

Adriatico	4.4.1931 / 4.1937	1976	81.5 x 12.3	14	2 x 1 - 102/45, 4 - 13.2, 60 mines	returned 1939, recommissioned 1940, sunk 1.12.1941
Arborea D5	1929 / 6.1940	4959	111.1 x 15.2	16	4 x 1 - 120/45, 6 - 13.2	captured 8.9.1943
Attilio Defenu	1929 / 1940	3510	98.8 x 13.4 x 5.3	14	2 x 1 - 102/45, 1 x 1 - 76/40, 6 - 13.2, 80 mines	sunk 25.11.1941
Barletta D16	12.9.1931 / 1936	1975	81.5 x 12.3	14	2 x 1 - 102/45, 4 - 13.2, 60 mines	returned 1939, recommissioned 5.1940, damaged 2.12.1943, repaired mercantile
Brindisi D15	15.6.1931 / 6.1940	1976	81.5 x 12.3	14	2 x 1 - 102/45, 4 - 13.2, 60 mines	sunk 6.8.1943
Brioni D13	4.2.1931 / 5.1940	1987	81.5 x 12.3	14	2 x 1 - 102/45, 4 - 13.2, 90 mines	sunk 2.11.1942
Capitano Antonio Cecchi	12.10.1933 / 1940	2321	91.0 x 12.4	15.5	2 x 1 - 100/27, 4 - 13.2	sunk 8.5.1941

ITALY

Name	Built/Comm.	Tons	Dimensions	Speed	Armament	Fate
Caralis D8	1929 / 5.1940	3510	95.9 x 13.3 x 7.0	14.5	4 x 1 - 102/45, 6 - 13.2	sunk 28.5.1943
Cattaro (ex-Jugoslavija) D26	1933 / 1942	1275	76.5 x 10.5	15.5	2 x 1 - 100/47, 1 x 1 - 76/40, 4 - 20/65, 2 DCT	captured 9.9.1943
Città di Bari	1928 / 1940	3220	96.7 x 13.7	13.5	2 x 1 - 120/45	fire 3.5.1941
Città di Catania	1910 / 1940	3262	110.8 x 12.8	20	4 x 1 - 120/47, 2 - 47/40	sunk 3.8.1943
Città di Genova D4	1930 / 1940	5413	125.5 x 15.5	19	4 x 1 - 120/45, 2 - 20/65, 2 - 13.2	sunk 21.1.1943
Città di Napoli D1	12.6.1929 / 1940	5418	119.2 x 15.5	17	4 x 1 - 120/45	sunk 28.11.1942
Città di Palermo D3	1930 / 1940	5413	125.5 x 15.6	19	4 x 1 - 120/45	sunk 5.1.1942
Città di Tunisi D2	1930 / 1940	5419	119.0 x 15.5	17	4 x 1 - 120/45	captured 9.9.1943
Egeo (ex-Città di Bari)	2.4.1927 / 6.1940	3220	96.0 x 13.7 x 7.3	15	2 x 1 - 102/45, 5 - 13.2	sunk 24.4.1941
Egitto D11	1928 / 7.1940	3220	96.7 x 13.7 x 7.3	12.5	2 x 1 - 102/45, 5 - 13.2	sunk 1.3.1942
Filippo Grimani D9	7.6.1928 / 7.1941	3431	100.4 x 13.5	16.5	2 x 1 - 102/45, 4 - 13.2, 60 mines	captured by Germany 9.9.1943
Francesco Morosini D12	3.10.1928 / 6.1940	2423	84.0 x 12.7	17	2 x 1 - 120/45, 2 - 20/65	captured 9.9.1943
Ipparco Baccich D17	1931 / 6.1941	1500	62.0 x 9.2 x 4.5	14	2 x 1 - 76/40, 2 - 13.2, 2 DCT	scuttled 8.9.1943
Lazzaro Mocenigo D21	1928 / 1940	1403	71.8 x 10.5 x 4.5	14	2 x 1 - 100/47, 2 - 20/65, 2 DCT	stricken 1945
Lew D25		1980			2 x 1 - 102/45	
Loredan D19	5.9.1936 / 1940	1357	72.2 x 10.9	14	2 x 1 - 102/45	sunk 10.4.1943
Lorenzo Marcello D20	1928 / 1941	1413	67.0 x 10.5	14	2 x 1 - 100/47, 4 - 20/65, 2 DCT	sunk 19.6.1943
Narenta D18	1934 / 7.1941	1362	72.2 x 10.9	12	2 x 1 - 100/47, 4 - 20/65	sunk 11.4.1943
Olbia D7	1929 / 1940	3514	95.9 x 13.3	14.5	4 x 1 - 102/45	sunk 20.6.1943
Piero Foscari D10	7.6.1928 / 8.1940	3423	100.4 x 13.6	16.5	2 x 1 - 102/45, 4 - 20/65, 80 mines	returned 1.1941, recommissioned 7.1941, sunk 9.9.1943
Ramb I	1937 / 6.1940	3667	116.8 x 15.1	17	4 x 1 - 120/40, 2 - 13.2	sunk 27.2.1941
Ramb II	7.6.1937 / 6.1940	3685	116.8 x 15.2	17	2 x 1 - 120/40, 2 - 13.2	scuttled 8.9.1943
Ramb III D6	1938 / 4.1940	3667	116.8 x 15.1	17	4 x 1 - 120/45, 2 - 13.2	scuttled 9.9.1943
Zara D14	4.7.1931 / 1940	1976	81.5 x 12.3	14		sunk 2.11.1942

Barletta 1942

Città di Catania 1911

Ramb II 1937

500-1000 grt capacity
Lago Tana D22 (1940 / 6.1940, 783 grt, 2 x 1 – 100/47 – sunk 20.11.1942)
Lago Zuai D23 (1940 / 7.1940, 783 grt, 2 x 1 – 100/47 – captured by Germany 9.9.1943)
Lubiana (*ex-Ljubljana*) D27 (1904 / 1941, 953 grt – returned 1945)
Mazara D24 (1934 / 1940, 984 grt, 2 x 1 – 76/40 – captured by Germany 9.9.1943)

100-500grt capacity
Requisitioned: 2 (1942)
Lost: 1 (1943)
Discarded: 1 (1945)

Merchant vessels converted to large patrols, smaller than the AMCs of other countries. Many of them were also used as minelayers.
1941, Adriatico: - 2 x 1 - 102/45, 2 x 1 - 13.2 MG; + 2 x 1 - 100/47, 2 x 1 - 20/65.
Adriatico was sunk 1.12.1941 by British cruisers *Aurora*, *Penelope*, and destroyer *Lively en route* from Argostoli to Bengasi. *Ipparco Baccich* was scuttled by her crew 8.9.1943 at La Spezia. *Brindisi* was torpedoed by British submarine *Uproar* 6.8.1943 *en route* from Bari to Teodo and sank while under tow at Brindisi. *Capitano A. Cecchi* was lost 8.5.1941 off Cyrenaica as a result of an explosion of ammunition. *Cattaro* was captured by German troops 9.9.1943 and in 1944 was damaged by Allied aircraft. *Città di Genova* was sunk *en route* from Patra to Bari 21.1.1943 by British submarine *Tigris*. *Attilio Defenu* was sunk by British submarines *Thunderbolt* and *Thrasher* 25.11.1941 *en route* from Taranto to Patra. *Egitto* was mined 1.3.1942 between Taranto and Messina. *Filippo Grimani* was captured by the Germans in September 1943 and after the war returned to mercantile service. *Lorenzo Marcello* was mined 19.6.1943 *en route* from Bari to Patra. *Francesco Morosini* was captured by German troops 9.9.1943. *Ramb I* was sunk 27.2.1941 by New Zealand cruiser *Leander* in the Indian Ocean off Addu Atoll. *Ramb III* was scuttled by the crew 9.9.1943 at Kobe, Japan. *Città di Catania* was sunk 3.8.1943 by British submarine *Unruffled* off Brindisi. *Arborea* was captured by German troops 8.9.1943. *Barletta* was damaged by German aircraft 2.12.1943 at Bari and repaired only in 1948 as a merchant vessel. *Brioni* was sunk by Allied aircraft 2.11.1942 at Tobruk. *Caralis* was sunk by US aircraft 28.5.1943 at Livorno. *Egeo* was sunk 24.4.1941 *en route* from Tunis to Palermo by British destroyers *Jervis*, *Juno*, and *Janus*. *Piero Foscari* was sunk by German MTBs 9.9.1943 off Cape Castiglioncello. *Narento* was bombed by Allied aircraft 6.4.1943 at Trapani and later capsized. *Ramb II* was scuttled 8.9.1943 at Kobe, Japan.

DESTROYERS AND TORPEDO BOATS

ALESSANDRO POERIO class destroyers

Alessandro Poerio	Ansaldo, Genova	25.6.1913	4.8.1914	25.5.1915	to Nationalist Spain 6.1938 (Huesca)
Guglielmo Pepe	Ansaldo, Genova	2.7.1913	17.9.1914	20.8.1915	to Nationalist Spain 6.1938 (Teruel)

ITALY

1028 / 1216 t, 85.0 x 8.0 x 2.8 m, 2 Beluzzo steam turbines, 3 Yarrow boilers, 20000 hp, 31.5 kts, 200 t oil, 2100 nm (13 kts), complement 129; 5 (*Alessandro Poerio*) or 6 (*Guglielmo Pepe*) x 1 – 102/45 Schneider 1917, 1 (*Alessandro Poerio*) or 2 (*Guglielmo Pepe*) x 1 – 40/39 Vickers 1917, 2 x 2 – 450 TT, 42 mines.

The first Italian leaders, officially rated as "light scouts".

Guglielmo Pepe 1937

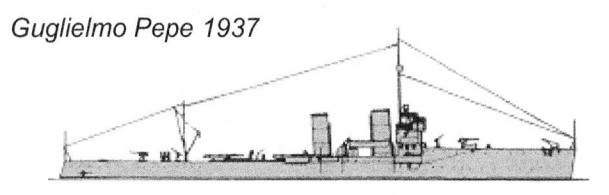

Rerated as destroyers in 1921.

CARLO MIRABELLO class destroyers

| **Carlo Mirabello** | Ansaldo, Genova | 21.11.1914 | 21.12.1915 | 24.8.1916 | sunk 21.5.1941 |
| **Augusto Riboty** | Ansaldo, Genova | 27.2.1915 | 24.9.1916 | 5.5.1917 | stricken 1950 |

1784 / 1972 t, 103.4 x 9.7 x 3.3 m, 2 Parsons steam turbines, 4 Yarrow boilers, 44000 hp, 35 kts, 386 t oil, 2300 nm (12 kts), complement 169; 8 x 1 – 102/45 Schneider-Canet 1917, 2 x 1 – 40/39 Vickers-Terni 1917, 2 x 1 – 6.5 MG, 2 x 2 – 450 TT, 100 (*Carlo Mirabello*) or 120 (*Augusto Riboty*) mines.

Augusto Riboty 1942

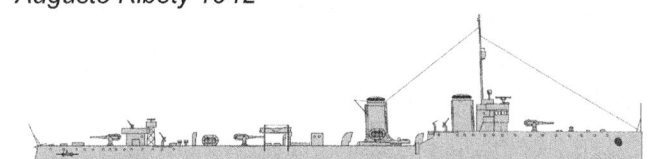

The ships, the appearance of which was directly related to the effect caused at one time by the British scout *Swift*. She did not receive further development in the homeland, but she made a great impression on the Italians, in whose opinion she was ideally suited for actions in the narrow Mediterranean region. In 1913-1915, the first scouts of the *Poerio* class were built. Before their completion, in 1913 the development of a design of a larger ship of this type was started. Initially, it was planned to create a fairly solid 5000-t scout with light armor, but for financial reasons this "almost cruiser" was abandoned in favor of designing a much more modest ship designed by Ansaldo, although at that time destroyers of similar dimensions served only in the Chilean and British Navies. The displacement increased by almost one and a half times compared to *Poerio* was spent on placing more powerful machinery, eight 102-mm/35 guns and 2 twin 450-mm TTs. The shortage of light cruisers forced the installation of heavy 152-mm guns on two ships of three built, but the experience was unsuccessful: 6" guns had a low rate of fire and also caused severe hull shaking. They were removed in 1919.

These ships were commissioned as scouts, two surviving were reclassified as light scouts in July 1921 and as destroyers in September 1938.

1942, *Augusto Riboty*: - 2 x 1 - 102/45, 2 x 1 - 6.5 MG; + 1 x 1 - 40/39 Vickers-Terni 1917, 2 x 1 – 8 MG.
1943, *Augusto Riboty*: - 2 x 1 - 102/45, 3 x 1 - 40/39, 2 x 2 - 450 TT; + 6 x 1 - 20/70 Oerlikon, DCTs.

Carlo Mirabello was sunk 21.5.1941 by a mine laid by British minelayer *Abdiel* in the Ionian Sea.

AQUILA class destroyers

| **Aquila** (ex-*Vifor*) | Pattison, Napoli | 11.3.1914 | 26.7.1917 | 8.2.1917 | to Nationalist Spain 10.1937 (Melilla) |
| **Falco** (ex-*Viscol*) | Pattison, Napoli | 19.8.1916 | 16.8.1919 | 20.1.1920 | to Nationalist Spain 10.1937 (Ceuta) |

1594 / 1733 (*Aquila*) or 1760 t, 94.7 x 9.5 x 3.6 m, 2 Tosi steam turbines, 5 Thornycroft boilers, 40000 hp, 34 kts, 270 t oil, 1700 nm (15 kts), complement 146; 2 x 2 – 120/45 Schneider-Armstrong 1918-1919, 2 x 1 – 76/40 Ansaldo 1917, 2 x 1 – 6.5 MG, 2 x 2 – 450 TT, 44 (*Aquila*) or 38 (*Falco*) mines.

Aquila 1937

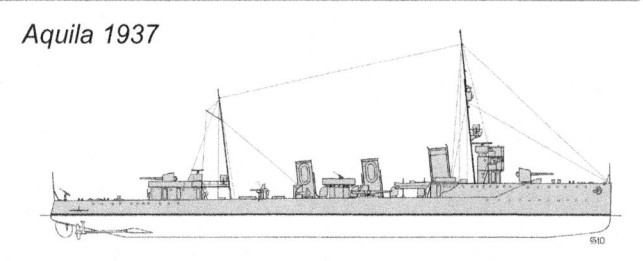

Ordered in 1913 by Romania, but requisitioned after Italy entered the war in June 1915 as scouts. They were among the strongest destroyers in the world. On trials, all exceeded the design speed, reaching 35.2-38.04 kts. The shortage of light cruisers forced the installation of old 152-mm guns on the first three ships. However, these guns proved too heavy for destroyers, and the last ship, *Falco*, received 120-mm/45 guns. Later, all ships of the class were rearmed with 120-mm guns.

Aquila and *Falco* were reclassified as destroyers in September 1938. Officially, they were transferred to Spain only 6.1.1939.

Ex-German PREMUDA destroyer

| **Premuda** *(ex-V116)* | Vulcan, Stettin, Germany | 1916 | 2.3.1918 | (31.7.1918) / 23.5.1920 | stricken 1.1939 |

Premuda 1920

2302 / 2555 t, 107.5 x 10.4 x 4.0 m, 2 Vulcan Marine steam turbines, 4 Marine boilers, 45000 hp, 34 kts, 660 t oil, 1900 nm (16 kts), complement 162; 4 x 1 – 149/42 TK C/16, 1 x 1 – 120/15 OTO 1933, 2 x 1 – 40/39 Vickers-Terni 1917, 2 x 1 – 6.5 MG, 1 x 2 – 450 TT, 40 mines. German destroyer leader transferred under reparations, entered service 1.8.1920 as a scout after partial rearming, was reclassified 15.9.1938 as a destroyer.

Ex-German CESARE ROSSAROL destroyer

| **Cesare Rossarol** *(ex-B97)* | Blohm & Voss, Hamburg, Germany | 1914 | 15.12.1914 | (13.2.1915) / 16.9.1920 | stricken 1.1939 |

Cesare Rossarol 1920

1655 / 1756 t, 98.0 x 9.4 x 4.0 m, 2 Marine steam turbines, 4 Marine boilers, 30000 hp, 30 kts, 527 t oil, 2600 nm (14 kts), complement 150; 1 x 2 - 120/45 Schneider-Canet-Armstrong 1918-19, 1 x 1 - 120/45 Schneider-Canet-Armstrong 1918, 2 x 1 - 76/40 Ansaldo 1917, 2 x 1 - 6.5 MG, 2 x 2 - 450 TT, 29 mines.
German destroyer leader transferred under reparations and entered service 1.12.1924 after rearming.

Ex-German ARDIMENTOSO destroyer

| **Ardimentoso** *(ex-S63)* | Schichau, Elbing, Germany | 1915 | 27.5.1916 | (12.1916) / 5.1920 | stricken 2.1939 |

Ardimentoso 1920

1050 / 1130 t, 83.1 x 8.4 x 3.7 m, 2 Schichau steam turbines + 1 Schichau cruising steam turbine, 3 Marine boilers (2 shafts), 24000 hp, 34 kts, 305 t oil, 1960 nm (17 kts), complement 111; 3 x 1 – 100/47 Škoda 1910, 2 x 1 – 40/39 Vickers-Terni 1917, 2 x 1 – 6.5 MG, 2 x 2 – 450 TT, 24 mines.
German destroyer transferred as a reparation and commissioned in October 1925 after the rearming, was used as a TS.

LEONE class destroyers

Leone	Ansaldo, Genova	23.11.1921	1.10.1923	1.7.1924	wrecked 1.4.1941
Pantera	Ansaldo, Genova	19.12.1921	18.10.1924	28.10.1924	scuttled 3-4.4.1941
Tigre	Ansaldo, Genova	23.1.1922	7.8.1924	10.10.1924	scuttled 3-4.4.1941

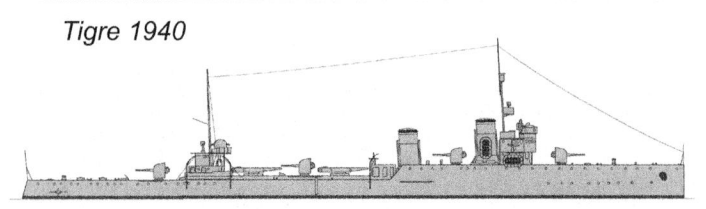

Tigre 1940

1745 / 2289 t, 113.4 x 10.3 x 3.2 m, 2 Parsons steam turbines, 4 Yarrow boilers, 42000 hp, 34 kts, 400 t oil, 2070 nm (15 kts), complement 204; 4 x 2 – 120/45 Schneider-Canet-Armstrong 1918-19, 2 x 1 – 40/39 Vickers-Terni 1917, 2 x 1 – 6.5 MG, 2 x 2 – 533 TT, 60 mines.

The development of the *Carlo Mirabello* class. In 1917, five ships were ordered, but due to a lack of materials, construction was not started. In 1920, three ships were reordered, but according to a modified design. The number of main guns remained the same, but the caliber was increased to 120 mm. The guns were placed in twin mounts on the centerline, as well as triple 450-mm TTs. Two 76-mm AA guns were also installed.

In 1936, the leaders, already considered obsolete, were arranged for colonial service in the Red Sea: the fuel supply was slightly increased and the 76-mm guns

ITALY

were removed. In 1938, they were re-rated from scouts to destroyers.
1938, all: + 2 x 2 - 13.2 MG, 2 x 1 - 6.5 MG, displacement was 2150 / 2605-2650 t, complement was 206.
1939, all: - 2 x 2 - 13.2 MG, 4 x 1 - 6.5 MG; + 2 x 2 - 20/65 Breda 1935.
Leone 1.4.1941 ran to an uncharted rock in the Red Sea and was lost. *Pantera* and *Tigre* were scuttled on the night of 3-4.4.1940 in shallow water off the coast of Saudi Arabia. The wrecks were destroyed by British aircraft and gunfire from British destroyer *Kingston*.

Pantera 1935

QUINTINO SELLA class destroyers

Francesco Crispi	Pattison, Napoli	10.1922	25.4.1925	4.1927	captured by Germany 9.9.1943 (TA15)
Quintino Sella	Pattison, Napoli	1.1923	12.9.1925	3.1926	sunk 11.9.1943
Bettino Ricasoli	Pattison, Napoli	1923	29.1.1926	10.1926	to Sweden 3.1940 (Puke)
Giovanni Nicotera	Pattison, Napoli	1923	24.6.1926	2.1927	to Sweden 3.1940 (Psilander)

1140 / 1457 t, 84.9 x 8.6 x 2.7 m, 2 sets Beluzzo (*Francesco Crispi*) or Parsons geared steam turbines, 3 Thornycroft boilers, 36000 hp, 35 kts, 250 t oil, 1800 nm (14 kts), complement 120-152; 1 x 2 – 120/45 Schneider-Canet-Armstrong 1918-19, 1 x 2 – 120/45 OTO 1926, 2 x 1 – 40/39 Vickers-Terni 1917, 2 x 1 – 13.2 MG, 2 x 2 – 533 TT, 2 DCT, 32 mines.
Designed by Pattison. The *Curtatone* class destroyers served as the starting point for the design. An increase in displacement by about 100 t made it possible to switch to 120-mm guns and 533-mm TTs and place more than one and a half times more powerful machinery. The design standard displacement of the new destroyers was 955 t, and the actual displacement exceeded 1100 t, the construction overload reached about 17%. Although on trials all 4 ships reached a speed of 38 kts, in real conditions, the speed at full load did not exceed 33 kts.
1938, all: - 2 x 1 - 13.2 MG; + 2 x 2 - 13.2 MG.
1941-1942, both remained: - 2 x 1 - 40/39; + 4 x 1 - 20/70 Scotti-Isotta Fraschini 1939, 2 DCT.
Quintino Sella was sunk 11.9.1943 by German MTBs *S54* and *S61* S off Venice.

Quintino Sella 1940

Francesco Crispi 1941

Francesco Crispi was captured by German troops in September 1943, renamed *TA15* and sunk 8.3.1944 by British aircraft N of Crete. Salvaged and towed to Piraeus, but 12.10.1944 scuttled in the same place.

NAZARIO SAURO class destroyers

Cesare Battisti	Odero, Sestri Ponente	2.1924	11.12.1926	4.1927	scuttled 3.4.1941
Daniele Manin	CNQ, Fiume	10.1924	15.6.1925	3.1927	sunk 3.4.1941
Francesco Nullo	CNQ, Fiume	10.1924	14.11.1925	4.1927	sunk 21.10.1940
Nazario Sauro	Odero, Sestri Ponente	2.1924	12.5.1926	9.1926	sunk 3.4.1940

1260 / 1575 t, 90.2 x 9.2 x 2.9 m, 2 sets Parsons geared steam turbines, 3 Thornycroft boilers, 36000 hp, 35 kts, 260 t oil, 2600 nm (12 kts), complement 155; 2 x 2 – 120/45 Vickers-Terni 1924, 2 x 1 – 40/39 Vickers-Terni 1917, 2 x 1 – 13.2 MG, 2 x 3 – 533 TT, 2 DCT, 52 mines.
Design of Odero. Development of the *Sella* class with

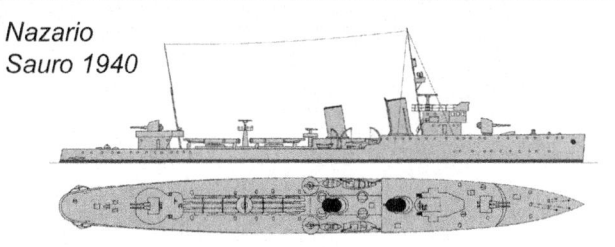

Nazario Sauro 1940

Nazario Sauro 1934

increased dimensions, triple TTs and 120-mm guns in twin mounts since completion (previous class originally had one twin and one single mount). They had larger bridge and conning tower. Due to the redevelopment of the boiler rooms, the resistance to damage of the machinery was increased: now each boiler was located in its own separate compartment. The design standard displacement was 1040 t, and the actual displacement was more than 1200 t. On trials, all destroyers exceeded the contract speed, but when fully loaded, they made just over 31kts. In addition, it turned out that the longitudinal strength of the hull was insufficient; and had to strengthen it.

Cesare Battisti was damaged by British aircraft 3.4.1941 off the Arabian coast of the Red Sea, ran ashore and was demolished by the crew. *Nazario Sauro* and *Daniele Manin* were sunk 3.4.1941 by British aircraft in the Red Sea. *Francesco Nullo* was torpedoed 20.10.1940 by British destroyer *Kimberly* in the Red Sea, ran aground and was destroyed by British aircraft the next day.

TURBINE class destroyers

Aquilone	Odero, Sestri Ponente	5.1925	3.8.1927	12.1927	sunk 17.9.1940
Borea	Ansaldo, Genoa	4.1925	28.1.1927	11.1927	sunk 17.9.1940
Espero	Ansaldo, Genoa	4.1925	31.8.1927	4.1928	sunk 28.6.1940
Euro	CT, Riva Trigoso	1.1925	7.7.1927	12.1927	sunk 1.10.1943
Nembo	CT, Riva Trigoso	1.1925	27.1.1927	10.1927	sunk 20.7.1940
Ostro	Ansaldo, Genoa	4.1925	2.1.1928	6.1928	sunk 20.7.1940
Turbine	Odero, Sestri Ponente	3.1925	21.4.1927	8.1927	captured by Germany 9.9.1943 (TA14)
Zeffiro	Ansaldo, Genoa	4.1925	27.5.1927	5.1928	sunk 5.7.1940

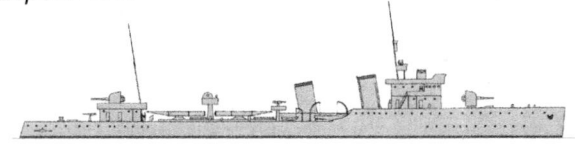

Espero 1940

1220 / 1670 t, 93.2 x 9.2 x 3.0 m, 2 sets Parsons geared steam turbines, 3 Thornycroft boilers, 40000 hp, 36 kts, 400 t oil, 3200 nm (14 kts), complement 142-179; 2 x 2 – 120/45 OTO 1926, 2 x 1 – 40/39 Vickers-Terni 1917, 1 x 2 – 13.2 MG, 2 x 3 – 533 TT, 52 mines.

Nembo 1931

Designed by Odero. The development of the *Sauro*, due to a slight increase in the hull, it was possible to install more powerful machinery, increasing the maximum speed by one knot. Additional side fuel tanks allowed to increase the fuel capacity. Like the previous classes, they had a significant overload: design standard displacement was 1073 t. On trials, all exceeded the contract speed, but at full load they reached no more than 33 kts.

1939-1940, *Euro, Turbine*: - 2 x 1 - 40/39; + 4 x 2 - 20/65 Breda 1935, 2 DCT.

1942, *Turbine*: - 1 x 3 - 533 TT; + 2 x 1 - 37/54 Breda 1939.

Espero was sunk by gunfire from Australian cruiser *Sydney* W of Crete 28.6.1940. *Zeffiro, Nembo* and *Ostro* 20.7.1940 were sunk by British aircraft at Tobruk. *Aquilone* 17.9.1940 was sunk by magnetic mines laid by British aircraft at Bengasi. *Borea* 17.9.1940 was sunk by British aircraft at Bengasi. *Euro* 1.10.1943 was badly damaged by German air bombs and sank off the coast of Leros, the Aegean. *Turbine* in September 1943 was captured by German troops, renamed *TA14* and sunk by US bombers at Salamis 15.10.1944.

ITALY

'NAVIGATORI' class destroyer leaders

Alvise da Mosto (ex-Alvise Cadamosto)	CNQ, Fiume	8.1928	1.7.1929	3.1931	sunk 10.12.1941
Antonio da Noli	CT, Riva Trigoso	7.1927	21.5.1929	12.1929	sunk 9.9.1943
Nicoloso da Recco	CNR, Ancona	12.1927	5.1.1930	5.1930	stricken 7.1954
Giovanni di Verazzano	CNQ, Fiume	8.1927	15.12.1928	9.1930	sunk 19.10.1942
Lanzerotto Malocello	Ansaldo, Genoa	8.1927	14.3.1929	1.1930	sunk 24.3.1943
Leone Pancaldo	CT, Riva Trigoso	7.1927	5.2.1929	11.1929	sunk 30.4.1943
Emanuele Pessagno	CNR, Ancona	10.1927	12.8.1929	3.1930	sunk 29.5.1943
Antonio Pigafetta	CNQ, Fiume	12.1928	10.11.1929	5.1931	scuttled 10.9.1943
Luca Tarigo	Ansaldo, Genoa	8.1927	9.12.1928	11.1929	sunk 16.4.1941
Antonio Usodimare	Odero, Sestri Ponente	6.1927	12.5.1929	11.1929	sunk 8.6.1942
Ugolini Vivaldi	Odero, Sestri Ponente	5.1927	9.1.1929	3.1930	sunk 10.9.1943
Nicoló Zeno	CNQ, Fiume	6.1927	12.8.1928	5.1930	scuttled 9.9.1943

1935 / 2580 t, 107.3 x 10.2 x 3.4 m, 2 sets Beluzzo (*Alvise da Mosto, Giovanni di Varazzano, Antonio Pigafetta, Nicoló Zeno*) or Parsons or Tosi (*Nicoloso da Recco, Emanuele Pessagno*) geared steam turbines, 4 Yarrow (*Alvise da Mosto, Giovanni di Varazzano, Antonio Pigafetta, Nicoló Zeno*) or Odero boilers, 50000 hp, 38 kts, 533 t oil, 3200 nm (18 kts), complement 173-224; 3 x 2 – 120/50 Ansaldo 1926, 2 x 1 – 40/39 Vickers-Terni 1917, 4 x 2 – 13.2 MG, 2 x 2 – 533 TT, 2 DCT, 56 mines; hydrophone.

Ordered in 1926 as a response to the new French leaders of the *Jaguar* and *Guépard* classes. They were named after famous Italian navigators, and the entire class is known as the "*Navigatori*". Whenn laid down, they were classified as destroyers, but even before they were commissioned, the ships were reclassified as scouts ('*esploratori*'). A feature of the '*Navigatori*' class was the machinery arrangement *en echelon*, which theoretically increased resistance to damage. Another important innovation was the transition to new 120-mm/50 guns. Due to the higher rate of fire, the new guns of the "*Navigatori*" with three twin mounts not only were not inferior, but also surpassed the previous *Leone* class with four twin mounts of the old brand. The TT banks on these ships were quite unusual in design: of the three tubes, the central one was intended for 450-mm torpedo, and the side tubes for 533-mm torpedoes.

On trials, traditionally caried out in Italy under standard load, the ships showed a phenomenal speed of up to 40 kts, and *Da Mosto* 43.5 kts. But, as is the case with other Italian destroyers, during the daily service the *Navigatori*' could rarely exceed 32 kts.

Operating experience revealed significant miscalculations in determining stability at the design stage. To eliminate this shortcoming, in the early thirties, all ships of this class underwent modernization, during which the superstructure was lowered by one level, the height of the funnels was reduced, and side oil fuel tanks were eliminated, instead of them for the fuel storage the double bottom space was used. To top it off, both TTs lost their central 450-mm tube. The above measures made it possible to somewhat improve the situation with stability, but did not eliminate another drawback characteristic of the '*Navigatori*', the poor seaworthiness, especially strong wetting of the bow deck in fresh weather.

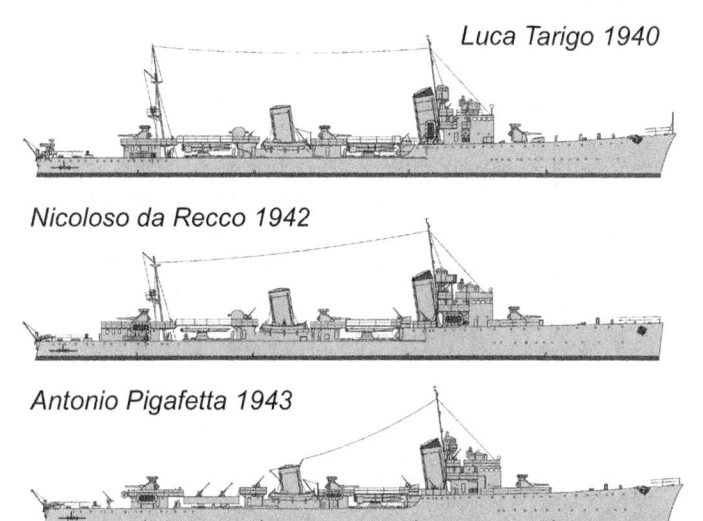

Luca Tarigo 1940

Nicoloso da Recco 1942

Antonio Pigafetta 1943

At the end of the thirties, after 10 years of service, the '*Navigatori*' underwent a second modernization aimed mainly at improving seaworthiness. The hull beam was increased by 1 m, and the bow was raised, giving it yacht-like lines and a noticeable rise to the stem. Due to the use of an increased volume of the hull, the fuel supply was increased to 680 t. The central torpedo tube was also installed again, now 533-mm. The increase in displacement and dimensions of the hull led to a drop in speed to 27-28 kts. In 1938, these ships were reclassified again as destroyers.

1939-1940, all except *Nicolosso da Recco* and *Antonio*

Leone Pancaldo 1938

Usodimare: the breadth was increased to 11.2 m, the stem was rebuilt (dimensions were 109.3 x 11.2 x 4.2 m, displacement 2125 / 2888 t, max speed 34 kts, 680 t of oil fuel); - 2 x 2 - 533 TT; + 2 x 2 - 13.2 MG, 2 x 3 - 533 TT, 2 DCT. 1939-1940, *Nicolosso da Recco*: - 56 mines; + 2 DCT. 1939-1940, *Antonio Usodimare*: + 2 DCT.
Mid-1940-late 1941, *Alvise da Mosto, Giovanni di Verazzano, Lanzerotto Malocello, Emanuele Pessagno, Luca Tarigo, Antonio Usodimare, Ugolini Vivaldi, Nicoló Zeno*: - 2 x 1 - 40/39, 4 x 2 - 13.2 MG; + 7 x 1 - 20/65 Breda 1940. Mid-1940-late 1941, *Antonio da Noli*: - 2 x 1 - 40/39, 4 x 2 - 13.2 MG; + 7 x 1 - 20/70 Scotti-Isotta Fraschini 1939. Mid-1940-late 1941, *Nicolosso da Recco, Antonio Pigafetta*: - 2 x 1 - 40/39, 4 x 2 - 13.2 MG; + 2 x 1 - 20/70 Scotti-Isotta Fraschini 1939, 7 x 1 - 20/65 Breda 1940. Mid-1940-late 1941, *Leone Pancaldo*: - 2 x 1 - 40/39, 4 x 2 - 13.2 MG; + 9 x 1 - 20/65 Breda 1940. 1941-1942, some survived: + S-Gerät sonar.

1942, *Antonio da Noli, Nicolosso da Recco, Lanzerotto Malocello, Leone Pancaldo, Antonio Pigafetta, Ugolini Vivaldi, Nicoló Zeno*: - 1 x 3 - 533 TT; + 2 x 1 - 37/54 Breda 1939. 1942-1943, *Leone Pancaldo, Nicolosso da Recco*: + EC.3/ter radar.
1943, *Lanzerotto Malocello*: + FuMO 39 radar.
Luca Tarigo 16.4.1941 was sunk by British destroyers *Nubian*, *Jervis* and *Janus* in the Mediterranean Sea. *Alvise da Mosto* 10.12.1941 was sunk by gunfire from British cruiser *Penelope* and destroyers *Lance* and *Lively* NW of Tripoli. *Antonio Usodimare* 8.6.1942 was mistakenly sunk by Italian submarine *Alagi* in the Strait of Sicily. *Giovanni di Varazzano* 19.10.1942 was sunk by British submarine *Unbending* S of Pantelleria. *Lanzerotto Malocello* 24.3.1943 was sunk by mines laid by British minelayer *Abdiel* off the coast of Tunisia. *Leone Pancaldo* 30.4.1943 was sunk by US aircraft off the coast of Tunisia. *Emanuele Pessagno* 29.5.1943 was sunk by British submarine *Turbulent* 75 nm NW of Bengasi. *Antonio da Noli* 9.9.1943 was badly damaged by German coastal guns off the N coast of Sardinia and was sunk 5 nm from a shore by a mine. *Ugolini Vivaldi* 9.9.1943 was badly damaged by German coastal guns and aircraft and sank 10.9.1943 at Sardinia. *Nicoló Zeno* 9.9.1943 was scuttled at Trieste while undergoing repairs after a collision with destroyer *da Noli*. *Antonio Pigafetta* was captured by German forces in September 1943, renamed *TA44* and scuttled by her crew at Trieste 17.2.1945.

FRECCIA class destroyers

Dardo	Odero, Sestri Ponente	1.1929	6.9.1930	1.1932	captured by Germany 9.9.1943 (TA31)
Freccia	CT, Riva Trigoso	2.1929	3.8.1930	10.1931	sunk 8.8.1943
Saetta	CT, Riva Trigoso	5.1929	17.1.1932	5.1932	sunk 3.2.1943
Strale	Odero, Sestri Ponente	2.1929	26.3.1931	2.1932	damaged 21.6.1942, repair incomplete

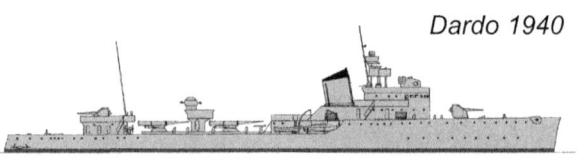

Dardo 1940

1400 / 2116 t, 94.1 (*Dardo, Strale*) or 96.2 x 9.8 x 3.2 m, 2 sets Parsons geared steam turbines, 3 Thornycroft boilers, 44000 hp, 38 kts, 630 t oil, 3600 nm (12 kts), complement 156-185; 2 x 2 – 120/50 Ansaldo 1926, 2 x 1 – 40/39 Vickers-Terni 1917, 2 x 2 – 13.2 MG, 2 x 3 – 533 TT, 2 DCT, 54 mines; hydrophone.

Strale prewar

They were built according to the 1928 Programme and were intended for joint operations with the *Zara* class cruisers, in connection with which they were subject to increased requirements for speed and cruising range. The design was based on the *Turbine* class, but with more powerful machinery, new 120-mm guns and additional side oil fuel tanks. All this led to an increase in the dimensions of the ship, mainly beam. From their predecessors *Dardo* and *Strale* with a straight stem differed from two other ships with more elegant yacht-like stem to decrease the bow deck wetness. At the early design stages, it was envisaged to have two funnels, as on *Turbine*, but in order to clear space for the more efficient placement of AA armament, the smoke ducts from all three boilers were combined into one massive funnel, which became the original look of all subsequent

ITALY

Italian destroyers and torpedo boats.

The main design flaw was low stability, caused both by the use of side oil fuel tanks and the increased weight of armament and fire control systems. It was especially bad when most of the fuel was consumed, so in practice it was necessary to leave part of the fuel supply in the tanks, which reduced the cruising range. Subsequently, they began to use the replacement of fuel with water, which, in turn, affected the quality of the fuel. In addition to liquid ballast, all four ships received 90-100 t of solid ballast and bilge keels, which, together with the building overload, led to an increase in the standard displacement from 1205 to almost 1400 t and a serious loss of speed. Under actual operating conditions, these destroyers rarely exceeded the speed of 30 kts.

1939-1940, all: - 2 x 1 - 40/39, 2 x 2 - 13.2 MG; + (5 - 6) x 1 - 20/65 Breda 1939/1940, 2 DCT.

1942-1943, *Dardo, Freccia, Saetta*: - 3 x 1 - 20/65, 1 x 3 - 533 TT; + 2 x 1 - 37/54 Breda 1939, 3 x 2 - 20/70 Scotti-Isotta Fraschini 1939.

Strale 21.6.1942, evading an aircraft attack, ran on the rocks off the coast of Tunisia. Finished off 6.8.1942 by British submarine *Turbulent*. *Saetta* 3.2.1943 was sunk by mines laid by British minelayer *Abdiel* in the central Mediterranean. *Freccia* 8.8.1943 was sunk by British bombers at Genoa. *Dardo* was captured by German forces at Genoa in September 1943, renamed *TA31* and scuttled there 24.4.1945.

FOLGORE class destroyers

Baleno	CNQ, Fiume	10.1929	22.3.1931	6.1932	foundered 17.4.1941
Folgore	OCP, Napoli	1.1930	26.4.1931	7.1932	sunk 2.12.1942
Fulmine	CNQ, Fiume	10.1929	2.8.1931	9.1932	sunk 9.11.1941
Lampo	OCP, Napoli	1.1930	26.7.1931	8.1932	sunk 30.4.1943

1450 / 2100 t, 96.1 x 9.2 x 3.3 m, 2 sets Beluzzo geared steam turbines, 3 Thornycroft boilers, 44000 hp, 38 kts, 510 t oil, 3600 nm (12 kts), complement 156-185; 2 x 2 – 120/50 Ansaldo 1926, 2 x 1 – 40/39 Vickers-Terni 1917, 2 x 2 – 13.2 MG, 2 x 3 – 533 TT, 2 DCT, 54 mines; hydrophone.

Baleno 1940

Folgore on trials

The *Folgore* class was sometimes referred to as the 2nd series of the *Dardo* class. An attempt to increase speed by reducing the hull beam to 9.2 m, was the main difference from the predecessors. A slight increase in speed came at the cost of a significant reduction in the cruising range, and the lack of stability found in the previous class, was exacerbated by an even smaller beam. It was necessary, as on the ships of the 1st series, to replace the fuel with water and lay about 100 t of solid ballast. The standard displacement increased from 1220 to 1450 t, the speed was reduced to about 31-32 kts.

1939-1940, all: - 2 x 1 - 40/39, 2 x 2 - 13.2 MG; + (5 - 6) x 1 - 20/65 Breda 1939/1940.

1942, *Folgore, Lampo*: - 1 x 3 - 533 TT; + 2 x 1 - 37/54 Breda 1939.

Baleno 16.4.1941 was badly damaged by gunfire from British destroyers *Nubian, Mohawk, Jervis,* and *Janus* in the central Mediterranean, ran aground, capsized 17.4.1941 and sank. *Fulmine* 9.11.1941 was sunk by British cruiser *Aurora* and destroyers *Lively* and *Lance* 130 nm W of Syracuse. *Folgore* 2.12.1942 was sunk by gunfire from British cruisers *Aurora, Argonaut* and *Sirius*, destroyer *Quentin* and Canadian *Quiberon* in the Sicilian Strait. *Lampo* 30.4.1943 was badly damaged by US aircraft off the coast of Tunisia, abandoned and sank.

MAESTRALE class destroyers

Grecale	CNR, Ancona	9.1931	17.6.1934	11.1934	stricken 5.1964
Libeccio	CT, Riva Trigoso	9.1931	4.7.1934	11.1934	sunk 9.11.1941
Maestrale	CNR, Ascona	9.1931	5.4.1934	9.1934	scuttled 9.9.1943
Scirocco	CT, Riva Trigoso	9.1931	22.4.1934	10.1934	foundered 23.3.1942

Libeccio 1940

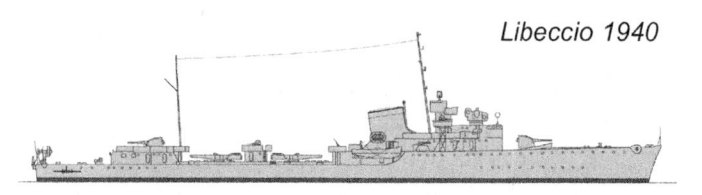

1615 / 2207 t, 106.7 x 10.2 x 3.3 m, 2 sets Parsons geared steam turbines, 3 3-drum boilers, 44000 hp, 38 kts, 520 t oil, 4000 nm (12 kts), complement 153-190; 2 x 2 – 120/50 OTO 1931, 2 x 1 – 40/39 Vickers-Terni 1917, 2 x 2 – 13.2 MG, 2 x 3 – 533 TT, 2 DCT, 52 mines; hydrophone.

Further development of the *Dardo* and *Folgore* classes. Dimensions were significantly increased to correct the main shortcomings of the predecessors. When designing, great attention was paid to the rational distribution of weight and increasing the strength of the hull. Although the power of the machinery did not increase compared to the previous classes, the successful hull lines allowed to maintain the design speed; moreover, the real speed, in comparison with *Dardo* and *Folgore*, was even increased by about 2 kts and reached 32 kts. The composition of the armament was not changed, with the exception of the installation of new 120-mm guns. Like the predecessors, the *Maestrales* could not avoid overload: the estimated standard displacement was 1449 t, and the actual one exceeded 1600 t.

1939-1940, all: - 2 x 1 - 40/39, 2 x 2 - 13.2 MG; + 6 x 1 - 20/65 Breda 1939/1940, 2 DCT.
1941-1942, all survived: + 1 x 1 - 120/15 OTO 1933/1934.
1942, *Maestrale*: - 1 x 1 - 120/15; + 1 x 1 - 120/50 Ansaldo 1940.
Early 1943, *Grecale*: - 6 x 1 - 20/65, 1 x 3 - 533 TT; + 2 x 1 - 37/54 Breda 1939, 6 x 2 - 20/65 Breda 1935.
Libeccio 9.11.1941 was badly damaged by British submarine *Upholder* and sank in tow in the Ionian Sea. *Scirocco* 23.3.1942 sank during a storm in the Ionian Sea. *Maestrale* 9.9.1943 was scuttled by her crew at Genoa, salvaged by the Germans but never repaired and scuttled again in April 1945.

Scirocco prewar

ALFREDO ORIANI class destroyers

Vittorio Alfieri	OTO, Livorno	4.1936	20.12.1936	12.1937	sunk 28.3.1941
Giosue Carducci	OTO, Livorno	2.1936	28.10.1936	11.1937	sunk 28.3.1941
Vincenzo Gioberti	OTO, Livorno	1.1936	19.9.1936	10.1937	sunk 9.8.1943
Alfredo Oriani	OTO, Livorno	10.1935	30.7.1936	7.1937	to France 8.1948 (D'Estaing)

Alfredo Oriani 1943

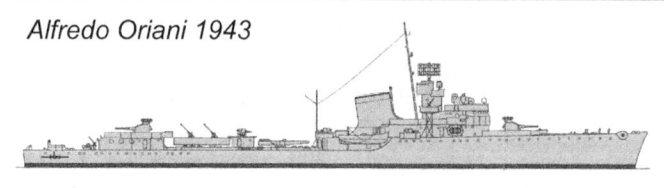

1675 / 2254 t, 106.7 x 10.2 x 3.4 m, 2 sets Parsons geared steam turbines, 3 3-drum boilers, 48000 hp, 38 kts, 520 t oil, 2190 nm (18 kts), complement 157-206; 2 x 2 – 120/50 OTO 1936, 4 x 2 – 13.2 MG, 2 x 3 – 533 TT, 2 DCT, 52 mines; hydrophone.

Repetition of the previous *Maestrale* class, but with a more powerful machinery. The increase in the 'official' speed appeared turned out to be insignificant, although the real speed increased to 33 kts. In addition to more powerful machinery, the obsolete 40-mm/39 Vickers machine guns disappeared from the specification of these ships. Instead, the number of 13.2-mm machine guns was doubled.

1939-1940, all: - 4 x 2 - 13.2 MG; + 8 x 1 - 20/65 Breda 1939/1940.
1941-1942, *Vincenzo Gioberti, Alfredo Oriani*: - 1 x 3 - 533 TT; + 1 x 1 - 120/15 OTO 1933/1934, 2 x 1 - 37/54 Breda 1939, 2 x 2 - 20/70 Scotti-Isotta Fraschini 1939, 2 DCT, S-Gerät sonar.
1943, *Alfredo Oriani*: + FuMO 21 radar.
Two ships were lost 28.3.1941 in the Battle of Matapan: *Vittorio Alfieri* was sunk by gunfire from British destroyers *Greyhound*, *Havock*, and *Stuart*; *Giosue Carducci* was sunk by gunfire from British destroyers *Jervis*, *Nubian* and *Hotspur*. *Vincenzo Gioberti* 9.8.1943 was sunk by British submarine *Simoom* off La Spezia.

Alfredo Oriani prewar

ITALY

'SOLDATI' class destroyers

1st group

Name	Builder	Laid down	Launched	Commissioned	Fate
Alpino	CNR, Ancona	5.1937	18.9.1938	4.1939	sunk 19.4.1943
Artigliere	OTO, Livorno	2.1937	12.12.1937	11.1938	sunk 12.10.1940
Ascari	OTO, Livorno	12.1937	31.7.1938	5.1939	sunk 24.3.1943
Aviere	OTO, Livorno	1.1937	19.9.1937	8.1938	sunk 17.12.1942
Bersagliere	CNR, Palermo	4.1937	3.7.1938	4.1939	sunk 7.1.1943
Camicia Nera, 7.1943- Artigliere	OTO, Livorno	1.1937	8.8.1937	6.1938	to the USSR 1.1949 (Lovkiy)
Carabiniere	CT, Riva Trigoso	2.1937	23.7.1938	12.1938	stricken 1.1965
Corazziere	OTO, Livorno	10.1937	22.5.1938	3.1939	scuttled 9.9.1943
Fuciliere	CNR, Ancona	5.1937	31.7.1938	1.1939	to the USSR 2.1950 (Lyogkiy)
Geniere	OTO, Livorno	8.1937	27.2.1938	12.1938	sunk 1.3.1943
Granatiere	CNR, Palermo	4.1937	24.4.1938	2.1939	stricken 7.1958
Lanciere	CT, Riva Trigoso	2.1937	18.12.1938	3.1939	foundered 23.3.1942

2nd group

Name	Builder	Laid down	Launched	Commissioned	Fate
Bombardiere	CNR, Ancona	10.1940	23.3.1942	7.1942	sunk 17.1.1943
Carrista	OTO, Livorno	9.1941	-	-	captured incomplete by Germany 9.9.1943 (TA34)
Corsaro	OTO, Livorno	1.1941	16.11.1941	5.1942	sunk 9.1.1943
Legionario	OTO, Livorno	10.1940	16.4.1941	3.1942	to France 8.1948 (Duchaffault)
Mitragliere	CNR, Ancona	10.1940	28.9.1941	2.1942	to France 7.1948 (Jurien de la Gravière)
Squadrista, 7.1943- Corsaro	OTO, Livorno	9.1941	12.9.1942	-	captured incomplete by Germany 9.9.1943 (TA33)
Velite	OTO, Livorno	4.1941	31.8.1941	8.1942	to France 7.1948 (Duperré)

1830 / 2460 t, 106.7 x 10.2 x 3.5 m, 2 sets Beluzzo (*Alpino, Bersagliere, Carabiniere, Fuciliere, Granatiere, Lanciere, Bombardiere, Mitragliere*) or Parsons geared steam turbines, 3 Yarrow boilers, 48000 hp, 38 kts, 517 t oil, 2200 nm (20 kts), complement 165-206; 2 x 2 – 120/50 Ansaldo 1936, 1 x 1 – 120/50 Ansaldo 1940 (*2nd group except Velite*), 1 x 1 – 120/15 OTO 1934 (*1st group except Carabiniere; Velite*), 4 x 2 – 20/65 Breda 1935 (*2nd group*), (4 x 2 + 4 x 1) – 13.2 MG (*1st group*), 2 x 3 – 533 TT, 2 (*1st group*) or 4 (*2nd group*) DCT, 48 mines (*1st group*); FuMO 21 (*Legionario*), EC.3/ter (*Velite*) radar, S-Gerät sonar (*Bombardiere, Corsaro, Mitragliere, Legionario, Velite*), hydrophone.

Camicia Nera 1940

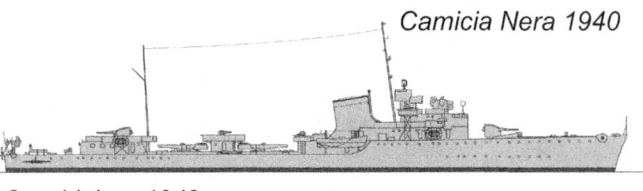

Carabiniere 1943

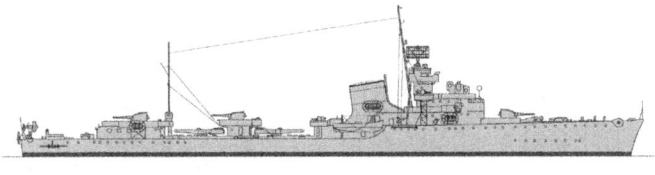

The most successful and numerous class of Italian destroyers. The first 12 ships were ordered in 1936 as repetition of the *Oriani*. Already during the construction, the design received some changes: the 120-mm guns of the new mark, as well as little changed machinery, which, with the same power, became more efficient and reliable. In addition to the new main guns, 120-mm/15 star-shell howitzer was installed and the number of 13.2-mm MGs was increased to 12. The overload after all the innovations became about 200 t, from 1620 to 1830 t, but despite this, destroyers of the "*Soldati*" class in real conditions were the fastest Italian destroyers: their speed reached 34-35 kts.

A second order for seven ships followed in 1940. All changes made to the design of the 1st "*Soldati*" group were extended to the ships of the 2nd group, in addition, after the appearance of a single 120-mm/50 mount, it began to be installed on new destroyers instead of a star-shell howitzer (except *Velite*).

Five 2nd group ships were commissioned before September 1943; *Squadrista* and *Carrista* remained incomplete, and work on the latter was suspended even earlier. The incomplete hull was used as a source of spare parts for the repair of damaged sister-ships: the

Legionario 1942

bow went to *Carabiniere*, and the stern to *Velite*.
1941-1942, all survived of 1st group: - (4 x 2 + 4 x 1) - 13.2 MG; + 4 x 2 - 20/65 Breda 1935, 2 DCT, S-Gerät sonar (some). 1941-1942, *Carabiniere*: + 1 x 1 - 120/50 Ansaldo 1940. 1941-1942, *Ascari, Camicia Nera, Geniere, Lanciere*: - 1 x 1 - 120/15; + 1 x 1 - 120/50 Ansaldo 1940.
1942, *Carabiniere, Fuciliere*: + EC3/ter radar.
1943, *Carabiniere, Granatiere, Legionario*: - 1 x 3 - 533 TT; + 2 x 1 - 37/54 Breda 1939. 1943, *Fucilirere*: - 1 x 1 - 120/15, 1 x 3 - 533 TT; + 2 x 1 - 37/54 Breda 1939. 1943, *Velite*: - 1 x 1 - 120/15, 1 x 3 - 533 TT; + 3 x 1 - 37/54 Breda 1939. 1943, all survived: + (4 - 5) x 1 - 20/65 Breda 1940.
Artigliere 12.10.1940 was sunk by British cruisers *York* and *Ajax* off Malta. *Lanciere* 23.5.1942 sank during a storm in the Ionian Sea. *Aviere* 17.12.1942 was sunk by two torpedoes from British submarine *Splendid* near Bizerte. *Bersagliere* 7.1.1943 was sunk by US aircraft at Palermo. *Corsaro* 9.1.1943 was sunk by two mines laid by British minelayer *Abdiel* near Bizerte. *Bombardiere* 17.1.1943 was sunk by British submarine *United* off the W coast of Sicily. *Geniere* 1.3.1943 was destroyed by US aircraft in the dock at Palermo. *Ascari* 24.3.1943 was sunk by three mines laid by British minelayer *Abdiel* off the coast of Tunisia. *Alpino* 19.4.1943 was sunk by British aircraft at La Spezia, salvaged but never recommissioned. Scuttled by the Germans 24.4.1945 at Genoa. *Camicia Nera* 30.7.1943 was renamed *Artigliere*. *Corazziere* 9.9.1943 was scuttled by her crew at Genoa, salvaged by the Germans but never repaired. Sunk 4.9.1944 by Allied aircraft at Genoa. *Squadrista* in July 1943 was renamed *Corsaro*, captured incomplete at Livorno by German troops in September 1943, renamed *TA33*. Sunk at Genoa by Allied aircraft 4.3.1944. *Carrista* was captured incomplete by German troops in September 1943, renamed *TA34* and broken up on the stocks.

Ex-Yugoslav SEBENICO class destroyers

Sebenico (ex-Beograd)	A C de la Loire, Nantes, France	1936	23.12.1937	(1.1939) / 4.1941	captured by Germany 9.1943 (TA43)
Lubiana (ex-Ljubljana)	Jadranske B G, Split, Yugoslavia	1937	28.6.1938	(12.1939) / 4.1941	sunk 1.4.1943

Sebenico 1941

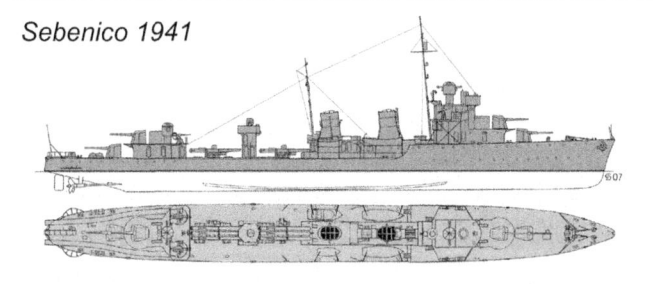

1210 / 1655 t, 98.0 x 9.5 x 3.2 m, 2 sets Curtis (*Sebenico*) or Parsons geared steam turbines, 3 Yarrow boilers, 40000 hp, 38 kts, 240 t oil, 2400 nm (16 kts), complement 183; 4 x 1 – 120/46 Škoda, 2 x 2 – 40/56 Bofors M36 (*Sebenico*), 1 x 1 – 37/54 Breda 1939 (*Lubiana*), 5 x 1 – 20/65 Breda 1940 (*Lubiana*), 2 x 3 – 533 TT, 2 DCT, 30 mines.
Yugoslavian destroyers surrendered 17.4.1941 and underwent modernization until August-October 1942.
Lubiana 1.4.1943 was sunk at Tunis by British aircraft. *Sebenico* in September 1943 was captured by German troops at Venice, renamed *TA43* and scuttled 1.5.1945 by the crew at Trieste.

Ex-Yugoslav PREMUDA destroyer

Premuda (ex-Dubrovnik)	Yarrow, Scotstoun, UK	6.1930	11.10.1931	(1932) / 4.1941	captured by Germany 8.9.1943 (TA32)

2100 / 2884 t, 113.2 x 10.7 x 3.6 m, 2 sets Parsons geared steam turbines, 3 Yarrow boilers, 48000 hp, 37 kts, 528 t oil, 4690 nm (18 kts), complement 204; 4 x 1 – 140/56 Škoda, 1 x 1 – 120/15 OTO 1934, 1 x 2 – 37/54 Breda 1938, 4 x 1 – 20/65 Breda 1940, 2 x 3 – 533 TT, 2 DCT; presumably sonar.
Yugoslavian destroyer *Dubrovnik* surrendered 17.4.1941 and underwent modernization until January 1942. In the mid-1943 she was again put in for repairs: it was supposed to replace the artillery with 135-mm/45 guns and 37-mm/54 and 20-mm/70 MGs. It was planned to remove one TT bank to compensate the overload.
Premuda was captured 8.9.1943 by German troops at Genoa during repairs, renamed *TA32* and 24-25.4.1945 scuttled at Genoa.

ITALY

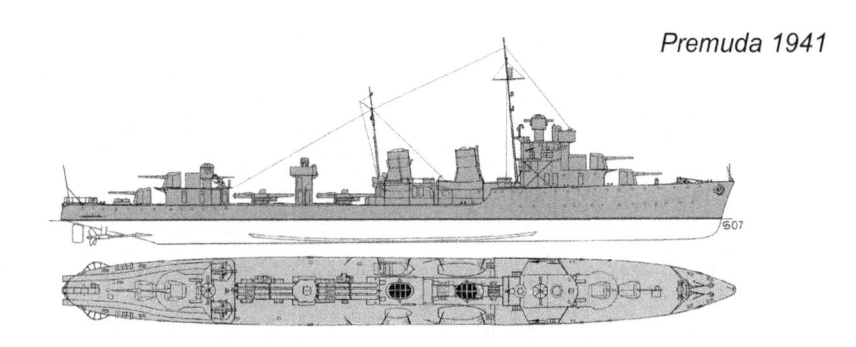

Premuda 1941

'COMANDANTI MEDAGLIE D'ORO' class destroyers

Comandante Baroni	OTO, Livorno	2.1943	-	- captured incomplete by Germany 8.9.1943
Comandante Borsini	OTO, Livorno	4.1943	-	- captured incomplete by Germany 8.9.1943
Comandante Botti	CRDA, Trieste	8.1943	-	- captured incomplete by Germany 8.9.1943
Comandante Casana	CNR, Ancona	2.1943	-	- captured incomplete by Germany 8.9.1943
Comandante De Cristofaro	CT, Riva Trigoso	2.1943	-	- captured incomplete by Germany 8.9.1943
Comandante Dell'Anno	CNR, Ancona	2.1943	-	- captured incomplete by Germany 8.9.1943
Comandante Fontana	OTO, Livorno	summer 1943	-	- captured incomplete by Germany 8.9.1943
Comandante Giobbe	CT, Riva Trigoso	10.1943	-	- captured incomplete by Germany 8.9.1943
Comandante Giorgis	CT, Riva Trigoso	9.1943	-	- captured incomplete by Germany 8.9.1943
Comandante Margottini	OTO, Livorno	3.1943	early 1944	- captured incomplete by Germany 8.9.1943
Comandante Moccagatta	OTO, Livorno	11.1943	-	- captured incomplete by Germany 8.9.1943
Comandante Rodocanacchi	OTO, Livorno	12.1943	-	- captured incomplete by Germany 8.9.1943
Comandante Ruta	CRDA, Trieste	8.1943	-	- captured incomplete by Germany 8.9.1943
Comandante Toscano	CT, Riva Trigoso	12.1942	-	- captured incomplete by Germany 8.9.1943

Comandante Toscano

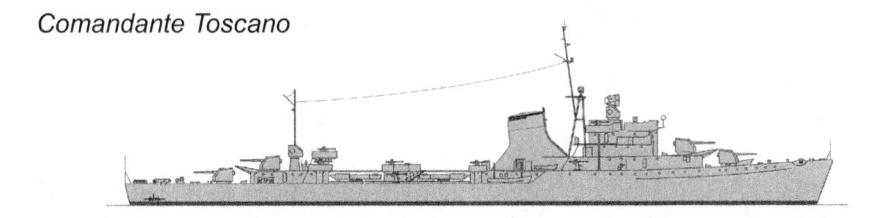

2067 / 2900 t, 120.7 x 12.3 x 3.6 m, 2 sets geared steam turbines, 3 boilers, 60000 hp, 35 kts, complement 272; 4 x 1 – 135/45 OTO/Ansaldo 1938, 12 x 1 – 37/54 Breda 1939, 2 x 3 – 533 TT, 4 DCT; EC.3/ter radar, S-Gerät sonar.

Unique Italian destroyers, the design of which took into account the experience of the war. Design work began in late 1940, and by mid-1942 the new destroyer was transformed from a slightly modified "*Soldati*" into a 2000-t ship with 135-mm main guns. At one stage of the design, 135-mm guns were placed in both single and twin mounts, but in the final version, preference was given to four single mounts. To maintain speed at an acceptable level, the power of the machinery was increased to 60000 hp. The general arrangement scheme repeated that adopted on earlier ships. The exception was to be one destroyer, which was supposed to be built with the machinery arrangement *en echelon* scheme instead of the linear one.

In total, 20 ships were assigned to the construction, but only 9 were laid down. All the ships laid down were captured by German troops in September 1943 on the stocks. The Germans did not make serious attempts to complete these ships, but it is known that one destroyer, *Comandante Margottini*, was launched during the German occupations, apparently only to clear the slipway.

Comandante Corsi, Comandante Esposito, Comandante Fiorelli, Comandante Gianattasio, Comandante Milano, Comandante Novaro (CRDA, Trieste) were ordered but never laid down.

Ex-French FR21 class destroyers

| **FR21** *(ex-Lion)* | A C de France, Dunkerque, France | 7.1927 | 5.8.1929 | (2.1931) / 1.1943 | scuttled 9.9.1943 |
| FR24 *(ex-Valmy)* | A C de St-Nazaire-Penhoët, France | 5.1927 | 19.5.1928 | (1.1930) | captured incomplete by Germany 9.9.1943 |

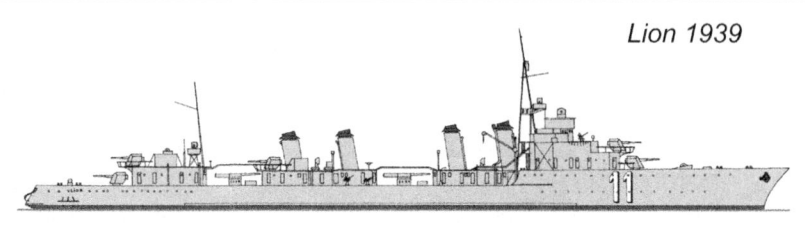

Lion 1939

2436 / 3200 t, 130.2 x 11.8 x 4.7 m, 2 sets Zoelly (*FR21*) or Parsons geared steam turbines, 4 Yarrow or Penhoët boilers, 64000 hp, 35.5 kts, 572 t oil, 2900 nm (16 kts), complement 230; 5 x 1 – 139/40 M1923, 1 x 2 – 37/50 M1933 (*FR24*), 4 x 1 – 37/50 M1925, 2 x 2 (*FR21*) or (2 x 2 + 2 x 1) (*FR24*) – 13.2 MG, 2 (*FR21*) or 1 (*FR24*) x 3 – 550 TT, 2 DCR (32).

French destroyers scuttled at Toulon 27.11.1942. Both were salvaged by the Italians. Only *FR21* was commissioned by the Italian Navy. Inoperable *FR24* was captured by the Germans but never repaired.
FR21 was scuttled by her own crew 9.9.1943 at La Spezia to avoid capture.

Ex-French FR22 class destroyers

| FR22 *(ex-Panthère)* | Arsenal de Lorient, France | 12.1922 | 27.10.1924 | (11.1926) | scuttled incomplete 8.9.1943 |
| FR23 *(ex-Tigre)* | A C de Bretagne, Nantes, France | 9.1923 | 2.8.1924 | (12.1925) | commissioned as personnel transport, returned to France 10.1943 (Tigre) |

Tigre 1940

2126 / 2950-3050 t, 126.8 x 11.3 x 4.1 m, 2 sets Rateau-Bretagne geared steam turbines, 5 Du Temple boilers, 50000 hp, 35.5 kts, 530 t oil, 2900 nm (16 kts), complement 195; 4 x 1 – 130/40 M1919, 4 x 2 – 13.2 MG, 2 x 3 – 550 TT, 4 DCT, 2 DCR (46).

French destroyers *Panthère* and *Tigre* were scuttled at Toulon 27.11.1942 but salvaged by the Italians and renamed *FR22* and *FR23*. The former was never repaired, the latter was commissioned by the Italian navy as an auxiliary personnel transport and returned to France after the surrender of Italy.

ITALY

Ex-French FR31 destroyer

FR31 (ex-Trombe)	F C de la Gironde, Bordeaux, France	3.1923	29.12.1925	(10.1927) / 1.1943	returned to France 10.1943 (Trombe)

1319 / 1900 t, 105.8 x 9.6 x 4.3 m, 2 sets Zoelly geared steam turbines, 3 Du Temple boilers, 33000 hp, 33 kts, 345 t oil, 2300 nm (14 kts), complement 142; 4 x 1 – 130/40 M1919, 2 x 1 – 37/50 M1925, 2 x 2 – 13.2 MG, 2 x 3 – 550 TT, 2 DCT, 2 DCR (32).
French destroyer *Trombe* was scuttled at Toulon 27.11.1942, later salvaged by the Italians and renamed *FR31*.

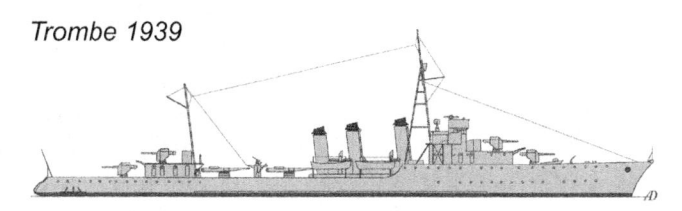

Trombe 1939

FR31 was returned to France after the surrender of Italy.

Ex-French FR32 class destroyers

FR32 (ex-Siroco, ex-Le Corsaire)	F C de la Méditerranée, La Seyne, France	3.1938	14.11.1939	(7.1941)	captured incomplete by Germany 9.9.1943
FR33 (ex-L'Adroit, ex-Epée)	F C de la Méditerranée, La Seyne, France	10.1936	26.10.1938	(6.1940)	captured incomplete by Germany 9.9.1943
FR34 (ex-Lansquenet)	F C de la Gironde, Bordeaux, France	12.1936	20.5.1939	-	captured incomplete by Germany 9.9.1943
FR35 (ex-Bison, ex-Le Filibustier)	F C de la Méditerranée, La Seyne, France	3.1938	14.12.1939	-	captured incomplete by Germany 9.9.1943
FR36 (ex-Le Foudroyant, ex-Fleuret)	F C de la Méditerranée, La Seyne, France	8.1936	28.7.1938	(6.1940)	captured incomplete by Germany 8.9.1943
FR37 (ex-Le Hardi)	A C de la Loire, Nantes, France	5.1936	4.5.1938	(6.1940)	captured incomplete by Germany 9.9.1943

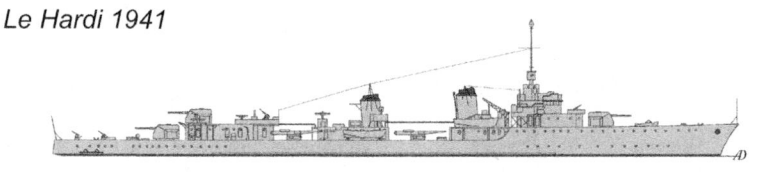

Le Hardi 1941

1772 / 2577 t, 117.2 x 11.1 x 4.2 m, 2 sets Rateau-Bretagne or Parsons (*FR32*) geared steam turbines, 4 Sural-Norguet boilers, 58000 hp, 37 kts, 470 t oil, 2760 nm (20 kts), complement 187; 3 x 2 – 130/45 M1935, 1 x 2 – 37/50 M1933, 4 x 2 – 13.2 MG, 5 x 1 – 8 MG, (1 x 3 + 2 x 2) – 550 TT, 1 DCR (8), 1 Ginocchio towed AS torpedo.

All these French destroyers were scuttled at Toulon and later salvaged by the Italians. *Le Hardi* was renamed *FR37*, *Foudroyant FR36*, *Epée FR33*, *Lansquenet FR34*, *Sirocco FR32* and *Bison FR35*. Later they all were captured by the Germans and scuttled. Only *FR33* was returned to France but in very bad condition.

Ex-Yugoslav SPALATO destroyer

Spalato (ex-Split)	Jadranska Brodogradilista, Split, Yugoslavia	7.1939	18.7.1943	(7.1958)	scuttled incomplete 20.9.1943

2040 / 2500 t, 121.0 x 12.0 x 3.5 m, 2 sets Tosi geared steam turbines, 3 Yarrow boilers, 55000 hp, 38 kts, 560 t oil, complement 214; 5 x 1 – 135/45 OTO/Ansaldo 1938, 10 x 1 – 37/54 Breda 1939, 4 x 2 – 20/65 Breda 1935, 1 x 3 – 533 TT, 2 DCT, 2 DCR, 40 mines; EC.3/ter radar, S-Gerät sonar.
Split was laid down in Split for the Yugoslavian Navy, captured by the Italians on the stocks 18.4.1941, renamed *Spalato* and launched 18.7.1943. The incomplete ship was scuttled in the dock 20.9.1943 by Yugoslav partisans, but then captured by the Germans and salvaged by them in 1944. The hull was scuttled again by the Germans in October 1944 but salvaged again after the war.

Split 1958

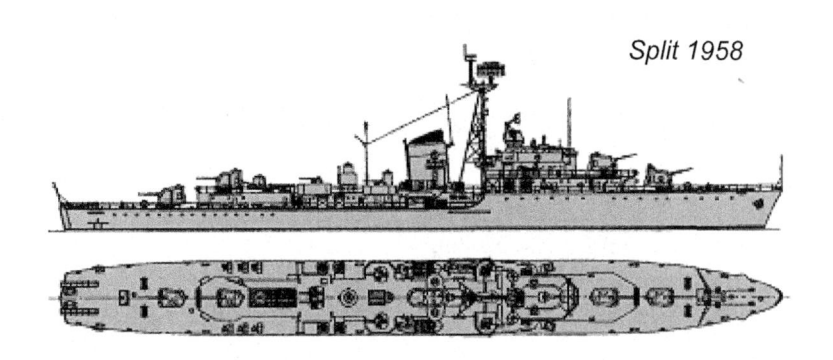

70OLT class torpedo boat

| **75OLT** | Orlando, Livorno | 6.1916 | 12.1.1918 | 9.1918 | stricken 11.1937 |

75OLT 1935

168 / 195 t, 45.7 x 4.6 x 1.8 m, 2 Orlando steam turbines, 2 Thornycroft boilers, 3500 hp, 27 kts, 23 t oil, 860 nm (14 kts), complement 31; 2 x 1 – 76/30 Armstrong 1914, 1 x 2 – 450 TT, 7 mines.
An obsolete small torpedo boat, the last presentative of a large series.

INDOMITO class torpedo boats

Indomito	Pattison, Napoli	6.1910	10.5.1912	1.1913	stricken 7.1937
Impavido	Pattison, Napoli	1.1911	22.3.1913	11.1913	stricken 9.1937
Insidioso	Pattison, Napoli	7.1912	30.9.1913	7.1914	stricken 9.1938, reinstated 3.1941, scuttled 10.9.1943
Irrequieto	Pattison, Napoli	6.1910	12.12.1912	6.1913	stricken 10.1937

Insidioso 1941

Insidioso 1941

672 / 900 t, 73.0 x 7.3 x 2.4 m, 2 Tosi steam turbines, 4 Thornycroft boilers, 16000 hp, 27-28 kts, 128 t oil, 1200 nm (14 kts), complement 69-79; 5 x 1 – 102/35 Schneider 1915-1915, 1 x 1 – 40/39 Vickers-Terni 1917, 2 x 2 – 450 TT, 10 mines.
The *Indomito* class design was developed by Pattison under the leadership of chief designer L. Scaglia in 1912 as a response to large dstroyers with 100-mm main guns that appeared in the Austro-Hungarian and French navies. The *Indomito* class ships were the first Italian rigorous destroyers to be equipped with steam turbines and exclusively oil-fired boilers. On trials, they made 33-35.5 kts. During the years of the First World War, 32 destroyers of this class were built in Italy in five groups (*Indomito* class and 4 more "improved" versions), which differed from each other mainly in the structure and arrangement of armament. All these destroyers were also known under the collective nickname "3-funnelers". 3.1941, *Insidioso*: had only 3 boilers with 2 funnels, 12000 hp, 24 kts, 758 / 890 t, armament consisted of 1 x 1 - 102/45 Schneider-Armstrong 1917, 2 x 2 - 20/70 Scotti-Isotta Fraschini 1939, 1 x 2 - 13.2 MG, 1 x 2 - 533 TT, 2 DCT, complement 75.

Insidioso, left in reserve since 1938, was recommissioned in March 1941 after modernization. Being rated as torpedo boat, she some time was used as a target ship for submariners, and then as an escort. *Insidioso* 10.9.1943 was captured at Pola by German troops, renamed *TA21 Wildfang*, damaged by British aircraft 9.8.1944 and 5.11.1944 sunk at Fiume by Allied bombers while being repaired.

ITALY

ROSOLINO PILO class torpedo boats

Name	Builder				
Rosolino Pilo	Odero, Sestri Ponente	8.1913	24.3.1915	5.1915	stricken 10.1954
Giuseppe Cesare Abba	Odero, Sestri Ponente	8.1913	25.5.1915	7.1915	stricken 9.1958
Giuseppe Dezza *(ex-Pilade Bronzetti)*	Odero, Sestri Ponente	9.1913	26.10.1915	1.1916	captured by Germany 16.9.1943 (TA35)
Giuseppe Missori	Odero, Sestri Ponente	1.1914	20.12.1915	3.1916	captured by Germany 10.9.1943 (TA22)
Antonio Mosto	Pattison, Napoli	10.1913	20.5.1915	7.1915	stricken 12.1958
Ippolito Nievo	Odero, Sestri Ponente	8.1913	24.7.1915	10.1915	stricken 4.1938
Fratelli Cairoli *(ex-Francesco Nullo)*	Pattison, Napoli	9.1913	12.11.1914	5.1915	sunk 23.12.1940
Simone Schiaffino	Odero, Sestri Ponente	9.1913	11.9.1915	11.1915	sunk 24.4.1941

770 / 912 t, 73.0 x 7.3 x 2.3 m, 2 Tosi steam turbines, 4 Thornycroft boilers, 16000 or 14800 (*Antonio Mosto, Frateli Cairoli*) hp, 30 or 29 (*Antonio Mosto, Fratelli Cairoli*) kts, 150 t oil, 1200 nm (14 kts), complement 69-79; 5 x 1 – 102/35 Schneider 1914-1915, 2 x 1 – 40/39 Vickers 1917, 2 x 1 – 6.5 MG, 4 x 1 – 450 TT, 10 mines. Development of the *Indomito* class with new guns, increased cruising range and cruising turbines. Re-rated as torpedo boats in 1929. By 1940, their speed did not exceed 25 kts.

1941-1942, all survived: - 3 x 1 - 102/35, 2 x 1 - 40/39, 2 x 1 - 450 TT; + 6 x 1 - 20/65 Breda 1940, 2 DCT.

Fratelli Cairoli 23.12.1940 was sunk by a mine laid by British submarine *Porpoise* off Tripoli. *Simone Schiaffino* 24.4.1941 was sunk by Italian mines off the coast of Tunisia. *Giuseppe Dezza* 16.9.1943 was captured by German troops at Fiume, renamed *TA35* and was mined 17.8.1944 off Pola. *Giuseppe Missori* 10.9.1943 was captured by German troops at Durazzo, renamed *TA22*, 25.6.1944 badly damaged by British aircraft SE of Trieste and scuttled there 2.5.1945.

Rosolino Pilo 1940

Rosolino Pilo prewar

GIUSEPPE SIRTORI class torpedo boats

Name	Builder				
Giuseppe Sirtori	Odero, Sestri Ponente	2.1916	24.11.1916	12.1916	wrecked 14.9.1943
Giovanni Acerbi	Odero, Sestri Ponente	2.1916	14.2.1917	2.1917	sunk 4.4.1941
Vincenzo Giordano Orsini	Odero, Sestri Ponente	2.1916	23.4.1917	5.1917	scuttled 8.4.1941
Francesco Stocco	Odero, Sestri Ponente	2.1916	5.5.1917	7.1917	sunk 24.9.1943

790 / 850 t, 73.5 x 7.3 x 2.8 m, 2 Tosi steam turbines, 4 Thornycroft boilers, 15500 hp, 30 kts, 150 t oil, 2000 nm (14 kts), complement 84-85; 6 x 1 – 102/45 Schneider-Armstrong 1917, 2 x 1 – 40/39 Vickers 1915, 2 x 1 – 6.5 MG, 2 x 2 – 450 TT, 10 mines.

Development of the *Pilo* class with an artillery caliber increased to 102 mm and twin TTs. All armament was arranged along the sides, outside the centerline. In 1929 they were re-rated as torpedo boats. 1942, *Giuseppe Sirtori, Francesco Stocco*: - 2 x 1 - 102/45; + 2 DCT.

Giovanni Acerbi 4.4.1941 was sunk by British aircraft

Giuseppe Sirtori 1940

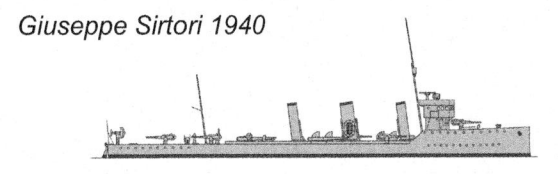

Giuseppe Sirtori prewar

at Massawa, Eritrea. *Vincenzo Giordano Orsini* 8.4.1941 was scuttled by crew at Massawa, Eritrea. *Giuseppe Sirtori* 14.9.1943 was badly damaged by German aircraft off Corfu, ran ashore and 25.9.1943 blown up by the crew. *Francesco Stocco* 24.9.1943 was sunk off Corfu by German aircraft.

AUDACE torpedo boat

Audace (ex-*Intrepido*, ex-*Kawakaze*)	Yarrow, Scotstoun, UK	10.1913	27.9.1916	3.1917	captured by Germany 12.9.1943 (TA20)

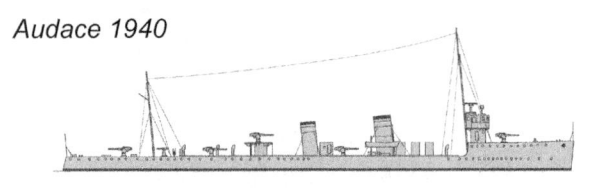

Audace 1940

Audace 1917

922 / 1170 t, 87.5 x 8.3 x 2.5 m, 2 Brown-Curtis steam turbines, 3 Yarrow boilers, 22000 hp, 30 kts, 248 t oil, 2180 nm (15 kts), complement 118; 7 x 1 – 102/35 Schneider 1914-1915, 2 x 1 – 40/39 Vickers 1915, 2 x 1 – 6.5 MG, 2 x 2 – 450 TT.

Audace was ordered by Japan in 1912 in the UK as *Kawakaze* together with the sister-ship *Urakaze*, but 3.7.1916 by agreement between Japan and Italy, she was transferred to the latter and renamed. At first, she was named *Intrepido*, but 25.9.1916 renamed *Audace*. The design provided for a mixed diesel-turbine machinery, however, since the order for cruising diesels was placed in Germany, the diesels were left in Germany, and the destroyer was commissioned with a conventional steam turbine machinery. On trials, the destroyer reached 34.5-kt speed. 120-mm and 76-mm guns and 533-mm TTs envisaged by the design were replaced by Italian 102-mm/35 guns and 450-mm TTs.

In September 1929, the ship was re-rated as torpedo boat. In 1938, she was converted to a command-and-control ship for the radio-controlled target *San Marco*. In this case both TT banks were removed. By the beginning of WWII, the maximum speed was 28 kts.
1938: - 2 x 2 - 450 TT
1942: - 5 x 1 - 102/35, 2 x 1 - 40/39; + 10 x 2 - 20/65 Breda 1935, 2 DCT.

Audace was captured by German troops in September 1943, renamed *TA20* and sunk 1.11.1944 by gunfire from British escort destroyers *Avon Vale* and *Wheatland* in the Adriatic Sea.

GIUSEPPE LA MASA class torpedo boats

Giuseppe La Masa	Odero, Sestri Ponente	9.1916	6.9.1917	9.1919	captured by Germany 9.9.1943
Angelo Bassini	Odero, Sestri Ponente	10.1916	28.3.1918	5.1918	sunk 28.5.1943
Enrico Cosenz (ex-*Agostino Bertani*)	Odero, Sestri Ponente	12.1917	6.6.1919	6.1919	scuttled 27.9.1943
Giacinto Carini	Odero, Sestri Ponente	9.1916	7.11.1917	11.1917	stricken 12.1958
Nicola Fabrizi	Odero, Sestri Ponente	9.1916	8.7.1918	7.1918	stricken 2.1957
Giuseppe La Farina	Odero, Sestri Ponente	12.1917	12.3.1919	3.1919	sunk 4.5.1941
Giacomo Medici	Odero, Sestri Ponente	10.1916	6.9.1918	9.1918	sunk 16.4.1943

Giuseppe La Masa 1942

785 / 851 t, 73.5 x 7.3 x 2.8 m, 2 Tosi steam turbines, 4 Thornycroft boilers, 15500 hp, 30 kts, 150 t oil, 2230 nm (12.5 kts), complement 78; 4 x 1 – 102/45 Schneider-Armstrong 1917, 2 x 1 – 76/40 Ansaldo 1917, 2 x 1 – 6.5 MG, 2 x 2 – 450 TT, 10 mines.

ITALY

The repeated *Sirtori* class differed from the latter with new 102-mm guns with a longer 45-cal bore instead of 35-cal one and the replacement of 40-mm AA MGs by 76-mm/40 guns. Due to the increased weight of the new artillery, the number of main guns had to be reduced from six to four, but due to the placement of some of them on the centerline, the side salvo did not decrease. In 1929, they all were re-rated as torpedo boats.

1940-1942, *Angelo Bassini, Enrico Cosenz, Nicola Fabrizzi, Giuseppe La Farina, Giacomo Medici*: - (1 - 2) x 1 - 102/45, 2 x 1 - 76/40, 2 x 1 - 6.5 MG, (0 - 1) x 2 - 450 TT; + 6 x 1 - 20/65 Breda 1940, 0 - 2 DCT 1942, *Giuseppe La Masa, Giacinto Carini*: - 3 x 1 - 102/45, 2 x 1 - 76/40, 2 x 1 - 6.5 MG, 1 x 2 - 450 TT; + 4 x 2 - 20/65 Breda 1935, 1 x 3 - 533 TT.

Giuseppe la Farina 4.5.1941 was sunk by Italian mines off the E coast of Tunisia. *Giacomo Medici* 16.4.1943 was sunk by US aircraft at Catania. *Angello Bassini* 28.5.1943 was sunk by US aircraft at Livorno. *Giuseppe la Masa* 9.9.1943 was captured by German troops and 11.9.1943 blown up at Naples. *Enrico Cosenz* 27.9.1943 was badly damaged by German aircraft and scuttled by her crew in the Adriatic Sea.

Ex-Austro-Hungarian GRADO class torpedo boats

Cortelazzo *(ex-Lika)*	Danubius, Porto Rè, Austria-Hungary	8.1916	8.5.1917	(9.1917) / 9.1920	stricken 1.1939
Grado *(ex-Triglav)*	Danubius, Porto Rè, Austria-Hungary	8.1916	24.2.1917	(7.1917) / 9.1920	stricken 9.1937
Monfalcone *(ex-Uzsok)*	Danubius, Porto Rè, Austria-Hungary	9.1916	16.9.1917	(1.1918) / 9.1920	stricken 1.1939

880 / 1045 t, 85.4 x 7.8 x 2.4 m, 2 AEG-Curtiss steam turbines, 6 Yarrow boilers, 22360 hp, 32.6 kts, 131 t coal + oil, 1600 nm (12 kts), complement 114; 2 x 1 – 100/47 G.K.10, 6 x 1 – 66/42 G. BAG, 2 x 1 – 6.5 MG, 2 x 2 – 450 TT. Austro-Hungarian destroyers transferred under reparations. Reclassified as torpedo boats in October 1929.

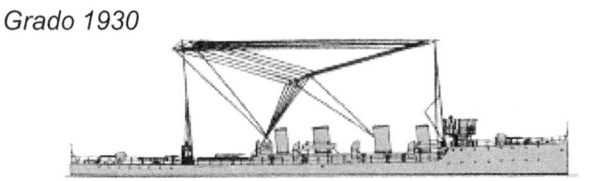

Grado 1930

PALESTRO class torpedo boats

Palestro	Orlando, Livorno	4.1917	23.3.1919	1.1921	sunk 22.9.1940
Confienza	Orlando, Livorno	5.1917	18.12.1920	4.1923	collision 20.11.1940
San Martino	Orlando, Livorno	4.1917	8.9.1920	10.1922	captured by Germany 9.9.1943 (TA18, later TA17)
Solferino	Orlando, Livorno	4.1917	28.4.1920	10.1921	captured by Germany 9.9.1943 (TA18)

875 / 1076 t, 81.9 x 8.0 x 2.7 m, 2 Zoelly steam turbines, 4 Thornycroft boilers, 18000 hp, 32 kts, 208 t oil, 1970 nm (14 kts), complement 118; 4 x 1 – 102/45 Schneider-Armstrong 1917, 2 x 1 – 76/40 Ansaldo 1917, 2 x 1 – 6.5 MG, 2 x 2 – 450 TT, 10 – 38 mines.

The design was developed by Orlando in 1915 on the basis of the earlier destroyer *Audace*. These ships differed from the *Indomito* classs in larger dimensions, a lengthened forecastle and two funnels instead of three. 18000-hp machinery provided an increase in speed increment up to 32 kts. In the rest, they were quite close to the last "three-funnelers" of the 3rd and 4th groups.

At the end of 1915, 8 ships of the *Palestro* class were ordered, but due to wartime shortages of shipbuilding steel and other strategic materials, the construction of four of them was suspended indefinitely. The remaining four, for the same reasons, were built slowly and entered service only in the early twenties. The *Palestro* class turned out to be more successful, than the "three-funnelers".

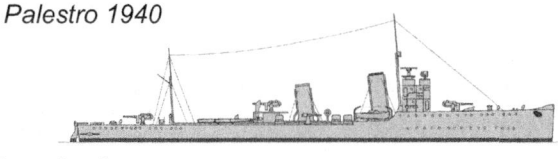

Palestro 1940

In 1938 they were re-rated as torpedo boats. Shortly before the outbreak of the Second World War, it was planned to strengthen the AA armament, replacing one 102-mm and both 76-mm guns with four 20-mm MGs,

San Martino prewar

but these plans were not implemented.
1942, San Martino, Solferino: - 2 x 1 - 102/45, 2 x 1 - 76/40; + 6 x 1 - 20/65 Breda 1940, 2 DCT.
Palestro 22.9.1940 was sunk by British submarine Osiris W of Durazzo. Confienza 20.11.1940 sank as result of a collision with auxiliary cruiser Capitano A. Cecchi off Brindisi. San Martino 9.9.1943 was captured by German troops at Piraeus, renamed TA18, then TA17, repeatedly damaged, stricken 12.10.1944 and scuttled. Solferino 9.9.1943 was captured by German troops at Suda, renamed TA18, 19.10.1944 badly damaged by gunfire from British destroyers Termagant and Tuscan near Skiathos Island, ran aground and destroyed.

GENERALE ANTONIO CANTORE class torpedo boats

Generale Antonio Cantore	Odero, Sestri Ponente	11.1919	23.4.1921	7.1921	sunk 22.8.1942
Generale Antonio Cascino	Odero, Sestri Ponente	3.1920	18.3.1922	5.1922	scuttled 9.9.1943
Generale Antonio Chinotto	Odero, Sestri Ponente	11.1919	7.8.1921	9.1921	sunk 28.3.1941
Generale Carlo Montanari	Odero, Sestri Ponente	6.1921	4.10.1922	11.1922	scuttled 9.9.1943
Generale Achille Papa	Odero, Sestri Ponente	12.1919	8.12.1921	2.1922	scuttled 9.9.1943
Generale Marcello Prestinari	Odero, Sestri Ponente	5.1921	4.7.1922	8.1922	sunk 31.1.1943

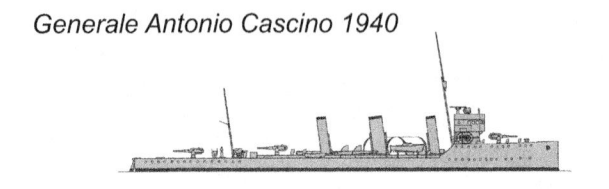

Generale Antonio Cascino 1940

730 / 870 t, 73.5 x 7.3 x 2.7 m, 2 Tosi steam turbines, 4 Thornycroft boilers, 15500 hp, 30 kts, 150 t oil, 2000 nm (14 kts), complement 118; 3 x 1 – 102/45 Schneider-Armstrong 1917, 2 x 1 – 76/40 Ansaldo 1917, 2 x 2 – 450 TT, 2 DCT, sweeps.
The last representatives of the Indomito family. An almost exact repetition of the La Masa class, but with the number of 102-mm guns reduced to three, located on the center line. In 1929, they were re-rated as torpedo boats.

1939, all: - 2 x 1 - 76/40; + 2 x 2 - 20 Breda 1935, (2 - 4) x 1 – 8 MG.
Generale Antonio Chinotto 28.3.1941 was sunk by a mine laid by British submarine Rorqual off Palermo. Generale Antonio Cantore 22.8.1942 was sunk by a mine laid by British submarine Porpoise off the coast of Cyrenaica. Generale Marcello Prestinari 31.1.1943 was sunk by a mine laid by British minelayer Welshman in the Strait of Sicily. Generale Antonio Cascino 9.9.1943 was scuttled by her crew at La Spezia. Generale Carlo Montanari 9.9.1943 was scuttled by the crew at La Spezia, salvaged by the Germans but never commissioned by them and 4.10.1944 sunk by Allied aircraft at La Spezia. Generale Achille Papa 9.9.1943 was scuttled by her crew at Genoa, salvaged by the Germans, originally named TA7, subsequently renamed SG20 but was never commissioned by them.

CURTATONE class torpedo boats

Calatafimi	Orlando, Livorno	12.1920	17.3.1923	5.1924	captured by Germany 9.9.1943 (TA19)
Castelfidardo	Orlando, Livorno	7.1920	4.6.1922	3.1924	captured by Germany 9.9.1943 (TA16)
Curtatone	Orlando, Livorno	1.1920	17.3.1922	6.1923	sunk 20.5.1941
Monzambano	Orlando, Livorno	1.1921	6.8.1923	6.1924	stricken 4.1951

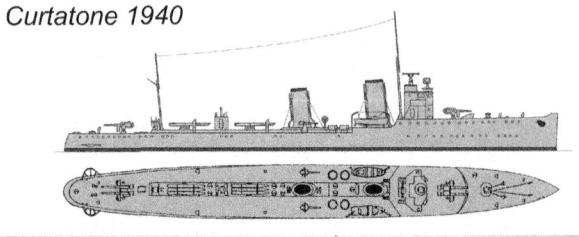

Curtatone 1940

Monzambano 1926

953 / 1214 t, 84.7 x 8.0 x 2.9 m, 2 Zoelly steam turbines, 4 Thornycroft boilers, 22000 hp, 32 kts, 206 t oil, 1800 nm (15 kts), complement 117; 2 x 2 – 102/45 Schneider-Armstrong 1919, 2 x 1 – 76/30 Armstrong 1914, 2 x 3 – 450 TT, 16 mines.
4 Curtatone class ships were ordered in 1915 and were originally the Palestro class, but their building was suspended until the end of the war. The laying of the keels took place only in 1920 according to a modified design, in which, in comparison with the prototype, many innovations was made regarding the structure and arrangement of the armament. The Curtatone class ships were the first Italian destroyers to have all of their armament placed on the centerline.

ITALY

For the first time in European practice, 102-mm guns were installed in twin mounts. In addition, these ships received triple TTs instead of paired ones. In 1938 they were re-rated as torpedo boats.
1939-1940, all: - 2 x 1 - 76/30; + 2 x 1 - 20/70 Scotti-Isotta Fraschini 1939, 2 x 1 – 8 MG.
1942-1943, *Castelfidardo*: + 1 x 2 - 20/65 Breda 1935.
1942-1943, *Calatafimi*: - 1 x 2 - 102/45, 2 x 3 - 450 TT; + 1 x 1 - 102/45 Schneider-Armstrong 1917, 2 x 2 - 20/65 Breda 1935, 1 x 2 - 533 TT. 1942-1943, *Monzambano*: - 1 x 2 - 102/45; + 1 x 1 - 102/45 Schneider-Armstrong 1917, 2 x 2 - 20/65 Breda 1935.

Curtatone 20.5.1941 was sunk by Greek mines at Piraeus. *Castelfidardo* 9.9.1943 was captured by German troops at Suda, renamed *TA16* and lost during a British air raid 1.6.1944. *Calatafimi* 9.9.1943 was captured by German troops at Piraeus, renamed *TA19* and 9.8.1944 was sunk by Greek submarine *Pipinos* at Samos.

ALBATROS torpedo boat

Albatros	CNR, Palermo	11.1931	27.5.1934	11.1934	sunk 27.9.1941

408 / 490 t, 70.5 x 6.9 x 1.7 m, 2 sets Beluzzo geared steam turbines, 2 3-drum boilers, 4300 hp, 24.5 kts, 72 t oil, 1420 nm (14 kts), complement 187; 2 x 1 – 102/35 Schneider-Armstrong 1914-15, 2 x 1 – 13.2 MG, 4 DCT, 2 DCR; hydrophone.

Albatros was the first attempt to create a purpose-built submarine chaser. The design was developed in 1931. It proved unsuccessful, and the construction of a sister ship was abandoned in favor of a larger ships of the future *Pegaso* class. In 1938 she was re-rated from a submarine chaser to a torpedo boat.
1939: + 2 x 1 - 37/54 Breda 1939.
Albatros 27.9.1941 was sunk by British submarine *Upright* off Messina.

Albatros 1939

Albatros prewar

SPICA class torpedo boats

Spica group					
Astore	BSN, Napoli	1933	22.4.1934	6.1935	to Sweden 3.1940 (Remus)
Spica	BSN, Napoli	5.1933	11.3.1934	5.1935	to Sweden 3.1940 (Romulus)
Climene group					
Canopo	CT, Riva Trigoso	12.1935	1.10.1936	3.1937	sunk 3.5.1941
Cassiopea	CT, Riva Trigoso	12.1935	22.11.1936	4.1937	discarded 10.1959
Castore	CNR, Ancona	1.1936	27.9.1936	1.1937	sunk 2.6.1943
Centauro	CNR, Ancona	5.1934	19.2.1936	6.1936	sunk 4.11.1942
Cigno	CNR, Ancona	3.1936	24.11.1936	4.1937	sunk 16.4.1943
Climene	CNR, Ancona	7.1934	7.1.1936	4.1936	sunk 28.4.1943
Perseo group					
Aldebaran	Ansaldo, Genoa	10.1935	14.6.1936	12.1936	sunk 20.10.1941
Altair	Ansaldo, Genoa	10.1935	26.7.1936	12.1936	sunk 20.10.1941
Andromeda	Ansaldo, Genoa	10.1935	28.6.1936	12.1936	sunk 17.3.1941
Antares	Ansaldo, Genoa	10.1935	19.7.1936	12.1936	sunk 28.5.1943
Perseo	CNQ, Fiume	11.1934	9.10.1935	2.1936	sunk 4.5.1943
Sagittario	CNQ, Fiume	11.1935	21.6.1936	10.1936	discarded 7.1964
Sirio	CNQ, Fiume	11.1934	16.11.1935	3.1936	discarded 10.1959
Vega	CNQ, Fiume	11.1935	21.6.1936	10.1936	sunk 10.1.1941
Alcione group					
Airone	Ansaldo, Genoa	10.1936	23.1.1938	5.1938	sunk 20.10.1941
Alcione	Ansaldo, Genoa	10.1936	23.12.1937	5.1938	sunk 11.12.1941
Aretusa	Ansaldo, Genoa	10.1936	6.2.1938	7.1938	discarded 8.1958

Ariel	Ansaldo, Genoa	10.1936	14.3.1938	7.1938	sunk 12.10.1940
Calipso	Ansaldo, Genoa	9.1937	12.6.1938	11.1938	sunk 5.12.1940
Calliope	Ansaldo, Genoa	5.1937	15.4.1938	10.1938	discarded 8.1958
Circe	Ansaldo, Genoa	9.1937	29.6.1938	10.1938	collision 27.11.1942
Clio	Ansaldo, Genoa	10.1936	3.4.1938	10.1938	discarded 10.1959
Libra	CNQ, Fiume	12.1936	3.10.1937	1.1938	discarded 4.1964
Lince	CNQ, Fiume	12.1936	15.1.1938	4.1938	sunk 28.8.1943
Lira	CNQ, Fiume	12.1936	12.9.1937	1.1938	scuttled 9.9.1943
Lupo	CNQ, Fiume	12.1936	7.11.1937	2.1938	sunk 2.12.1942
Pallade	BSN, Napoli	2.1937	19.12.1937	10.1938	sunk 5.8.1943
Partenope	BSN, Napoli	3.1937	27.2.1938	11.1938	scuttled 11.9.1943
Pleiadi	BSN, Napoli	1.1937	5.9.1937	7.1938	damaged 13.10.1941, never repaired
Polluce	BSN, Napoli	2.1937	24.10.1937	8.1938	sunk 4.9.1942

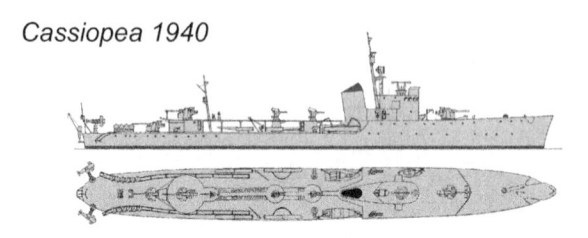

Cassiopea 1940

638 / 885 (*Spica group*) or 780 / 995 (*Climene group*) or 775 / 1005 (*Perseo group*) or 785 / 1035 (*Alcione group*) t, 80.4 (*Spica group, Canopo, Cassiopea, Perseo, Sagittario, Sirio, Vega, Alcione group*) or 82.0 x 8.2 (*Spica, Climene, Perseo groups*) or 7.9 x 2.8-3.1 m, 2 sets Tosi geared steam turbines, 2 Yarrow boilers, 19000 hp, 34 kts, 207 t oil, 1900-1960 nm (15 kts), complement 99; 3 x 1 – 100/47 OTO 1931 (*Spica, Climene, Perseo groups*) or 3 x 1 – 100/47 OTO 1937 (*Alcione group*), 2 x 2 – 40/39 Vickers-Terni 1917 (*Spica group*), 2 x 2 (*Spica group*) or 4 x 2 (*Climene, Perseo, Alcione groups*) – 13.2 MG, 4 x 1 (*Spica group, Climene group except Centauro and Climene, Libra, Lince, Lira, Lupo*) or (1 x 2 + 2 x 1) (*Centauro, Climene*) or 2 x 2 (*Perseo group, Alcione group except Libra, Lince, Lira, Lupo*) – 450 TT, 2 DCT, 18 – 28 mines.

In the early 1930s, to replace obsolete torpedo boats, it was decided to build a series of new ships of this

Ariel 1939

Vega 1941

type, while their standard displacement was limited to 600 t. It allowed to use one of the articles of the total document of the London Naval Conference of 1930, according to which the ships with a displacement of up to 600 t were not subject to restrictions and could be built in any quantity. According to naval shipbuilding experts, it was impossible to create anything other than a coastal torpedo boat with low seaworthiness and a short cruising range. For Italy, whose interests were focused in the Mediterranean Sea with its relatively short distances and good weather conditions, the endurance and seaworthiness faded into the background. It was understandable that the Italians wanted to use this article to upgrade their torpedo flotillas, without wasting precious contract tonnage and leaving it on full-fledged destroyers.

It is interesting that the decision to build 600-t ships had, in addition to economic, also political overtones, since Italy, following France, did not ratify the final documents of the London conference and formally had the full right not to comply with any restrictions.

The first two torpedo boats, laid down in 1933, were structurally a much smaller version of the *Freccia* class destroyer with 100-mm main guns and 450-mm torpedoes. In total, 32 ships were completed, differing from each other in the arrangement of torpedo tube banks. On trials, many exceeded 37 kts, but after commissioning, the speed was significantly reduced due to 115-150-t overload to the 630-670-t design standard displacement and averaged 30 kts.

Successful from the point of view of the naval theory, the design of a 600-t torpedo boat, however, was of dubious practical value, since it was not very suitable for solving many of the tasks facing the destroyer. For operations against enemy destroyers, the ships were too small and poorly armed. For torpedo attacks on enemy surface ships, on the contrary, they were too large and had only 2-4 weak 450-mm torpedoes in a side salvo. To a much greater extent, 600-t torpedo boats were suitable for patrol and escort duties, but even in this case their anti-aircraft and anti-submarine armaments

ITALY

were too weak.
1939-1941, all survived: were armed with 3 x 1 - 100/47 OTO 1931/1937, 3 x 2 - 20/65 Breda 1935, 1 x 2 - 13.2 MG, 2 x 2 - 450 TT, 2 DCT, 18 - 28 mines, hydrophone.
1941-1942, all survived: + 2 DCT (40 DC at all).
1942-1943, all survived: - 1 x 2 - 13.2 MG; + 4 x 1 - 20/70 Scotti-Isotta Fraschini 1939.
Airone and *Ariel* 12.10.1940 were sunk by British cruiser *Ajax* E of Malta. *Calipso* 5.12.1940 was sunk by mines laid by British submarine *Rorqual* E of Tripoli. *Andromeda* 18.3.1941 was sunk by British aircraft off the coast of Albania. *Canopo* was sunk 3.5.1941 by British aircraft at Tripoli. *Pleiadi* 31.5.1941 was mistakenly damaged by Italian aircraft at Tobruk, towed to Tripoli, 13.10.1941 badly damaged by British aircraft and not repaired. *Aldebaran* and *Altair* 20.10.1941 were sunk by mines laid by British submarine *Rorqual* off Piraeus. *Alcione* 11.12.1941 was sunk by British submarine *Truant* N of Crete. *Vega* 10.1.1942 was damaged by gunfire from British cruiser *Bonaventure* off Pantelleria and sunk by a torpedo from British destroyer *Hereward*. *Polluce* 4.9.1942 was sunk by British aircraft N of Tobruk. *Centauro* 4.11.1942 was sunk by US aircraft at Bengasi. *Circe* 27.11.1942 was sunk in a collision with armed merchant cruiser *Città di Tunisi* off Sicily. *Lupo* 2.12.1942 was sunk by British cruisers *Aurora*, *Argonaut*, and *Sirius* off Kirkenah. *Cigno* 16.4.1943 was sunk by gunfire and torpedoes from British destroyers *Paladin* and *Pakenham* W of Sicily. *Climene* 28.4.1943 was sunk by British submarine *Unshaken* W of Sicily. *Perseo* 4.5.1943 was sunk by British destroyers *Nubian*, *Paladin*, and *Petard* off the coast of Tunisia. *Antares* 28.5.1943 was sunk by US air raid on Livorno. *Castore* was sunk 2.6.1943 by gunfire from British destroyer *Jervis* and Greek destroyer *Vasilissa Olga* off Calabria. *Lince* 4.8.1943 ran aground at Taranto and 28.8.1943 was finished by British submarine *Ultor*. *Pallade* 5.8.1943 was sunk by US aircraft at Naples. *Lira* was captured by German troops in September 1943, renamed *TA49* and sunk 4.11.1944 by Allied aircraft at La Spezia. *Partenope* was captured by German troops in September 1943 and 11.9.1943 blown up at Naples.

Centauro 1942

PEGASO class torpedo boat - escort destroyers

Pegaso	BSN, Napoli	2.1936	8.12.1936	3.1938	scuttled 11.9.1943
Procione	BSN, Napoli	2.1936	31.1.1937	3.1938	scuttled 9.9.1943
Orione	CNR, Palermo	4.1936	21.4.1937	3.1938	discarded 1.1965
Orsa	CNR, Palermo	4.1936	21.3.1937	3.1938	discarded 7.1964

1000 / 1575 t, 89.3 x 9.7 x 3.7 m, 2 sets Tosi geared steam turbines, 2 3-drum boilers, 16000 hp, 28 kts, 520 t oil, 5100 nm (14 kts), complement 154-168; 2 x 1 – 100/47 OTO 1937, (3 x 2 + 2 x 1) – 13.2 MG, 2 x 2 – 450 TT, 6 DCT; hydrophone.

The escorts based on the design of the *Spica* class torpedo boats. Due to increase in the dimensions and decrease in the machinery power, the fuel supply was increased by more than 2.5 times; which provided the cruising range greater than that of destroyers. The artillery was reduced to two 100-mm guns, but the anti-submarine armament was increased to 6 DCTs, and the DC stowage was significantly increased.

Although the design speed was reduced by 6 kts compared to the prototype, on the high seas *Pegaso* was practically not inferior to *Spica* class torpedo boats and easily reached speed of up to 27 kts.

In 1938, shortly after commissioning, the ships were re-rated from escort vessels to torpedo boats.
1940-1941, all: - (3 x 2 + 2 x 1) - 13.2 MG; + 4 x 2 - 20/65 Breda 1935.
1942-1943, all: + 3 x 1 - 20/70 Scotti-Isotta Fraschini

Pegaso 1940

1939.
Procione and *Pegaso* were scuttled by their crews to avoid capture by German troops: the first 9.9.1943 at La Spezia, the second 11.9.1943 at Mallorca.

Orsa postwar

Ex-Yugoslav T1 class torpedo boats

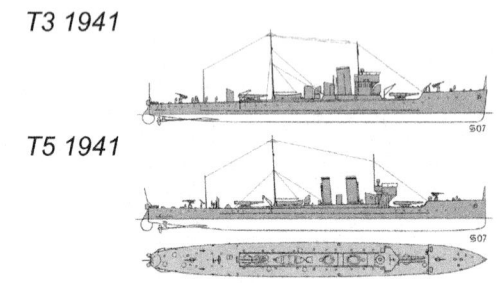

T1 group					
T1 *(ex-T1, ex-76T)*	STT, Trieste, Austria-Hungary	6.1913	15.12.1913	(7.1914) / 4.1941	to Yugoslavia 12.1943 (Golešnica)
T3 *(ex-T3, ex-78T)*	STT, Trieste, Austria-Hungary	10.1913	4.3.1914	(8.1914) / 4.1941	captured by Germany 16.9.1943 (TA48)
T5 group					
T5 *(ex-T5, ex-87F)*	Danubius, Porto Ré / Bergudi, Austria-Hungary	3.1914	20.3.1915	(10.1915) / 4.1941	to Yugoslavia 12.1943 (Cer)
T6 *(ex-T6, ex-93F)*	Danubius, Porto Ré / Bergudi, Austria-Hungary	1.1915	25.11.1915	(4.1916) / 4.1941	scuttled 11.9.1943
T7 *(ex-T7, ex-96F)*	Danubius, Porto Ré / Bergudi, Austria-Hungary	2.1915	7.7.1916	(11.1916) / 4.1941	captured by Germany 9.9.1943 (TA34)
T8 *(ex-T8, ex-97F)*	Danubius, Porto Ré / Bergudi, Austria-Hungary	3.1915	20.8.1916	(12.1916) / 4.1941	sunk 10.9.1943

T3 1941

T5 1941

T3

262 / 320 (*T1 group*) or 266 / 330 (*T5 group*) t, 58.2 (*T1 group*) or 58.8 (*T5 group*) x 5.7 (*T1 group*) or 5.8 (*T5 group*) x 1.5 m, 2 Parsons (*T1 group*) or AEG-Curtis steam turbines, 2 Yarrow boilers, 5000 hp, 28 kts, 24 t coal + 18 t oil (*T1 group*) or 20 t coal + 34 t oil (*T5 group*), 1200 nm (16 kts), complement 52; 1 (*T1 group*) or 2 (*T5 group*) x 1 – 66/42 SFK, 1 x 1 – 66/27 TAK K.09 (*T1 group*), 1 x 1 – 15 MG, 2 x 2 – 450 TT.

In April 1941, after the surrender of Yugoslavia, six obsolete 230-t torpedo boats of the Austro-Hungarian construction during the First World War were commissioned by the Regia Marina.

1942, *T3*: - 1 x 1 - 66/42, 1 x 1 - 66/27; + 2 x 1 - 76/30 Armstrong 1914.

1942, *T5*: - 2 x 1 - 66/42; + 2 x 1 - 76/30 Armstrong 1914.

T3 was captured by Germans at Rijeka 16.9.1943, commissioned by them as *TA48*, transferred by them to the Croatian Navy and sunk by Allied bombers 20.2.1945. *T6* was scuttled by the crew off Casenatico, the Adriatic. *T7* was captured by Germans 8.9.1943 off Gruz, commissioned by them as *TA34*, transferred to the Croatian Navy 17.6.1944 as *T7* and sunk by British MTBs 24.6.1944. *T8* was sunk by German aircraft 10.9.1943 NW of Dubrovnik.

CICLONE class torpedo boat - escort destroyers

Aliseo	Navalmeccanica, Castellammare di Stabia	9.1941	20.9.1942	2.1943	to Yugoslavia 5.1949 (Biokovo)
Animoso	Ansaldo, Genoa	4.1941	15.4.1942	8.1942	to the USSR 3.1949 (Ladnyy)
Ardente	Ansaldo, Genoa	4.1941	27.5.1942	9.1942	collision 12.1.1943
Ardimentoso	Ansaldo, Genoa	4.1941	28.6.1942	12.1942	to the USSR 10.1949 (Liutyy)
Ardito	Ansaldo, Genoa	4.1941	14.3.1942	6.1942	captured by Germany 16.9.1943 (TA26)
Ciclone	CRDA, Trieste	5.1941	1.3.1942	5.1942	sunk 8.3.1943
Fortunale	CRDA, Trieste	5.1941	18.4.1942	8.1942	to the USSR 3.1949 (Liotnyy)
Ghibli	Navalmeccanica, Castellammare di Stabia	8.1941	28.2.1943	7.1943	scuttled 9.9.1943
Groppo	Navalmeccanica, Castellammare di Stabia	6.1941	19.4.1942	8.1942	sunk 25.5.1943

ITALY

Impavido	CT, Riva Trigoso	8.1941	24.2.1943	4.1943	captured by Germany 16.9.1943 (TA23)
Impetuoso	CT, Riva Trigoso	8.1941	20.4.1943	7.1943	scuttled 11.9.1943
Indomito	CT, Riva Trigoso	1.1942	6.7.1943	8.1943	to Yugoslavia 4.1949 (Triglav)
Intrepido	CT, Riva Trigoso	1.1942	8.9.1943	(1.1944)	completed for Germany as TA25
Monsone	Navalmeccanica, Castellammare di Stabia	6.1941	7.6.1942	11.1942	sunk 1.3.1943
Tifone	CRDA, Trieste	6.1941	31.3.1942	7.1942	scuttled 7.5.1943
Uragano	CRDA, Trieste	6.1941	3.5.1942	9.1942	sunk 3.2.1943

1113 / 1683 t, 87.8 x 9.9 x 3.8 m, 2 sets Tosi or Parsons geared steam turbines, 2 Yarrow boilers, 16000 hp, 26 kts, 442 t oil, 4000 nm (14 kts), complement 177; 2 (*Aliseo, Ardente, Ardimentoso, Ardito, Ciclone, Fortunale, Groppo, Impetuoso, Uragano*) or 3 (*Animoso, Ghibli, Impavido, Indomito, Intrepido, Monsone*) x 1 – 100/47 OTO 1937, 4 x 2 (*Aliseo, Ardente, Ardimentoso, Ardito, Ciclone, Fortunale, Groppo, Impetuoso, Uragano*) or (3 x 2 + 2 x 1) (*Animoso, Ghibli, Impavido, Indomito, Intrepido, Monsone*) – 20/70 Scotti-Isotta Fraschini 1939, 2 x 2 – 450 TT, 4 (*Aliseo, Ardente, Ardimentoso, Ardito, Ciclone, Fortunale, Groppo, Impetuoso, Uragano*) or 4 - 6 (*Animoso, Ghibli, Impavido, Indomito, Intrepido, Monsone*) DCT, 20 mines (*Animoso, Ghibli, Impavido, Indomito, Intrepido, Monsone*); presumably S-Gerät sonar, hydrophone.

Further development of the *Pegaso* class. The decision to build a class of 16 ships was made in early 1941 to compensate for the loss of destroyers. Dimensions, in comparison with the prototype, were slightly increased to increase stability, for the same purpose side oil fuel tanks were eliminated. In May 1943 they were all reclassified from torpedo boats to escort torpedo boats. Mid-1943, all completed and survived: + (4 - 5) x 1 - 20/70 Scotti-Isotta Fraschini 1939.

Ardente 12.1.1943 was sunk in a collision with destroyer *Grecale* off Sicily. *Uragano* 3.2.1943 was sunk by a mine laid by British minelayer *Abdiel* off Bizerte. *Monsone* 1.3.1943 was sunk by US aircraft at Naples. *Ciclone* 7.3.1943 was sunk by a mine laid by British minelayer *Abdiel* NE of Bizerte. *Tifone* 6.5.1943 was damaged by US aircraft off the coast of Tunisia and 7.5.1943 sank. *Groppo* 25.5.1943 was sunk by US aircraft at Messina.

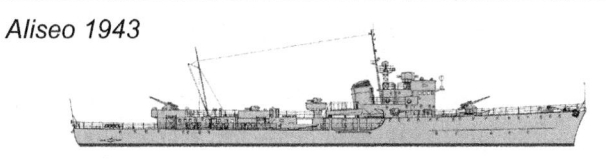

Ghibli and *Impetuoso* were scuttled by their crews to avoid capture by German troops: the first 9.9.1943 at La Spezia and the second 11.9.1943 off Mallorca. *Ghibli* subsequently was salvaged by the Germans, but was never commissioned by them. *Ardito* and *Impavido* were captured by German troops in September 1943 and renamed *TA26* and *TA23* respectively. *TA26* was sunk 15.6.1944 by British MTBs. *TA23* 25.4.1944 was damaged by a mine laid by torpedo boat *Sirio* off Corsica and sunk by torpedo from *TA29*.

Incomplete *Intrepido* was captured by German troops in September 1943, renamed *TA25*, completed by the Germans and sunk 21.6.1944 by British MTBs.

Aliseo 1943

Aliseo 1945

Ex-French FR41 class torpedo boats

FR41 (ex-*Bombarde*)	A C de la Loire, Nantes, France	2.1935	23.3.1936	(8.1937) / 12.1942	to Germany 4.1943 (TA9)
FR42 (ex-*La Pomone*)	A C de la Loire, Nantes, France	11.1933	25.1.1935	(12.1936) / 12.1942	to Germany 4.1943 (TA10)
FR43 (ex-*L'Iphigénie*)	A C de la Loire, Nantes, France	12.1933	18.4.1935	(11.1936) / 12.1942	to Germany 4.1943 (TA11)

680 / 895 t, 80.7 x 8.0 x 3.1 m, 2 sets Parsons or Rateau-Bretagne geared steam turbines, 2 Indret boilers, 22000 hp, 34.5 kts, 170 t oil, 1000 nm (20 kts), complement 105; 2 x 1 – 100/45 M1932, 2 x 2 – 13.2

Pomone 1939

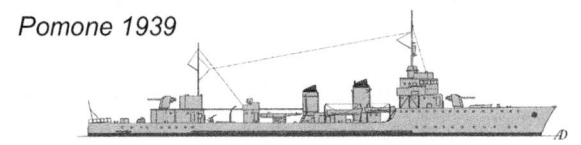

MG, 1 x 2 – 550 TT, 1 DCR, 1 Gincocchio towed AS torpedo.
After the Allied landing in North Africa in November 1942, German troops captured French ships at Bizerte and transferred three torpedo boats of the 600-t class to Italy 28.12.1942 as F*R41 (ex-Bombarde), FR42 (ex-La Pomone)* and *FR43 (ex-L'Iphigenie)*.
All were returned to Germany 6.4.1943.

ARIETE class torpedo boats

Alabarda	CRDA, Trieste	3.1943	7.5.1944	(11.1944)	captured incomplete by Germany 9.1943 (TA42)
Ariete	Ansaldo, Genoa	7.1942	6.3.1943	8.1943	to Yugoslavia 4.1949 (Durmitor)
Arturo	Ansaldo, Genoa	7.1942	27.3.1943	(10.1943)	captured incomplete by Germany 9.1943 (TA24)
Auriga	Ansaldo, Genoa	7.1942	15.4.1943	(12.1943)	captured incomplete by Germany 9.1943 (TA27)
Balestra	CNQ, Fiume	9.1942	4.10.1947	(1949)	captured incomplete by Germany 9.1943 (TA47), completed for Yugoslavia (Uchka)
Daga	CRDA, Trieste	1.1943	14.8.1943	(3.1944)	captured incomplete by Germany 9.1943 (TA39)
Dragone	Ansaldo, Genoa	7.1942	14.8.1943	(4.1944)	captured incomplete by Germany 9.1943 (TA30)
Eridano	Ansaldo, Genoa	7.1942	12.7.1943	(3.1944)	captured incomplete by Germany 9.1943 (TA29)
Fionda	CNQ, Fiume	8.1942	31.1.1943	-	captured incomplete by Germany 9.1943 (TA46)
Gladio	CRDA, Trieste	1.1943	15.6.1943	(1.1944)	captured incomplete by Germany 9.1943 (TA37)
Lancia	CRDA, Trieste	3.1943	7.5.1944	(9.1944)	captured incomplete by Germany 9.1943 (TA41)
Pugnale	CRDA, Trieste	1.1943	1.8.1943	(7.1944)	captured incomplete by Germany 9.1943 (TA40)
Rigel	Ansaldo, Genoa	7.1942	22.5.1943	(1.1944)	captured incomplete by Germany 9.1943 (TA28)
Spada	CRDA, Trieste	1.1943	1.7.1943	(2.1944)	captured incomplete by Germany 9.1943 (TA38)
Spica	CNQ, Fiume	1.1942	30.1.1944	(9.1944)	captured incomplete by Germany 9.1943 (TA45)
Stella Polare	CNQ, Fiume	4.1942	11.7.1943	(1.1944)	captured incomplete by Germany 9.1943 (TA36)

Ariete 1943

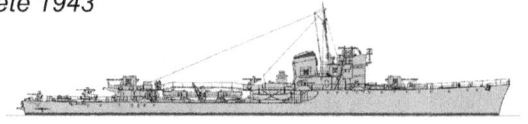

745 / 1110 t, 83.5 x 8.6 x 3.2 m, 2 sets Parsons geared steam turbines, 2 3-drum boilers, 22000 hp, 31.5 kts, 210 t oil, 1500 nm (16 kts), complement 150; 2 x 1 – 100/47 OTO 1937, 3 x 2 – 20/65 Breda 1935, 4 x 1 – 20/65 Breda 1940, 2 x 3 – 450 TT, 2 DCT; hydrophone (presumably).

42 torpedo boats of the improved *Spica* class were ordered in 1942 to compensate for the heavy losses of escort ships during convoys to Africa to supply Rommel's Corps and the Italian Army in Tripolitania. Ships of the improved class differed from the prototype in more powerful machinery and a shorter cruising range. The number of 100-mm guns was also reduced from three to two, but the torpedo salvo was increased due to the use of triple TTs. In addition, antiaircraft armament was significantly strengthened. According to the design, it was supposed to install on each ship 14 AA guns: one twin 37-mm/54, 2 twin and 8 single 20-mm/65, however, due to the lack of 37-mm guns, new torpedo boats did not receive them.

Due to increasing supply problems, only 16 ships out of 42 ordered were laid down, and until September 1943 only the lead *Ariete* was commissioned; the remaining 15 incomplete ships passed into the hands of the Germans. *Alabarda* was completed as German *TA42* and 21.3.1945 was sunk by British aircraft at Venice. *Arturo* was completed as German *TA24* and 18.3.1945 was sunk by torpedo from British destroyer *Meteor* S of Genoa. *Auriga* was completed as German *TA27* and 9.6.1944 was sunk by

ITALY

British aircraft at Porto Ferraio. *Daga* was completed as German *TA39* and 16.10.1944 was sunk by drifting mine S of Thessaloniki. *Dragone* was completed as German *TA30* and 16.5.1944 was sunk by US MTBs *PT550*, *558* and *559* W of La Spezia. *Eridano* was completed as German *TA29* and 18.3.1945 was sunk by gunfire from British destroyers *Meteor* and *Lookout* S of Genoa. *Gladio* was completed as German *TA37* and 7.10.1944 was sunk by gunfire from British destroyers *Termagant* and *Tuscan* in Thessaloniki Bay. *Lancia* was completed as German *TA41*, 20.2.1945 badly damaged by British aircraft and 1.5.1945 blown up by the crew at Trieste. *Pugnale* was completed as German *TA40* and 4.5.1945 was scuttled by the crew at Trieste. *Rigel* was completed as German *TA28* and 4.9.1944 destroyed by US aircraft in the drydock at Genoa. *Spada* was completed as German *TA38*, ran aground 9.10.1944 and 13.10.1944 was scuttled by the crew. *Spica* was completed as German *TA45* and 13.4.1945 was sunk by British MTBs *MTB670* and *697* in the Morlacca Strait off Fiume. *Stella Polare* was completed as German *TA36* and 18.3.1944 mined SW of Fiume. *Fionda* and *Balestra* were renamed *TA46* and *TA47* respectively, were never completed by the Germans and both were scuttled 3.5.1945.

SUBMARINES

H1 class small submarines

H1	Canadian Vickers, Montreal, Canada	5.1916	16.10.1916	12.1916	stricken 3.1947
H2	Canadian Vickers, Montreal, Canada	5.1916	19.10.1916	12.1916	stricken 3.1947
H4	Canadian Vickers, Montreal, Canada	8.1916	17.4.1917	5.1917	stricken 3.1947
H6	Canadian Vickers, Montreal, Canada	11.1916	23.4.1917	7.1917	captured by Germany 14.9.1943
H8	Canadian Vickers, Montreal, Canada	11.1916	24.5.1917	6.1918	sunk 5.6.1943

364 / 475 t, 45.8 x 4.7 x 3.8 m, 2 NLSE diesels / 2 Dynamic Electric electric motors, 480 / 620 hp, 12 / 11 kts, 16 t diesel oil, 2640 nm (11 kts) / 110 nm (5 kts), complement 22, 50 m; 1 x 1 – 76/30 Armstrong 1914, 4 – 450 TT (bow, 6); hydrophone (presumably)

Famous Holland's boats built in the USA and assembled in Canada in 1916-1917. One of the most successful designs of that time. Single-hulled.
H8 was sunk at La Spezia 5.6.1943 by Allied aircraft. *H6* was captured by German troops in September 1943 and scuttled by them.

H1 1943

H2 1941

PIETRO MICCA class large submarine

| **Luigi Galvani** | R. Arsenale di La Spezia | 9.1915 | 26.1.1918 | 6.1918 | stricken 1.1938 |

842 / 1244 t, 63.2 x 6.2 x 4.3 m, 2 Fiat diesels / 2 Ansaldo or Savigliano electric motors, 2600-2900 / 1300-1800 hp, 11 / 10.9 kts, 60 t diesel oil, 945 nm (11 kts) / 94 nm (5 kts), complement 40, 50 m; 1 x 1 – 76/40 Ansaldo 1916, 1 x 1 – 76/30 Armstrong 1914, 6 – 450 TT (4 bow, 2 stern, 8).

Pietro Micca class boats were the largest Italian submarines of the First World War. They were ordered from La Spezia NYd in 1914, but completion was delayed until the end of the war. Refitted in 1923 with new engines and better maneuverability.

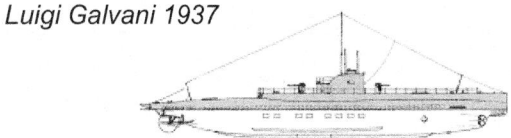

Luigi Galvani 1937

X2 class submarine minelayers

| X2 | Ansaldo, Sestri Ponente | 8.1916 | 25.4.1917 | 2.1918 | laid up 9.1940 |
| X3 | Ansaldo, Sestri Ponente | 8.1916 | 29.12.1917 | 8.1918 | laid up 9.1940 |

X2 1937

403 / 468 t, 42.6 x 5.5 x 3.2 m, 2 Sulzer diesels / 2 Ansaldo electric motors, 650 / 325 hp, 8.2 / 6.3 kts, 1200 nm (8 kts) / 70 nm (3 kts), complement 22-25, 40 m; 1 x 1 – 76/30 Armstrong 1914, 2 – 450 TT (bow, 2), 18 mines.

Small submarine minelayers, designed on the model of the captured Austro-Hungarian submarine *U24*, former German *UC12*. Saddle-tank hull. "German" scheme of the minelaying: nine vertical trunks with two mines each. Unsuccessful boats, too slow and poorly controlled. Since 1936, both have been used for training.
In September 1940, both submarines were disarmed and converted to hulks.

BALILLA class large submarines

Balilla	OTO, Muggiano	1.1925	20.2.1927	7.1928	hulk 4.1941
Domenico Millelire	OTO, Muggiano	1.1925	19.9.1927	8.1928	hulk 4.1941
Antonio Sciesa	OTO, Muggiano	10.1925	12.8.1928	4.1929	scuttled 12.11.1942
Enrico Toti	OTO, Muggiano	1.1925	14.4.1928	9.1928	laid up 4.1943

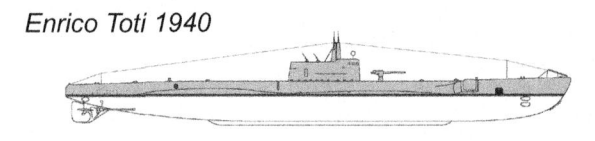

Enrico Toti 1940

Domenico Millelire 1935

1427 / 1874 t, 86.5 x 7.8 x 4.7 m, 2 Fiat diesels + 1 auxiliary Fiat diesel-generator / 2 Savigliano electric motors, 4900 + 425 / 2200 hp, 16 / 7 kts, 140 t diesel oil, 13000 nm (7 kts) / 110 nm (3 kts), complement 77, 90 m; 1 x 1 – 120/45 OTO 1931, 2 x 2 – 13.2 MG, 6 – 533 TT (4 bow, 2 stern, 16), 4 mines (*except Antonio Sciesa*); presumably hydrophone.

Cruiser submarines for service in the Red Sea and the Indian Ocean. Designed by the builder on the basis of the German submarine *U120*, received by Italy after the First World War. Double-hulled. To increase, an auxiliary 425-hp diesel-generator was introduced into the composition of the machinery for recharging battery and cruising speed. Initially, the gun was placed on the CT. In 1934, to improve stability, the gun was moved from the CT to the deck. The disadvantages of this class included low stability and the impossibility of achieving the design speed of 17.5 / 8.9 kts.

Too large for service in the Mediterranean, *Balilla* and *Domenico Millelire* were disarmed in April 1941 and used as oil hulks. *Enrico Toti* and *Antonio Sciesa* served as transport submarines from 1942 to supply of troops in Africa. *Antonio Sciesa* was damaged 6.9.1942 at Tobruk by US aircraft and scuttled by her crew 12.11.1942. *Enrico Toti* was disarmed 1.4.1943.

GOFFREDO MAMELI class medium submarines

Pier Capponi	Tosi, Taranto	8.1925	19.6.1927	1.1929	sunk 31.3.1941
Giovanni da Procida	Tosi, Taranto	9.1925	1.4.1928	1.1929	discarded 2.1948
Goffredo Mameli (ex-Masaniello)	Tosi, Taranto	8.1925	9.12.1926	1.1929	discarded 2.1948
Tito Speri	Tosi, Taranto	9.1925	25.5.1928	8.1929	discarded 2.1948

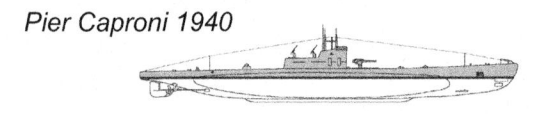

Pier Caproni 1940

810 / 993 t, 64.6 x 6.5 x 4.3 m, 2 Tosi diesels / 2 CGE electric motors, 3000 / 1100 hp, 15 / 7.5 kts, 48 t diesel oil, 3500 nm (8 kts) / 110 nm (3 kts), complement 49, 100 m; 1 x 1 – 102/35 Schneider-Armstrong 1914-15, 2 x 1 – 13.2 MG, 6 – 533 TT (4 bow, 2 stern, 10); hydrophone. The design was developed by the builder using the experience of the service of former German submarines, received by Italy after the First World War. Partially double-hulled. Successful boats that became the standard for subsequent submarines of the Italian Navy. The only noticeable drawback of this class was the lack of stability. To correct this, shortly after completion all

ITALY

four boats received external bulges. Speed reduced from 17.2 / 7.7 to 15 / 7.5 kts.
1942, all survived: diesels were replaced by new Tosi engines (4000 hp, 17 kts surfaced)

Pier Capponi was sunk 31.3.1941 S of Stromboli by British submarine *Rorqual*.

VETTOR PISANI class medium submarines

Giovanni Bausan	CNT, Monfalcone	1.1926	24.3.1928	9.1929	floating oil depot 4.1942
Marcantonio Colonna	CNT, Monfalcone	12.1925	26.12.1927	7.1929	hulk 4.1942
Des Geneys	CNT, Monfalcone	2.1926	14.11.1928	10.1929	floating charging station 4.1942
Vettor Pisani	CNT, Monfalcone	11.1925	24.11.1927	6.1929	discarded 3.1947

866 / 1040 t, 68.2 x 6.1 x 4.9 m, 2 Tosi diesels / 2 CGE electric motors, 3000 / 1100 hp, 15 / 8.2 kts, 70 t diesel oil, 5000 nm (8 kts) / 70 nm (4 kts), complement 48, 50 m; 1 x 1 – 102/35 Schneider-Armstrong 1914-15, 2 x 1 – 13.2 MG, 6 – 533 TT (4 bow, 2 stern, 9); hydrophone.

The design was developed by the builder according to the same technical requirements as *Mameli* class. Single-hulled. In terms of the cruising range, they exceeded the *Mameli* class, but, like the latter, they had insufficient stability. Shortly after commissioning, external bulges

Vettor Piani 1940

were fitted: stability increased, but speed fell from 17.3 / 8.8 to 15 / 8.2 kts.

By the beginning of the war, they were considered obsolete, and since 1942, three boats were disarmed and converted to battery recharging stations and fuel oil hulks.

ETTORE FIERAMOSCA large submarine

Ettore Fieramosca	Tosi, Taranto	7.1926	15.4.1929	4.1930	disarmed 4.1941

1530 / 1934 t, 84.0 x 8.3 x 5.1 m, 2 Tosi diesels / 2 Marelli electric motors, 5200 / 2300 hp, 15 / 8 kts, 150 t diesel oil, 5000 nm (9 kts) / 90 nm (3 kts), complement 78, 90 m; 1 x 1 – 120/45 OTO 1931, 2 x 2 – 13.2 MG, 8 – 533 TT (4 bow, 4 stern, 14); hydrophone.

Submarine cruiser for service in the Red Sea and the Indian Ocean. Designed by the builder. Single-hulled, with external bulges. According to the design, *Ettore Fieramosca* was supposed to carry the seaplane in a watertight hangar. For some reason, the aircraft was never created, and in 1931 the hangar was liquidated, due to the presence of which the dive time turned out to be unreasonably long. After that, the submerged displacement was reduced from 2094 to 1934t and the

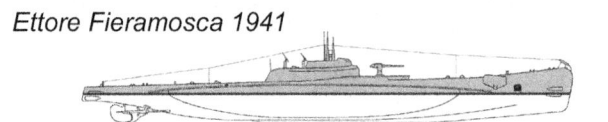

Ettore Fieramosca 1941

dive time decreased somewhat, although it continued to be considered excessive.

Ettore Fieramosca, like the *Balilla* class, could not reach design speed of 19 / 10 kts, but, unlike the latter, she had better stability due to bulges.

Too large for service in the Mediterranean, *Ettore Fieramosca* was laid up to reserve after a battery explosion in the mid-1940, disarmed in April 1941 and broken up in 1946.

FRATELLI BANDIERA class medium submarines

Fratelli Bandiera	CNT, Monfalcone	2.1928	7.8.1929	9.1930	discarded 2.1948
Luciano Manara	CNT, Monfalcone	2.1928	5.10.1929	6.1930	discarded 2.1948
Ciro Menotti	OTO, Muggiano	5.1928	29.12.1929	8.1930	discarded 2.1948
Santorre Santarosa	OTO, Muggiano	5.1928	22.10.1929	7.1930	scuttled 20.1.1943

925 / 1080 t, 69.8 x 7.3 x 5.3 m, 2 Tosi (*Fratelli Bandiera, Luciano Manara*) or Fiat diesels / 2 Savigliano electric motors, 3000 / 1300 hp, 15 / 8 kts, 4750 nm (8.5 kts) / 60 nm (4 kts), complement 53, 90 m; 1 x 1 – 102/35 Schneider-Armstrong 1914-15, 2 x 1 – 13.2 MG, 8 – 533 TT (4 bow, 4 stern, 12); hydrophone.

An enlarged *Pisani* with more powerful engines, two extra TTs and slightly longer cruising range. Single-

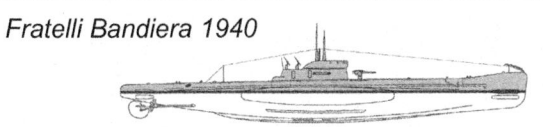

Fratelli Bandiera 1940

hulled. They had insufficient stability; to correct it, shortly after the completion of the submarines, they received external bulges which reduced the speed from 17.5 / 9 to 15 / 8 kts. Then, at the fore end, for about 5 m aft of the stem, the deck was lengthened to improve seaworthiness.

In 1942, *Luciano Manara* (and possibly others) was refitted, receiving a smaller CT.

1942, *Ciro Menotti*: - 1 x 1 - 102/35; + 1 x 1 - 100/47 OTO 1938
Santore Santarosa ran aground near Tripoli 20.1.1943, torpedoed by British *MTB260* and then scuttled.

SQUALO class medium submarines

Delfino	CRDA, Monfalcone	10.1928	27.4.1930	6.1931	collision 23.3.1943
Narvalo	CRDA, Monfalcone	10.1928	15.3.1930	12.1930	scuttled 14.1.1943
Squalo	CRDA, Monfalcone	10.1928	15.1.1930	10.1930	discarded 2.1948
Tricheco	CRDA, Monfalcone	11.1928	11.9.1930	6.1931	sunk 18.3.1942

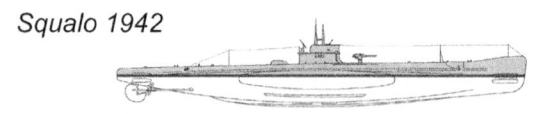

Squalo 1942

920 / 1125 t, 69.8 x 7.2 x 5.2 m, 2 Fiat diesels / 2 CRDA electric motors, 3000 / 1300 hp, 15 / 8 kts, 5650 nm (8 kts) / 100 nm (3 kts), complement 53, 90 m; 1 x 1 – 102/35 Schneider-Armstrong 1914-15, 2 x 1 – 13.2 MG, 8 – 533 TT (4 bow, 4 stern, 12); hydrophone.
Development of the *Bandiera* class. Differences from the prototype were minor and mainly of a technological nature. Just like the *Bandiera*, they initially suffered from insufficient stability during diving-surfacing, to correct that, they received external bulges soon after completion. The shape of the bow was also changed to improve seaworthiness.

During the war years, the size of CT on *Squalo* (and possibly others) was reduced.
Tricheco was sunk 18.3.1942 near Brindisi by British submarine *Upholder*. *Narvalo* was scuttled by her crew 14.1.1943 near Tripoli after being attacked by British destroyer *Pakenham* and escort destroyer *Hursley*. *Delfino* sank 23.3.1943 near Taranto after colliding with a pilot vessel.

MARCANTONIO BRAGADIN class medium submarine minelayers

| **Marcantonio Bragadin** (ex-*Marcantonio Bragadino*) | Tosi, Taranto | 2.1927 | 21.7.1929 | 11.1931 | discarded 2.1948 |
| **Filippo Corridoni** | Tosi, Taranto | 7.1927 | 30.3.1930 | 11.1931 | discarded 2.1948 |

Marcantonio Bragadin 1940

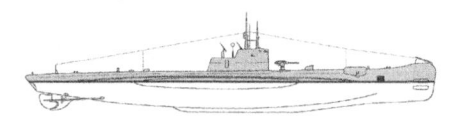

965 / 1068 t, 68.0 x 7.1 x 5.0 m, 2 Tosi diesels / 2 Marelli electric motors, 1500 / 1000 hp, 11.5 / 7 kts, 41 t diesel oil, 9000 nm (8 kts) / 72 nm (4 kts), complement 55, 90 m; 1 x 1 – 102/35 Schneider-Armstrong 1914-15, 2 x 1 – 13.2 MG, 4 – 533 TT (bow, 6), 16 – 24 mines; hydrophone.

Submarine minelayers designed on the basis of the *Pisani* class. Single-hulled. Mines were stored in two horizontal tubes at the stern. During trials, it turned out that the mine tubes were unsuccessfully located, and in 1935 the submarines were put on modernization. During this modernization, the hull was shortened from 71.5 to 68.0 m due to the aft end, external bulges were installed, increasing the breadth was increased from 6.2 to 7.1 m, the shape of the bow was modified as in the *Bandiera* class.

LUIGI SETTEMBRINI class medium submarines

| **Luigi Settembrini** | Tosi, Taranto | 4.1928 | 28.9.1930 | 1.1932 | sunk 15.11.1944 |
| **Ruggiero Settimo** | Tosi, Taranto | 6.1928 | 29.3.1931 | 4.1932 | discarded 3.1947 |

Luigi Settembrini 1941

938 / 1135 t, 69.1 x 6.6 x 4.5 m, 2 Tosi diesels / 2 Ansaldo electric motors, 3000 / 1400 hp, 17.5 / 7.7 kts, 52 t diesel oil, 9000 nm (8 kts) / 80 nm (4 kts), complement 56, 90 m; 1 x 1 – 102/35 Schneider-Armstrong 1914-15, 2 x 1 – 13.2 MG, 8 – 533 TT (4 bow, 4 stern, 12); hydrophone.

An evolution of the *Mameli* class that fixed a lack of stability. In addition, the cruising range was more than doubled, and the number of TTs was increased to 8. Partially double-hulled.

In 1943, both received the new smaller CT.
Luigi Settembrini was mistakenly sunk by ramming of US destroyer escort *Frament* 15.11.1944 E of Bermuda during anti-submarine maneuvers.

ITALY

ARGONAUTA class medium submarines

Argonauta	CRDA, Monfalcone	11.1929	19.1.1931	1.1932	sunk 28.6.1940
Fisalia	CRDA, Monfalcone	11.1929	2.5.1931	6.1932	sunk 28.9.1941
Jalea	OTO, Muggiano	1.1930	15.6.1932	3.1933	discarded 2.1948
Jantina	OTO, Muggiano	1.1930	16.5.1932	3.1933	sunk 5.7.1941
Medusa	CRDA, Monfalcone	11.1929	10.12.1931	9.1932	sunk 30.1.1942
Salpa	Tosi, Taranto	4.1930	8.5.1932	12.1932	sunk 27.6.1941
Serpente (ex-Nautilus)	Tosi, Taranto	4.1930	28.2.1932	11.1932	scuttled 12.9.1943

650 / 800 t, 61.5 x 5.7 x 4.7 m, CRDA or Fiat (*Jalea, Jantina*) or Tosi (*Salpa, Serpente*) diesels / CRDA or Marelli (*Salpa, Serpente*) electric motors, 1200 / 800 hp, 14 / 8 kts, 28 t diesel oil, 5000 nm (8 kts) / 74 nm (4 kts), complement 44, 80 m; 1 x 1 – 102/35 Schneider-Armstrong 1914-15, 2 x 1 – 13.2 MG, 6 – 533 TT (4 bow, 2 stern, 12).

Medium submarines of the so-called 600-ton class, the most numerous in the Italian Navy. The design was based on the *Squalo* class. Single-hulled with external bulges.

Argonauta was sunk 28.6.1940 off Sicily by British aircraft. *Salpa* was sunk 27.6.1941 in the Mediterranean by British submarine *Triumph*. *Jantina* was sunk 5.7.1941 in the Aegean Sea by British submarine *Torbay*. *Fisalia* was sunk 28.9.1941 near Jaffa by DCs from British corvette *Hyacinth*. *Medusa* was sunk 30.1.1942 in the Adriatic Sea by British submarine *Thorn*. *Serpente* was scuttled by her crew 12.9.1943 near Ancona.

Argonauta 1940

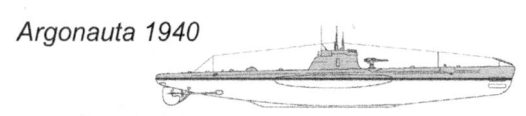

Jalea and Jantina during outfitting

SIRENA class medium submarines

Ametista	OTO, Muggiano	9.1931	26.4.1933	4.1934	scuttled 12.9.1943
Anfitrite	CRDA, Monfalcone	7.1931	5.8.1933	3.1934	sunk 6.3.1941
Diamante	Tosi, taranto	5.1931	21.5.1933	11.1933	sunk 20.6.1940
Galatea	CRDA, Monfalcone	7.1931	5.10.1933	6.1934	discarded 2.1948
Naiade	CRDA, Monfalcone	5.1931	27.3.1933	11.1933	sunk 14.12.1940
Nereide	CRDA, Monfalcone	5.1931	25.5.1933	2.1934	sunk 13.7.1943
Ondina	CRDA, Monfalcone	7.1931	2.12.1933	9.1934	sunk 11.7.1942
Rubino	CNQ, Fiume	9.1931	29.3.1933	3.1934	sunk 29.6.1940
Sirena	CRDA, Monfalcone	5.1931	26.1.1933	10.1933	scuttled 9.9.1943
Smeraldo	Tosi, Taranto	5.1931	23.7.1933	11.1933	sunk about 16.9.1941
Topazio	CNQ, Fiume	9.1931	15.5.1933	4.1934	sunk 12.9.1943
Zaffiro	OTO, Muggiano	9.1931	28.6.1933	6.1934	sunk probably 9.6.1942

680 / 837 t, 60.2 x 6.5 x 4.7 m, 2 Fiat or Tosi (*Diamante, Rubino, Smeraldo, Topazio*) diesels / 2 CRDA or Marelli (*Diamante, Rubino, Smeraldo, Topazio*) electric motors, 1200 / 800 hp, 14 / 7.7 kts, 80 t diesel oil, 2280 nm (12 kts) / 72 nm (4 kts), complement 45, 80 m; 1 x 1 – 100/47 OTO 1931, 2 x 2 – 13.2 MG, 6 – 533 TT (4 bow, 2 stern, 12); hydrophone.

A development of the 600-t *Argonauta* class, with a slightly larger displacement and reshaped hull, shorter and wider. The obsolete 102mm/35 gun was replaced with a more modern 100-mm/47. Otherwise, they differed little from their predecessors a little.

Ametista 1940

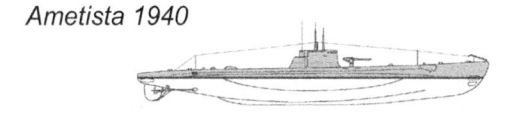

Diamante was sunk 20.6.1940 near Tobruk by British submarine *Parthian*. *Rubino* was sunk 29.6.1940 in the Ionian Sea by British aircraft. *Naiade* was sunk 14.12.1940 near Bardia by DCs from British destroyers *Hereward* and *Hyperion*. *Anfitrite* was sunk 6.3.1941 off Crete by DCs and gunfire from British destroyer *Greyhound*. *Zaffiro* lost in June 1942, probably sunk 9.6.1942 by British aircraft. *Ondina* was

Ondina 1942 sunk 11.7.1942 near Beirut by South African armed whalers *Protea* and *Southern Maid*. *Nereide* was sunk 13.7.1943 near Augusta by DCs and gunfire from British destroyers *Echo* and *Ilex*. *Smeraldo* was lost in September 1943 in the Mediterranean of unknown cause. *Sirena* was scuttled by the crew 9.9.1943 in the harbor of La Spezia. *Topazio* was mistakenly sunk 12.9.1943 off the SE coast of Sardinia by British aircraft. *Ametista* was scuttled by the crew 12.9.1943 near Ancona.

ARCHIMEDE class large submarines

Galileo Ferraris	Tosi, Taranto	10.1931	11.8.1934	1.1935	to Nationalist Spain 10.1937-1.1938 (General Sanjurjo II), sunk 25.10.1941
Galileo Galilei	Tosi, Taranto	10.1931	19.3.1934	10.1934	to Nationalist Spain 10.1937-1.1938 (General Mola II), captured by Britain 19.6.1940 (X2)

Galileo Ferraris 1940

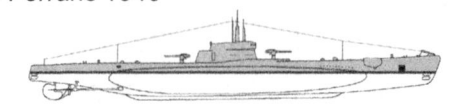

Galileo Galileo 19.6.1940

970 / 1239 t, 70.5 x 6.9 x 4.1 m, 2 Tosi diesels / 2 Marelli electric motors, 3000 / 1100 hp, 17 / 8 kts, 100 t diesel oil, 10500 nm (8 kts) / 105 nm (3 kts), complement 55, 90 m; 2 x 1 – 100/43 OTO 1927, 2 x 1 – 13.2 MG, 8 – 533 TT (4 bow, 4 stern, 16); hydrophone.

Slightly enlarged version of the *Settembrini* class with increased fuel capacity and enhanced armament; the second main gun was added, the number of spare torpedoes was increased. Partially double-hulled.

The two sister-boats, *Archimede* and *Evangelista Torricelli*, were given to the Spanish Nationalists in April 1937 as *General Sanjurjo* and *General Mola* respectively; two other submarines bore these names when the first pair were undergoing repairs in Italy. *Galileo Ferraris* was sunk 25.10.1941 in the Atlantic E of Madeira by British aircraft and escort destroyer *Lamerton*. *Galileo Galilei* was captured 19.6.1940 in the Red Sea by British armed trawler *Moonstone* after poisoning the crew of the submarine with gases coming from the ventilation system. She was later commissioned by the Royal Navy as *X2*.

GLAUCO class large submarines

Glauco (ex-*Delfim*)	CRDA, Monfalcone	10.1932	5.1.1935	9.1935	scuttled 27.6.1941
Otaria (ex-*Espadarte*)	CRDA, Monfalcone	11.1932	20.3.1935	10.1935	discarded 2.1948

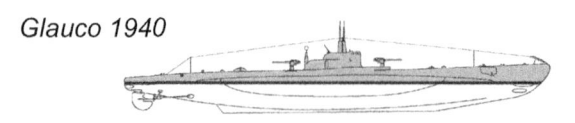

Glauco 1940

1054 / 1305 t, 73.0 x 7.2 x 5.1 m, 2 Fiat diesels / 2 CRDA electric motors, 3000 / 1200 hp, 17 / 8 kts, 59 t diesel oil, 9760 nm (8 kts) / 110 nm (3 kts), complement 58, 90 m; 2 x 1 – 100/47 OTO 1931, 2 x 1 – 13.2 MG, 8 – 533 TT (4 bow, 4 stern, 14); hydrophone.

This pair was ordered by Portugal in 1931 as *Delfim* and *Espadarte*, but the contract was cancelled that year. In 1932, they were re-ordered by the Italian Government for their own Navy. The design was based on the *Squalo* class. Single-hulled, with external bulges. A successful design, distinguished by easy maneuverability both on the surface and in the underwater position, fast and well-armed.

Otaria was damaged by DCs and gunfire from British destroyer *Wishart* and scuttled by her own crew as inoperable 27.6.1941 W of Gibraltar.

PIETRO MICCA large submarine minelayer

Pietro Micca	Tosi, Taranto	10.1931	31.3.1935	10.1935	sunk 29.7.1943

1545 / 1940 t, 90.3 x 7.7 x 5.3 m, 2 Tosi diesels / 2 Marelli electric motors, 3000 / 1500 hp, 15.5 / 8.5 kts, 67 t diesel oil, 12000 nm (8 kts) / 80 nm (4 kts), complement 72, 90 m; 2 x 1 – 120/45 OTO 1931, 2 x 2 – 13.2 MG, 6 – 533 TT (4 bow, 2 stern, 10), 20 mines; hydrophone.

Cruiser submarine minelayer. The design was

ITALY

developed by the builder. Partially double-hulled. The mines were stored in vertical trunks, in the lower part of the pressure hull amidships. Minelaying was carried out, as in German submarines, down under the own keel. Although this did not cause such problems with trim as when using the horizontal tubes, this scheme had two significant lacks. Firstly, minelaying could only be carried out if there was sufficient clearance between the keel of the submarine and seabed; and undermining a mine laid "under herself", secondly, was possible.

In general, the submarine turned out to be successful, with the exception of the dubious method of minelaying, she had good seaworthiness and good maneuverability for her dimensions.

Pietro Micca 1940

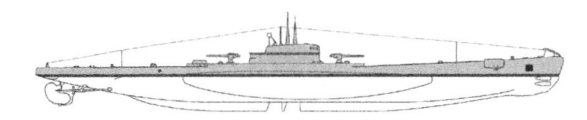

Late 1940: submarine was converted to transport of ammunition and petrol.
Too large for service in the Mediterranean, *Pietro Micca* was from the late 1940 used in transport service between Italy and Africa. In 1941 *Pietro Micca* was badly damaged by a torpedo hit but repaired. *Pietro Micca* was sunk 29.7.1943 in the Strait of Otranto by British submarine *Trooper*.

PIETRO CALVI class large submarines

Pietro Calvi	OTO, Muggiano	7.1932	31.3.1935	10.1935	scuttled 15.7.1942
Giuseppe Finzi	OTO, Muggiano	8.1932	29.6.1935	1.1936	captured by Germany 9.9.1943 (UIT21)
Enrico Tazzoli	OTO, Muggiano	9.1932	14.10.1935	4.1936	lost probably 16.5.1943

1525 / 2028 t, 84.3 x 7.7 x 5.2 m, 2 Fiat diesels / 2 San Giorgio electric motors, 4400 / 1800 hp, 16.8 / 7.4 kts, 249 t diesel oil, 13400 nm (8 kts) / 80 nm (4 kts), complement 77, 100 m; 2 x 1 – 120/45 OTO 1931, 2 x 2 – 13.2 MG, 8 – 533 TT (4 bow, 4 stern, 16), 14 mines (*Enrico Tazzoli*); hydrophone.

Submarine cruisers for service in the Red Sea and the Indian Ocean, improved *Balillas*. Double-hulled. An auxiliary diesel engine was not installed on these boats, and a greater cruising range was obtained by increasing the volume of fuel tanks volume and installing more efficient main diesels with a slightly lower power. The hull lines were modified to improve stability, which in turn resulted in a slight increase in speed compared to the predecessors, despite the lower engine power. The abandonment of the auxiliary diesel made it possible to noticeably strengthen the armament: the number of 120-mm guns was increased to two, and the TTs to eight. In 1943, *Enrico Tazzoli* and *Giuseppe Finci* were converted

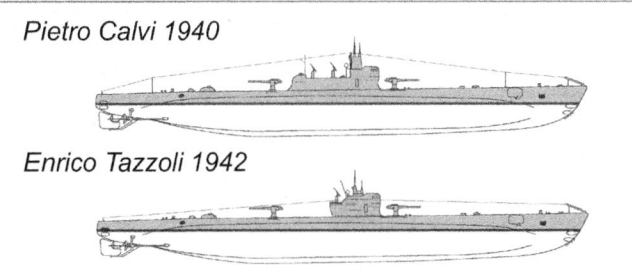

Pietro Calvi 1940

Enrico Tazzoli 1942

to transport submarines for voyages to Japan.
1943, *Enrico Tazzoli*: was converted to transport of ammunition and petrol (*Giuseppe Finzi* was converted after 8.9.1943 by the Germans).
Pietro Calvi was sunk 15.7.1942 S of the Azores by British sloop *Lulworth*. *Enrico Tazzoli* was lost in May 1943 in the Bay of Biscay, cause unknown, probably sunk 16.5.1943 by Allied aircraft. *Giuseppe Finci* was captured by German forces 9.9.1943, renamed *UIT21* and scuttled at Bordeaux 25.8.1944.

PERLA class medium submarines

Ambra	OTO, Muggiano	8.1935	28.5.1936	8.1936	scuttled 9.9.1943
Berillo	CRDA, Monfalcone	9.1935	14.6.1936	8.1936	sunk 2.10.1940
Corallo	CRDA, Monfalcone	9.1935	2.8.1936	9.1936	sunk 13.12.1942
Diaspro	CRDA, Monfalcone	9.1935	5.7.1936	8.1936	discarded 2.1948
Gemma	CRDA, Monfalcone	9.1935	21.5.1936	7.1936	sunk 8.10.1940
Iride	OTO, Muggiano	9.1935	30.7.1936	11.1936	to Nationalist Spain 10.1937-1.1938 (González López), sunk 22.8.1940
Malacite	OTO, Muggiano	8.1935	15.7.1936	11.1936	sunk 9.2.1943

Onice	OTO, Muggiano	8.1935	15.6.1936	9.1936	to Nationalist Spain 10.1937-1.1938 (Aguilar Tablada), discarded 3.1947
Perla	CRDA, Monfalcone	8.1935	3.5.1936	7.1936	captured by the UK 9.7.1942 (Greek Matrozos)
Turchese	CRDA, Monfalcone	9.1935	19.7.1936	9.1936	discarded 2.1948

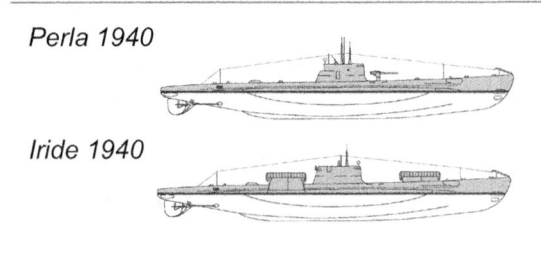

Perla 1940

Iride 1940

Iride prewar

680 / 844 t, 60.2 x 6.5 x 4.7 m, 2 Tosi (*Ambra, Malachite*) or Fiat or CRDA (*Corallo, Diaspro, Turchese*) diesels / 2 Marelli (*Ambra, Malachite*) or CRDA electric motors, 1200 / 800 hp, 14 / 7.5 kts, 80 t diesel oil, 2500 nm (12 kts) / 74 nm (4 kts), complement 45, 80 m; 1 x 1 – 100/47 OTO 1935, 2 x 1 or 2 x 2 – 13.2 MG, 6 – 533 TT (4 bow, 2 stern, 12); hydrophone.

A repeat of the *Sirena* class with slightly increased fuel capacity.

Iride and *Ambra* were converted to carry human torpedoes in 1940 and 1942, respectively. 100-mm/47 gun was removed, and four (*Iride*) or three (*Ambra*) cylindrical transportation containers were installed on the deck.
1940, *Iride*: - 1 x 1 - 100/47; + 4 SLC human torpedoes.
1942, *Ambra*: - 1 x 1 - 100/47; + 3 SLC human torpedoes.
Iride 22.8.1940 was sunk by a torpedo from an air group of British carrier *Eagle* near Tobruk. *Berillo* was sunk 2.10.1940 in the Mediterranean by DCs from British destroyers *Hasty* and *Havock*. *Gemma* was mistakenly sunk 8.10.1940 in the Aegean Sea by Italian submarine *Tricheco*. *Perla* was captured 9.7.1942 near Beirut by British corvette *Hyacinth*, transferred to Greece and renamed *Matrozos*. *Corallo* was sunk 13.12.1942 near Bougie, Algeria by gunfire from British sloop *Enchantress*. *Malacite* was sunk 9.2.1943 S of Sardinia by Dutch submarine *Dolfijn*. *Ambra* was scuttled by the crew 9.9.1943 in the harbor of La Spezia.

ADUA class medium submarines

Adua	CRDA, Monfalcone	2.1936	13.9.1936	11.1936	sunk 30.9.1941
Alagi	CRDA, Monfalcone	2.1936	15.11.1936	2.1937	discarded 5.1947
Aradam	CRDA, Monfalcone	2.1936	18.10.1936	1.1937	scuttled 9.9.1943
Ascianghi	OTO, Muggiano	1.1937	5.12.1937	3.1938	sunk 23.7.1943
Axum	CRDA, Monfalcone	2.1936	27.9.1936	12.1938	scuttled 28.12.1943
Beilul	OTO, Muggiano	7.1937	22.5.1938	9.1938	captured by Germany 9.9.1943
Dagabur	Tosi, Taranto	4.1936	22.11.1936	4.1937	sunk 12.8.1942
Dessié	Tosi, Taranto	4.1936	22.11.1936	4.1937	sunk 28.11.1942
Durbo	OTO, Muggiano	3.1937	6.3.1938	7.1938	sunk 18.10.1940
Gondar	OTO, Muggiano	1.1937	3.10.1937	2.1938	scuttled 30.11.1940
Lafolé	OTO, Muggiano	6.1937	10.4.1938	8.1938	sunk 20.10.1940
Macallé	OTO, Muggiano	3.1936	29.10.1936	3.1937	wrecked 15.6.1940
Neghelli	OTO, Muggiano	1.1937	7.11.1937	2.1938	sunk 19.1.1941
Sciré	OTO, Muggiano	1.1937	6.1.1938	3.1938	sunk 10.8.1942
Tembien	OTO, Muggiano	2.1937	6.2.1938	7.1938	sunk 2.8.1941
Uarsciek	Tosi, Taranto	12.1936	19.9.1937	12.1937	sunk 15.12.1942
Uebi Scebeli	Tosi, Taranto	1.1937	3.10.1937	12.1937	scuttled 29.6.1940

Adua 1940

680 / 844 t, 60.2 x 6.5 x 4.7 m, 2 CRDA (*Adua, Alagi, Aradam, Axum*) or Fiat or Tosi (*Dagabur, Dessié, Uarsciek, Uebi Scebeli*) diesels / 2 CRDA (*Adua, Alagi, Aradam, Axum*) or Marelli electric motors, 1200 / 800 hp, 14 / 7.5 kts, 80 t diesel oil, 2200 nm (14 kts) / 74 nm (4 kts), complement 45, 80 m; 1 x 1 – 100/47 OTO 1935, 2

ITALY

x 1 or 2 x 2 – 13.2 MG, 6 – 533 TT (4 bow, 2 stern, 12); hydrophone.

Repetition of the *Perla* class without significant differences. Three more submarines of this class, the first *Ascianghi*, *Gondar* and *Neghelli*, were sold to Brazil in March 1937 soon after the laying of the keels.

On *Adua*, *Alagi*, *Gondar*, *Sciré* and *Tembien* during the war years the CT was reduced. *Gondar* and *Sciré* in 1940-1941 were converted to human torpedo carriers. 100-mm/47 gun was removed, and three cylindrical transportation containers were installed on the deck.
1940-1941, *Gondar, Sciré*: - 1 x 1 - 100/47; + 3 SLC human torpedoes.

Macallé was wrecked on the reefs 15.6.1940 near Port Sudan after the entire crew was poisoned by halon from the air-conditioning system. *Uebi Scebeli* was scuttled 29.6.1940 W of Crete after an attack by British destroyers *Dainty* and *Ilex*. *Gondar* was scuttled by her crew 30.9.1940 near Alexandria after being attacked by British destroyers *Diamond* and *Stuart*. *Durbo* was sunk 18.10.1940 E of Gibraltar by British destroyers *Firedrake* and *Wrestler*. *Lafolé* was sunk 20.10.1940 N of Melilla by British destroyers *Gallant*, *Griffin* and *Hotspur*. *Neghelli* was sunk 19.1.1941 off the coast of Greece by British destroyer *Greyhound*. *Tembien* was sunk 2.8.1941 by ramming by British cruiser *Hermione* off the coast of Tunisia. *Adua* was sunk 30.9.1941 E of Cartagena by British destroyers *Gurkha* and *Legion*. *Sciré* was sunk

Sciré 1942

10.8.1942 near Haifa by British armed trawler *Islay*. *Dagabur* was rammed and sank 12.8.1942 by British destroyer *Wolverine*. *Dessié* was sunk 28.11.1942 off Cape Bon by British destroyers *Quiberon* and *Quentin*. *Uarsciek* was sunk 15.12.1942 S of Malta by British destroyer *Petard* and Greek destroyer *Vasilissa Olga*. *Ascianghi* was sunk 23.7.1943 S of Sicily by British destroyers *Eclipse* and *Laforey*. *Aradam* was scuttled by her crew 9.9.1943 at Genoa, salvaged by the Germans but never commissioned by the Kriegsmarine and sunk by Allied aircraft 4.9.1944. *Axum* ran aground at W coast of Greece and was scuttled by the crew 28.12.1943. *Beilul* was captured 9.9.1943 by German troops in the harbor of Monfalcone but never commissioned by the Kriegsmarine and was sunk by Allied aircraft in May 1945.

Macallé prewar

FOCA class large submarine minelayers

Atropo	Tosi, Taranto	7.1937	20.11.1938	2.1939	discarded 3.1947
Foca	Tosi, Taranto	1.1936	26.6.1937	11.1937	lost presumably 15.10.1940
Zoea	Tosi, Taranto	2.1936	5.12.1937	2.1938	discarded 3.1947

1305 / 1625 t, 82.9 x 7.2 x 5.2 m, 2 Fiat diesels / 2 Ansaldo electric motors, 2880 / 1250 hp, 16 / 8 kts, 63 t diesel oil, 8500 nm (8 kts) / 106 nm (4 kts), complement 60, 100 m; 1 x 1 – 100/43 OTO 1927, 2 x 2 – 13.2 MG, 6 – 533 TT (bow, 8), 36 mines; hydrophone.

The design was developed by the builder on the basis of the earlier *Archimede* and *Pietro Micca*. Partially double-hulled. Minelayers of this class were notable for the fact that they used two fundamentally different minelaying systems at once, horizontal and vertical. 8 mines were carried in two stern horizontal tubes and another 20 were carried in vertical trunks, as on *Pietro Micca*. Another distinguishing feature of the class was the massive CT, carrying a 102-mm/43 gun in the aft

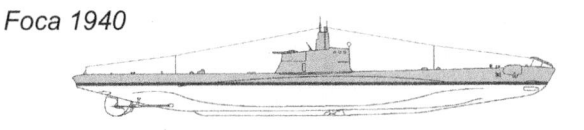

Foca 1940

part, theoretically capable of firing in fresh weather dur to its high position. In 1941, on *Atropo* and *Zoea* new main gun was moved to the deck fwd of the CT.
1941, *Atropo, Zoea*: - 1 x 1 - 100/43; + 1 x 1 - 100/47 OTO 1938.

Foca was lost in November 1940 in the Eastern Mediterranean. Probably mined near Haifa 15.10.1940. *Zoea* sank in an accident in the summer 1942 at Taranto but was quickly salvaged and recommissioned.

ARGO class medium submarines

| **Argo** | CRDA, Monfalcone | 10.1931 | 27.11.1936 | 8.1937 | scuttled 11.9.1943 |
| **Velella** | CRDA, Monfalcone | 10.1931 | 12.12.1936 | 9.1937 | sunk 7.9.1943 |

FIGHTING SHIPS OF WORLD WAR TWO

Argo 1941

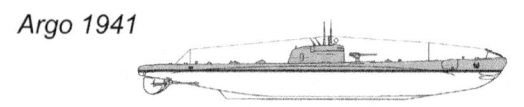

780 / 1000 t, 63.2 x 6.9 x 4.5 m, 2 Fiat diesels / 2 CRDA electric motors, 1500 / 800 hp, 14 / 8 kts, 60 t diesel oil, 5300 nm (14 kts) / 100 nm (3 kts), complement 46, 90 m; 1 x 1 – 100/47 OTO 1931, 2 x 2 – 13.2 MG, 6 – 533 TT (4 bow, 2 stern, 10); hydrophone.
Ordered by Portugal in 1931, but the order was cancelled soon after, and in 1935 it was purchased by the Italian Government for the own Navy. The design was developed by the builder as a moderated version of the *Balilla* class. Partially double-hulled.

Successful medium submarines with a long cruising range and easy maneuverability. A noticeable drawback was the relatively low speed. They served as the prototypes for wartime-built *Flutto* class submarines.
Velella was sunk 7.9.1943 in Salerno Bay by British submarine *Shakespeare*. *Argo* was scuttled 11.9.1943 at Monfalcone DYd.

MARCELLO and COMANDANTE CAPPELLINI classes large submarines

Marcello class

Name	Builder	Laid down	Launched	Completed	Fate
Barbarigo	CRDA, Monfalcone	2.1937	13.6.1938	9.1938	sunk probably 17-19.6.1943
Dandolo	CRDA, Monfalcone	6.1937	20.11.1937	3.1938	discarded 3.1947
Emo	CRDA, Monfalcone	2.1937	26.6.1938	10.1938	scuttled 10.11.1942
Marcello	CRDA, Monfalcone	1.1937	20.11.1937	3.1938	sunk probably 22.2.1941
Mocenigo	CRDA, Monfalcone	1.1937	20.11.1937	8.1938	sunk 13.5.1943
Morosini	CRDA, Monfalcone	3.1937	28.7.1938	11.1938	sunk probably 11.8.1942
Nani	CRDA, Monfalcone	1.1937	16.1.1938	9.1938	sunk probably 7.1.1941
Provana	CRDA, Monfalcone	2.1937	16.3.1938	6.1938	sunk 17.6.1940
Veniero	CRDA, Monfalcone	1.1937	12.2.1938	6.1938	sunk probably 7.6.1942

Comandante Cappellini class

Name	Builder	Laid down	Launched	Completed	Fate
Comandante Cappellini	OTO, Muggiano	4.1938	14.5.1939	9.1939	captured by Japan 10.9.1943 (German UIT24)
Comandante Faà di Bruno	OTO, Muggiano	4.1938	18.6.1939	10.1939	sunk probably 8.11.1940

Barbarigo 1940

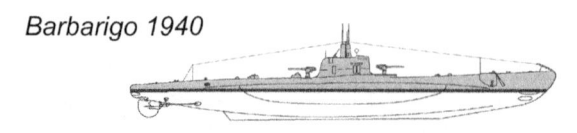

1043 / 1290 t, 73.0 x 7.2 x 5.1 m, 2 CRDA or Fiat (*Mocenigo, Veniero, Comandante Cappellini, Comandante Faà di Bruno*) diesels / 2 CRDA electric motors, 3600 / 1100 hp, 17.4 / 8 kts, 108 t diesel oil, 8000 nm (8 kts) / 120 nm (3 kts), complement 57, 100 m; 2 x 1 – 100/47 OTO 1938, 2 x 2 – 13.2 MG, 8 – 533 TT (4 bow, 4 stern, 16); hydrophone.

Development of the *Glauco* class. Single-hulled with external bulges. The best Italian large submarines of the Second World War: fast, with good underwater maneuverability. The weak point, common to all Italian submarines of that time, was the lack of stability during surfacing / diving.

1943, *Barbarigo, Comandante Cappellini*: were converted to transport submarines for voyages to Japan, carrying 50 t of ammunition and 80 t of petrol.
Provana was rammed 17.6.1940 near Oran by French sloop *La Curieuse*. *Comandante Faà di Bruno* was lost in November 1940 in the Atlantic, probably sunk by British destroyer *Havelock*. *Nani* was sunk in the North Atlantic 7.1.1941 by British corvette *Anemone*. *Marcello* was sunk in the North Atlantic by Allied escorts

Comandante Cappellini as German UIT24 1944

ITALY

22.2.1942. *Veniero* was sunk in the Mediterranean 7.6.1942, possibly by aircraft. *Morosini* was lost in August-September 1942 in the Bay of Biscay. *Emo* was sunk N of Alger by British armed trawler *Lord Nuffield* 10.11.1942. *Mocenigo* was sunk 15.5.1943 at Cagliari by US bombers. *Barbarigo* was sunk 16 or 19.6.1943 in the Bay of Biscay by Allied aircraft. *Comandante Cappellini* was captured 10.9.1943 by Japan at Sabang, transferred to Germany, renamed *UIT24*, 10.5.1945 recaptured by Japan, commissioned as *UIT24* (later *I503*), surrendered at Kobe 2.9.1945 and broken up in 1946.

BRIN class large submarines

Archimede	Tosi, Taranto	12.1937	5.3.1939	4.1939	sunk 15.4.1943
Brin	Tosi, Taranto	2.1936	3.4.1938	6.1938	discarded 2.1948
Galvani	Tosi, Taranto	12.1936	22.5.1938	7.1938	sunk 24.6.1940
Guglielmotti	Tosi, Taranto	12.1936	11.9.1938	10.1938	sunk 17.3.1942
Torricelli	Tosi, Taranto	12.1937	26.3.1939	5.1939	scuttled 23.6.1940

1000 / 1245 t, 72.5 x 6.7 x 4.5 m, 2 Tosi diesels / 2 Ansaldo electric motors, 3400 / 1300 hp, 17.3 / 8 kts, 61 t diesel oil, 9000 nm (7.8 kts) / 90 nm (4 kts), complement 58, 110 m; 2 x 1 – 100/43 OTO 1927, 4 x 1 – 13.2 MG, 8 – 533 TT (4 bow, 4 stern, 14); hydrophone.

Repetition of the *Archimede* class. Partially double-hulled. They differed from the prototype in slightly more powerful diesels and a larger CT, as in the *Foca* class, with a 100-mm/43 gun mounted on it.

The construction of the two last boats of this class, *Archimede* and *Toricelli*, was carried out in a confidential manner in order to hide the fact of transfer of two submarines of the same names to Franco.

In 1941-1942, on *Brin*, *Archimede* and, probably, *Guiglemotti*, the new gun was moved from the CT to the deck.

Brin 1941

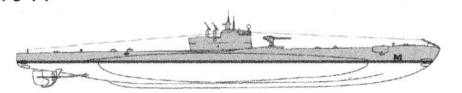

1941-1942, *Arcimede, Brin, Guglielmotti*: - 1 x 1 - 100/43; + 1 x 1 - 100/47 OTO 1938.

Toricelli after an artillery battle with British sloop *Shoreham* and destroyers *Khartoum*, *Kandahar*, and *Kingston* 23.6.1940 in the Red Sea was badly damaged and was scuttled by the crew. *Galvani* was sunk 26.4.1940 in the Persian Gulf by British sloop *Falmouth*. *Guglielmotti* was sunk 17.3.1942 S of Calabria by British submarine *Unbeaten*. *Archimede* was sunk 15.4.1943 off the coast of Brazil by US aircraft.

CONSOLE GENERALE LIUZZI class large submarines

Alpino Bagnolini	Tosi, Taranto	12.1938	28.10.1939	12.1939	captured by Germany 10.9.1943 (UIT22)
Reginaldo Giuliani	Tosi, Taranto	3.1939	3.12.1939	2.1940	captured by Japan 10.9.1943 (German UIT23)
Console Generale Liuzzi	Tosi, Taranto	11.1938	17.9.1939	11.1939	scuttled 27.6.1940
Capitano Tarantini	Tosi, Taranto	4.1939	7.1.1940	3.1940	sunk 15.12.1940

1148 / 1460 t, 76.1 x 7.0 x 4.6 m, 2 Tosi diesels / 2 Ansaldo electric motors, 2500 / 1500 hp, 18 / 8 kts, 135 t diesel oil, 11300 nm (8 kts) / 108 nm (3 kts), complement 58, 90 m; 2 x 1 – 100/47 OTO 1938, 2 x 2 – 13.2 MG, 8 – 533 TT (4 bow, 4 stern, 12); hydrophone.

An enlarged version of the *Brin* class. Partially double-hulled. Compared to their predecessors, they had better stability and, due to the new bow lines, higher speed. The gun was moved from the CT to the fore part of the deck.

1943, *Alpino Bagnolini*, *Reginaldo Guilliani*: converted to transports for voyages to Japan with an ammunition and petrol.

Capitano Tarantini was sunk in the Bay of Biscay 15.12.1940 by British submarine *Thunderbolt*. *Console*

Console Generale Liuzzi 1940

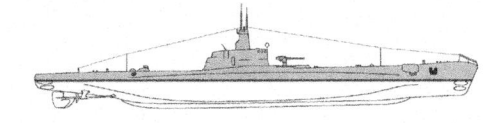

Generate Liuzzi was sunk 27.6.1940 S of Crete by British destroyers *Dainty*, *Ilex* and *Defender*. *Reginaldo Guilliani* was captured by the Japanese in Singapore 10.9.1943, transferred to Germany and renamed *UIT23*. She was sunk 14.2.1944 in the Strait of Malacca by British submarine *Tally Ho*. *Alpino Bagnolini* 10.9.1943 was captured by German forces at Bordeaux, renamed *UIT22* and sunk 11.3.1944 S of the Cape Good Hope by SAAF Catalina flying boat.

GUGLIELMO MARCONI class large submarines

Maggiore Baracca	OTO, Muggiano	3.1939	21.4.1940	7.1940	sunk 8.9.1941
Michele Bianchi	OTO, Muggiano	2.1939	3.12.1939	4.1940	sunk 7.8.1941
Leonardo da Vinci	CRDA, Monfalcone	9.1938	16.9.1939	4.1940	sunk 23.5.1943
Alessandro Malaspina	OTO, Muggiano	3.1939	18.2.1940	6.1940	sunk 21.9.1941
Guglielmo Marconi	CRDA, Monfalcone	9.1938	30.7.1939	2.1940	sunk ~ 11.1941
Luigi Torelli	OTO, Muggiano	2.1939	6.1.1940	5.1940	captured by Japan 10.9.1943 (German UIT25)

Guglielmo Marconi 1940

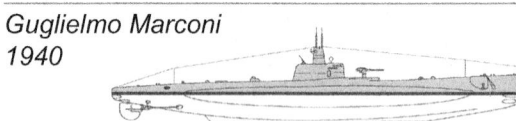

Leonardo da Vinci 1942

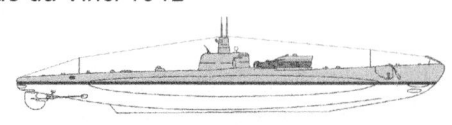

Leonardo da Vinci

1175 / 1465 t, 76.5 x 6.8 x 4.7 m, 2 CRDA diesels / 2 Marelli electric motors, 3600 / 1500 hp, 17.8 / 8.2 kts, 118 t diesel oil, 10500 nm (8 kts) / 110 nm (3 kts), complement 57, 90 m; 1 x 1 – 100/47 OTO 1938, 2 x 2 – 13.2 MG, 8 – 533 TT (4 bow, 4 stern, 12); hydrophone.

Development of the *Marcello* class. Single-hulled, with external bulges. To increase underwater speed, the hull was made narrower and longer than of the *Marcello*, for the same purpose more powerful electric motors were installed, but the increase in speed was insignificant. In addition, the fuel supply was increased slightly. In order to avoid a decrease in stability due to the smaller hull beam, the number of 100-mm/47 guns was reduced to one and the CT was made smaller.

1942, *Leonardo da Vinci*: - 1 x 1 - 100/47; + 1 CA midget submarine (for trials only).

1943, *Luigi Torelli*: was converted to transport for voyages to Japan.

Michele Bianchi was sunk 7.8.1941 W of Gibraltar by British submarine *Severn*. *Maggiore Baracca* was rammed 8.9.1941 by British escort destroyer *Croome* NE of the Azores. *Alessandro Malaspina* was lost in September 1941 in the Atlantic, probably sunk by British destroyer *Vimy*. *Guiglielmo Marconi* was lost in October 1941 in the Atlantic. *Leonardo da Vinci* was sunk 23.5.1943 NE of the Azores by British destroyer *Active* and frigate *Ness*. *Luigi Torelli* was captured by the Japanese 10.9.1943 in Singapore, transferred to Germany and renamed *UIT25*. She was subsequently handed over to the Japanese, later renamed *I504*, and scuttled after the war by the Americans.

AMMIRAGLIO CAGNI class large submarines

Ammiraglio Cagni	CRDA, Monfalcone	9.1939	20.7.1940	4.1941	discarded 2.1948
Ammiraglio Caracciolo	CRDA, Monfalcone	10.1939	16.10.1940	6.1941	scuttled 11.12.1941
Ammiraglio Millo	CRDA, Monfalcone	10.1939	31.8.1940	5.1941	sunk 14.3.1942
Ammiraglio Saint-Bon	CRDA, Monfalcone	9.1939	6.6.1940	3.1941	sunk 5.1.1942

Almirante Caracciolo 1941

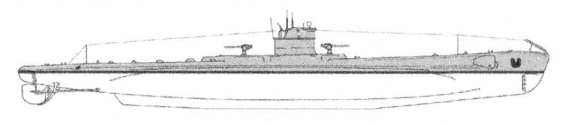

1653 / 2136 t, 87.9 x 7.8 x 5.7 m, 2 CRDA diesels / 2 CRDA electric motors, 4370 / 1800 hp, 17 / 8.5 kts, 180 t diesel oil, 10700 nm (12 kts) / 107 nm (3.5 kts), complement 85, 100 m; 2 x 1 – 100/47 OTO 1938, 2 x 2 – 13.2 MG, 14 – 450 TT (8 bow, 6 stern, 36); hydrophone.

The largest attack submarines of the Italian Navy during World War II. Designed by the builder. Single-hulled, with external bulges. Submarines of this class were intended, first of all, for operations against the merchant shipping on ocean routes. In this regard, the caliber of the torpedoes was reduced, but the number of spare torpedoes was greatly increased. Due to their

ITALY

large dimensions, the *Cagni* class submarines had good seaworthiness and habitability, while they were distinguished by good maneuverability.

1943, *Ammiraglio Cagni*: was converted to transport submarine for voyages to Japan.

Ammiraglio Caracciolo was scuttled by her crew 11.12.1941 near Bardia, having been heavily damaged by an attack by British escort destroyer *Farndale*. *Ammiraglio Saint-Bon* was commissioned in March 1941 incomplete and acquired combat readiness during an official service. She was sunk 5.1.1942 N of Sicily by British submarine *Upholder*. *Ammiraglio Millo* was sunk 14.3.1943 in the Ionian Sea by British submarine *Ultimatum*.

ACCIAIO class medium submarines

Acciaio	OTO, Muggiano	11.1940	20.7.1941	1.1942	sunk 13.7.1943
Alabastro	CRDA, Monfalcone	3.1941	18.12.1941	5.1942	sunk 14.9.1942
Argento	Tosi, Taranto	4.1941	22.2.1942	5.1942	sunk 3.8.1943
Asteria	CRDA, Monfalcone	10.1940	25.6.1941	11.1941	sunk 17.2.1943
Avorio	CRDA, Monfalcone	11.1940	6.9.1941	3.1942	sunk 9.2.1943
Bronzo	Tosi, Taranto	12.1940	28.9.1941	1.1942	captured by the UK 12.7.1943 (P714)
Cobalto	OTO, Muggiano	11.1940	20.7.1941	1.1942	sunk 12.8.1942
Giada	CRDA, Monfalcone	10.1940	10.7.1941	12.1941	discarded 1.1966
Granito	CRDA, Monfalcone	11.1940	7.8.1941	1.1942	sunk 9.11.1942
Nichelio	OTO, Muggiano	7.1941	12.4.1942	7.1942	to the USSR 2.1949 (I-42)
Platino	OTO, Muggiano	11.1940	1.6.1941	10.1941	discarded 2.1948
Porfido	CRDA, Monfalcone	11.1940	23.8.1941	1.1942	sunk 6.12.1942
Volframio *(ex-Stronzio)*	Tosi, Taranto	12.1940	9.11.1941	2.1942	scuttled 8.9.1943

697 / 850 t, 60.2 x 6.4 x 4.8 m, 2 Fiat or Tosi (*Argento, Bronzo, Volframio*) diesels / 2 CRDA or Ansaldo (*Argento, Bronzo, Volframio*) or Marelli (*Argento, Bronzo, Volframio*) electric motors, 1400 or 1500 (*Argento, Bronzo, Volframio*) / 800 hp, 14 or 14.7 (*Argento, Bronzo, Volframio*) / 7.7 kts, 78 t diesel oil, 2300 nm (14 kts) / 80 nm (4 kts), complement 45, 80 m; 1 x 1 – 100/47 OTO 1938, 2 or 1 x 1 – 20/70 Scotti-Isotta Fraschini 1939 or 2 x 1 or 2 x 2 – 13.2 MG, 6 – 533 TT (4 bow, 2 stern, 10) or 4 – 533 TT (bow, 8) (*Argento, Bronzo, Volframio*); hydrophone.

The last, 5th class of 600-ton submarines. Repetition of the *Adua* class with a moderately sized CT to improve stability and reduce visibility. Diesel power was also increased. Three boats, due to the use of even more powerful engines than on the other boats of the class, did not have stern TTs.

Cobalto was rammed 12.8.1942 N of Bizerte by British destroyer *Ithuriel*. *Alabastro* was sunk 14.9.1942 on approaches to Philippeville, Algeria by British aircraft. *Granito* was sunk 9.11.1942 near Cape St. Vito, Sicily by British submarine *Saracen*. *Porfido* was sunk 6.12.1942 near Cape Bon by British submarine *Tigris*. *Avorio* was sunk 9.2.1943 off Bougie by Canadian corvette *Regina*. *Asteria* was scuttled by her crew 17.2.1943 NW of Bougie after an attack by British escort destroyers *Easton* and *Wheatland*. *Bronzo* surrendered 12.7.1943 near Syracuse after a battle with British minesweepers *Boston*, *Cromarty*, and *Poole*, renamed *P714*, later transferred to France and named *Narval*. *Acciaio* was sunk 13.7.1943 N of the Strait of Messina by British submarine *Unruly*. *Argento* was sunk 3.8.1943 S of Pantelleria by US escort destroyer *Buck*. *Volframio* was scuttled by her crew 8.9.1943 in the harbor of La Spezia, salvaged by the Germans but never commissioned by them and sunk by Allied bombers in 1944.

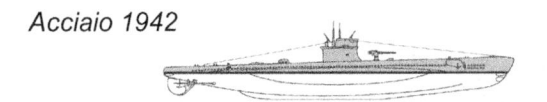

Acciaio 1942

Avorio 1942

Ex-Yugoslav N1 class medium submarines

N1 *(ex-Osvetnik)*, 4.1941- **Francesco Rismondo**	A C de la Loire, Nantes, France	1927	14.2.1929	(1929) / 4.1941	captured by Germany 14.9.1943
N2 *(ex-Smeli)*, 4.1941- **Antonio Bajamonti**	A C de la Loire, Nantes, France	1927	1.12.1928	(12.1929) / 4.1941	scuttled 9.9.1943

N2 1941

Francesco Rismondo 1941

630 / 809 t, 66.5 x 5.4 x 3.8 m, 2 MAN diesels / 2 CGE (Nancy) electric motors, 1480 / 1100 hp, 14.5 / 9.2 kts, 25 t diesel oil, 5000 nm (9 kts) / 100 nm (4.5 kts), complement 43, 80 m; 1 x 1 – 100/45 M1925, 1 x 1 – 40/67 Škoda, 6 – 533 TT (4 bow, 2 stern, 12).

In April 1941, after the surrender of Yugoslavia, two former Yugoslav submarines, *Osvetnik* and *Smeli*, were commissioned by the Regia Marina and renamed *Francesco Rismondo* and *Antonio Bajamonti* respectively. In 1941, they underwent repairs, during which the armament was partly modified; the form of the CT was changed.

Francesco Rismondo was 18.9.1943 scuttled by the Germans, *Antonio Bajamonti* was scuttled by her own crew 9.9.1943.

Ex-Yugoslav N3 medium submarine

N3 (ex-*Hrabri*, ex-*L67*)	Vickers-Armstrong, Elswick, UK	8.11.1917	15.6.1927	(2.1928) / 4.1941	never commissioned, BU 1941

N3 1941

975 / 1164 t, 72.1 x 7.3 x 4.0 m, 2 Vickers diesels / 2 electric motors, 2400 / 1600 hp, 15.7 / 10 kts, 5000 nm (9 kts) /, complement 47, 50 m; 2 x 1 – 102/40 QF Mk IV, 1 x 1 – 13.2 MG, 6 – 533 TT (bow, 12); presumably Type 113C sonar.

The Yugoslav submarine, captured 17.4.1941 but never commissioned by the Italian Navy as she was considered inoperable.

FLUTTO class medium submarines, 1st series

Cernia	Tosi, Taranto	7.1943	-	-	cancelled 1.1944
Dentice	Tosi, Taranto	8.1943	-	-	cancelled 1.1944
Flutto	CRDA, Monfalcone	12.1941	19.11.1942	3.1943	sunk 11.7.1943
Gorgo	CRDA, Monfalcone	5.1941	31.1.1942	11.1942	sunk 21.5.1943
Grongo	OTO, Muggiano	4.1942	6.5.1943	-	scuttled incomplete 9.9.1943
Marea	CRDA, Monfalcone	12.1941	10.12.1942	5.1943	to the USSR 2.1949 (I-41)
Murena	OTO, Muggiano	4.1942	11.4.1943	8.1943	scuttled 9.9.1943
Nautilo	CRDA, Monfalcone	1.1942	20.3.1943	7.1943	scuttled 10.9.1943
Sparide	OTO, Muggiano	4.1942	21.2.1943	8.1943	scuttled 9.9.1943
Spigola	Tosi, Taranto	6.1943	-	-	suspended 11.1943, BU 2.1948
Tritone	CRDA, Monfalcone	5.1941	3.1.1942	10.1942	sunk 19.1.1943
Vortice	CRDA, Monfalcone	1.1942	23.2.1943	6.1943	discarded 8.1967

Flutto 1943

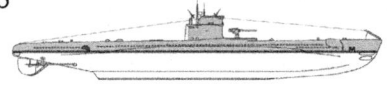

930 / 1093 t, 63.2 x 7.0 x 4.9 m, 2 Fiat diesels / 2 CRDA electric motors, 2400 / 800 hp, 16 / 8 kts, 52 t diesel oil, 5400 nm (8 kts) / 80 nm (4 kts), complement 50, 120 m; 1 x 1 – 100/47 OTO 1938, 2 x 1 – 20/70 Scott-Isotta Fraschini 1939, 1 x 2 – 13.2 MG (*some*), 6 – 533 TT (4 bow, 2 stern, 12), 4 SLC human torpedoes (*Grongo, Murena*)

Development of the *Argo* class with greater dive depth. Due to the use of more powerful diesels, the speed was increased to 16kts. The size of the CT was reduced. 8 submarines of the class of 12 were commissioned, one was scuttled incomplete and three were broken up on

ITALY

the stocks. Partially double-hulled, dive time was 30 sec.

Gorgo and *Murena* each received four cylindrical containers for transporting human torpedoes, located abreast of the CT. Unlike a similar assignment on 600-t submarines, they retained the main gun.

The incomplete *Cernia*, *Dentice* and *Spigola* were broken up on the stocks. The incomplete but highly completed *Grongo* was scuttled 9.9.1943 at La Spezia, salvaged by the Germans, renamed *UIT20* but never completed and sunk by Allied bombers at Genoa 4.9.1944.

Tritone was sunk 19.1.1943 NE of Algiers by DCs and gunfire from British destroyer *Antelope* and Canadian corvette *Port Arthur*. *Gorgo* was sunk 21.5.1943 near Oran by US destroyer *Nields*. *Flutto* was sunk 11.7.1943 off the E coast of Sicily by British *MTB640*, *MTB651* and *MTB670*.

Nautilo 1942

Three submarines were scuttled by their crews in September 1943: *Murena* and *Sparide* at La Spezia and *Nautilo* at Venice. They were salvaged by the Germans and renamed *UIT16*, *UIT15* and *UIT19* respectively. They were never commissioned by the Kriegsmarine and were sunk at Genoa by British aircraft 4.9.1944, 6.9.1944 and 9.1.1944 respectively.

Ex-French FR111 class large transport submarines

FR111 *(ex-Phoque)*	Arsenal de Brest, France	1924	16.3.1926	(5.1928) / 1.1943	sunk 28.2.1943
FR113 (ex-Requin)	Arsenal de Cherbourg, France	1923	19.7.1924	(5.1926)	scuttled during conversion 9.9.1943
FR114 (ex-Espadon)	Arsenal de Toulon, France	1924	28.5.1926	(12.1927)	scuttled during conversion 13.9.1943
FR115 (ex-Dauphin)	Arsenal de Toulon, France	1923	2.4.1925	(11.1927)	scuttled during conversion 15.9.1943

1150 / 1441 t, 78.3 x 6.8 x 5.1 m, 2 Sulzer or Schneider diesels / 2 electric motors, 2900 / 1800 hp, 15 / 9 kts, 167 t diesel oil, 7700 nm (9 kts) / 70 nm (5 kts), complement 51, 80 m; 2 x 1 – 13.2 MG, 50 t of dry cargo, 145 t of petrol.

After the Allied landing in North Africa in November 1942, German forces captured French ships based at Bizerte and transferred nine submarines to Italy in December 1942.

The French Requin class submarines *Phoque*, *Requin*, *Espadon* and *Dauphin* were renamed *FR111*, *FR113*, *FR114* and *FR115* respectively. They were

Requin 1939

immediately were put for conversion to transports. All original armament was removed, leaving only two 13.2-mm AA MGs. Submarines had to be able to carry 50 t of dry cargo and 145 t of fuel. Only *FR111* was commissioned by the Italians. The remaining three boats in September 1943 were scuttled by crews in shipyards or sunk by the Germans.

28.2.1943 *FR111* was sunk by Allied bombers.

Ex-French FR112 class medium submarine minelayers

FR112 (ex-Saphir)	Arsenal de Toulon, France	11.1925	20.12.1928	(9.1930)	repair incomplete, recharging station 4.1943
FR116 (ex-Turquoise)	Arsenal de Toulon, France	1926	16.5.1929	(9.1930)	repair incomplete, scuttled 6.5.1943

761 / 925 t, 65.9 x 7.2 x 4.3 m, 2 Normand-Vickers diesels / 2 electric motors, 1300 / 1000 hp, 12 / 9 kts, 75 t diesel oil, 7000 nm (7.5 kts) / 80 nm (4 kts), complement 42, 80 m; 1 x 1 – 75/35 M1928, 1 x 2 – 13.2 MG, 2 – 550 TT (bow, 4), 1 x (1 – 533 + 2 – 400) TT (1 + 2), 32 mines.

French Saphir class submarines *Saphir*, *Turquoise* and *Nautilus* were transferred by the Germans to the Italians in 1942, the first two were renamed *FR112* and *FR116*

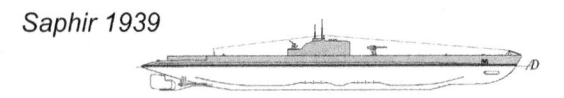

Saphir 1939

respectively but never commissioned by the Italians. *Nautilus* was sunk at Bizerte by Allied aircraft in January 1943. *FR112* was towed to Naples and used as a battery charging station from April 1943. *FR116* was scuttled at Bizerte 6.5.1943. *Nautilus* was never delivered to the Navy.

Ex-French FR117 medium submarine

FR117 (ex-Circé)	Schneider, Chalon-sur-Saône, France	2.1923	29.10.1925	(6.1929)	repair incomplete, scuttled 6.5.1943

Circé 1940

615 / 776 t, 62.5 x 6.2 x 4.0 m, 2 Schneider diesels / 2 electric motors, 1250 / 1000 hp, 14 / 7.5 kts, 60 t diesel oil, 2000 nm (10 kts) / 90 nm (5 kts), complement 41, 80 m; 1 x 1 – 75/35 M1925, 2 x 1 – 8 MG, 7 – 550 TT (2 bow, 2 ext bow, 1 ext stern, 1 x 2 ext turnable, 13).

The French 600-ton submarines *Circé* and *Calypso* were transferred to Italy by the Germans, the former was renamed *FR117* but was never commissioned by the Italians. *Calypso* was sunk at Bizerte by Allied aircraft 30.1.1943, *FR117* was scuttled by her crew at Bizerte 6.5.1943.

Ex-French FR118 large submarine

FR118 (ex-Henri Poincaré)	Arsenal de Lorient, France	1925	10.4.1929	(12.1931)	repair incomplete, captured by Germany 9.9.1943

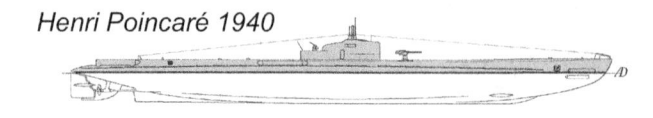

Henri Poincaré 1940

1570 / 2084 t, 92.3 x 8.2 x 4.7 m, 2 Sulzer or Schneider diesels / 2 electric motors, 6000 / 2000 hp, 17 / 10 kts, 108 t diesel oil, 10000 nm (10 kts) / 100 nm (5 kts), complement 61, 80 m; 1 x 1 – 100/45 M1925, 1 x 2 – 13.2 MG, 10 – 550 TT (4 bow, 2 x 3 ext, 12).

French 1500-ton submarine *Henri Poincaré* was scuttled at Toulon in November 1942. The Italians managed to salvage and tow her to Genoa in early 1943 for repairs. *Henri Poincaré* was renamed *FR118*. Still under repair at Genoa by September 1943, she was 9.9.1943 captured by Germans and sunk by Allied bombers 9.9.1944.

ROMOLO class large transport submarines

Remo	Tosi, Taranto	9.1942	28.3.1943	6.1943	sunk 15.7.1943
Romolo	Tosi, Taranto	7.1942	21.3.1943	6.1943	sunk 18.7.1943
R3	Tosi, Taranto	3.1943	7.9.1946	-	delivered incomplete 11.1946, BU
R4	Tosi, Taranto	3.1943	30.9.1946	-	delivered incomplete 11.1946, BU
R5	Tosi, Taranto	3.1943	-	-	cancelled 1.1944
R6	Tosi, Taranto	3.1943	-	-	cancelled 1.1944
R7	CRDA, Monfalcone	3.1943	21.10.1943	-	captured incomplete by Germany 10.9.1943 (UIT4)
R8	CRDA, Monfalcone	3.1943	28.12.1943	-	captured incomplete by Germany 10.9.1943 (UIT5)
R9	CRDA, Monfalcone	3.1943	27.2.1944	-	captured incomplete by Germany 10.9.1943 (UIT6)
R10	OTO, Muggiano	2.1943	12.7.1944	-	captured incomplete by Germany 9.9.1943 (UIT1)
R11	OTO, Muggiano	3.1943	6.8.1944	-	captured incomplete by Germany 9.9.1943 (UIT2)
R12	OTO, Muggiano	5.1943	29.9.1944	-	captured incomplete by Germany 9.9.1943 (UIT3)

Remo 1943

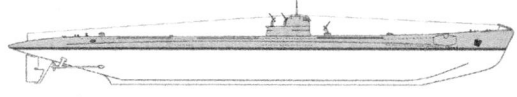

2155 / 2560 t, 86.5 x 7.9 x 5.3 m, 2 Tosi diesels / 2 Marelli electric motors, 2600 / 900 hp, 14 / 6.5 kts, 200 t diesel oil, 12000 nm (9 kts) / 90 nm (4 kts), complement 63, 100 m; 3 x 1 – 20/65 Breda 1940, 2 – 450 TT (bow, 2) (*some incomplete boats*); 600 t of dry cargo, liquid cargo; hydrophone.

Transport submarines specially designed for voyages to Japan. Partially double-hulled. They had four watertight cargo holds with a total capacity of 610 m³. The maximum weight of the cargo was 600 t. Defensive

ITALY

armament originally consisted of three AA MGs, already after the laying of the submarines they received two 450-mm TTs, but they were not installed on all units. So, both completed submarines did not have TTs. In total, two submarines of this class were completed.

R3 and *R4* were taken by the Italian Navy 14.11.1946 at 77% and 71% readiness and were broken up. The construction of *R5* and *R6* never started really, the order was cancelled 1.8.1944. The remaining six submarines were captured by German forces at Monfalcone (*R7*, *R8* and *R9*) and La Spezia (*R10*, *R11* and *R12*) in September 1943. They were renamed *UIT4, 5, 6, 1, 2* and *3* respectively. The Germans tried to complete these boats, the submarines were even launched, but none of them could be completed. Three incomplete submarines at Monfalcone were sunk

Romolo 1943

by Allied aircraft: *UIT4* 25.5.1944, *UIT6* 20.4.1944 and *UIT5* 16.3.1945. The rest were scuttled by the Germans 24.4.1945 at La Spezia (*UIT1* and *UIT3*) and Genoa (*UIT2*).

Remo was sunk 15.7.1943 in the Bay of Taranto by British submarine *United*. *Romolo* was sunk 18.7.1943 near Augusta by British aircraft.

Ex-German S1 class medium submarines

S1 (ex-U428)	Danziger Werft, Danzig, Germany	8.1942	11.3.1943	(6.1943) / 6.1943	captured by Germany 8.9.1943 (U428)
S2 (ex-U746)	Schichau, Danzig, Germany	7.1942	16.4.1943	7.1943	captured by Germany 8.9.1943 (U746)
S3 (ex-U747)	Schichau, Danzig, Germany	8.1942	13.5.1943	7.1943	captured by Germany 8.9.1943 (U747)
S4 (ex-U429)	Danziger Werft, Danzig, Germany	9.1942	30.3.1943	(7.1943) / 7.1943	captured by Germany 8.9.1943 (U429)
S5 (ex-U748)	Schichau, Danzig, Germany	8.1942	13.5.1943	7.1943	captured by Germany 8.9.1943 (U748)
S6 (ex-U430)	Danziger Werft, Danzig, Germany	10.1942	22.4.1943	(8.1943) / 8.1943	captured by Germany 8.9.1943 (U430)
S7 (ex-U749)	Schichau, Danzig, Germany	9.1942	10.6.1943	8.1943	captured by Germany 8.9.1943 (U749)
S8 (ex-U1161)	Danziger Werft, Germany	10.1942	8.5.1943	8.1943	captured by Germany 8.9.1943 (U1161)
S9 (ex-U750)	Schichau, Danzig, Germany	9.1942	10.6.1943	8.1943	captured by Germany 8.9.1943 (U750)
S10 (ex-U1162)	Danziger Werft, Germany	11.1942	29.5.1943	(9.1943)	captured by Germany 8.9.1943 (U1162), never really transferred
S11 (ex-U745)	Schichau, Danzig, Germany	7.1942	16.4.1943	(6.1943)	captured by Germany 8.9.1943 (U745), never really transferred

769 / 1070 t, 67.1 x 6.2 x 4.7 m, 2 Germania diesels / 2 SSW (*S1, 4, 6, 8, 10*) or AEG electric motors, 2800-3200 / 750 hp, 17-17.7 / 7.6 kts, 114 t diesel oil, 8500 nm (10 kts) / 80 nm (4 kts), complement 44-56, 100 m; 1 x 1 – 37/69 FlaK M/42, 2 x 2 – 20/65 C/38, 5 – 533 TT (4 bow, 1 stern, 14) (*S1 – 7, 9, 11*), 5 – 533 TT (4 bow, 1 stern, 14 torpedoes or 36 mines) (*S8, 10*); FuMO 30 radar, S-Gerät sonar, GHG hydrophone, FuMB 1 Metox ECM suite.

In 1943, Germany transferred to Italy 9 submarines of the VIIC and VIIC/41 series in exchange for Italian oceangoing submarines, which were supposed

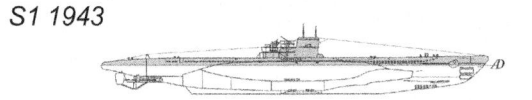

S1 1943

to be converted to transports for voyages to the Far East. In September 1943, all 9 submarines (*S1-9*) were taken over by Italian crews in Germany and, after the signing of an armistice between Italy and the Allies, were commissioned by the Kriegsmarine. Two more boats, *S10* and *S11*, were never actually handed over.

S1-11 were recommissioned by the German Navy 9.9.1943.

CM1 class small submarines

CM1	CRDA, Monfalcone	6.1943	5.9.1943	(1.1945) / 1.1945	captured by Germany 9.9.1943 (UIT17), to Italy 1.1945, discarded 2.1948
CM2	CRDA, Monfalcone	8.1943	4.1945	-	captured by Germany 9.9.1943 (UIT18)

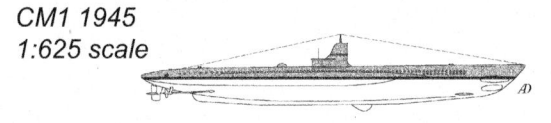

CM1 1945
1:625 scale

90 / 112 t, 33.0 x 2.9 x 2.8 m, 2 Fiat-Spa diesels / 2 CRDA electric motors, 600 / 120 hp, 14 / 6 kts, 2000 nm (9 kts) / 70 nm (4 kts), complement 8, 80 m; 2 x 1 – 13.2 MG, 3 – 450 TT (bow, 3)

Coastal boats for the harbor protection. Prototypes were ordered in 1943 from Caproni (CC) and CRDA (CM). Until September 1943, an order was issued for 16 CM and 8 CCs in addition to prototypes.

After comparative trials of the prototypes, it was supposed to establish a mass building of a better sample under the CU index (unified).

Prior to the armistice, only one submarine of the CC class and two of the CM class were laid down, one of which, *CM1*, was launched. For *CC2*, *CC3* and *CM3*, preparation of materials has begun, but in reality, they were not laid down. Incomplete boats in September 1943 were captured by the Germans. It was decided to complete *CM1* and *CM2*, renamed *UIT17* and *UIT18* respectively. *CM1* (*UIT17*) was commissioned in January 1945 and *CM2* (*UIT18*) was damaged on the stock by Allied aircraft in May 1944. *CM1* was transferred by the Germans to the RSI. Shortly thereafter, the Italian crew brought the boat to the Royal Italian Navy.

CC1 small submarine

CC1	Caproni, Milano	1943	-	-	suspended 9.1943, BU 4.1945

CC1
1:625 scale

98 / 115 t, 33.0 x 2.7 x 2.2 m, 2 Fiat diesels / 2 CRDA electric motors, 700 / 120 hp, 16 / 9 kts, 1200 nm (10 kts) / 70 nm (4 kts), complement 8, 80 m; 2 x 1 – 13.2 MG, 3 – 450 TT (bow, 3)

FLUTTO class medium submarines, 2nd series

Alluminio	OTO, Muggiano	12.1942	-	-	captured incomplete by Germany 9.9.1943
Antimonio	OTO, Muggiano	12.1942	-	-	captured incomplete by Germany 9.9.1943
Bario	CRDA, Monfalcone	3.1943	23.1.1944 / 21.6.1959	16.12.1961	captured incomplete by Germany 9.9.1943 (UIT7), recommissioned as Pietro Calvi 1961, discarded 1.1972
Cromo	CRDA, Monfalcone	9.1943	-	-	captured incomplete by Germany 10.9.1943
Ferro	CRDA, Monfalcone	6.1943	-	-	captured incomplete by Germany 10.9.1943 (UIT12)
Fosforo	OTO, Muggiano	12.1942	-	-	captured incomplete by Germany 9.9.1943
Litio	CRDA, Monfalcone	3.1943	19.2.1944	-	captured incomplete by Germany 10.9.1943 (UIT8)
Manganese	OTO, Muggiano	12.1942	-	-	captured incomplete by Germany 9.9.1943
Piombo	CRDA, Monfalcone	8.1943	-	-	captured incomplete by Germany 10.9.1943 (UIT13)
Potassio	CRDA, Monfalcone	5.1943	-	-	captured incomplete by Germany 10.9.1943 (UIT10)

ITALY

Rame	CRDA, Monfalcone	6.1943	-	-	captured incomplete by Germany 10.9.1943 (UIT11)
Silicio	OTO, Muggiano	12.1942	-	-	captured incomplete by Germany 9.9.1943
Sodio	CRDA, Monfalcone	5.1943	16.3.1944	-	captured incomplete by Germany 10.9.1943 (UIT9)
Zinco	CRDA, Monfalcone	8.1943	-	-	captured incomplete by Germany 10.9.1943 (UIT14)
Zolfo	OTO, Muggiano	12.1942	-	-	captured incomplete by Germany 9.9.1943

As designed: 913 / 1113 t, 64.2 x 7.0 x 4.9 m, 2 Fiat diesels / 2 CRDA electric motors, 2400 / 800 hp, 16 / 8 kts, 52 t diesel oil, 5400 nm (8 kts) / 80 nm (4 kts), complement 50, 120 m; 1 x 1 – 100/47 OTO 1938, 2 x 1 – 20/70 Isotta-Fraschini 1939, 6 – 533 TT (4 bow, 2 stern, 12); hydrophone.

Pietro Calvi as completed: 905 / 1107 t, 66.0 x 7.0 x 4.0 m, 2 MAN diesels / 3 electric motors (1 shaft), 2700 / 2700 hp, 14 / 14 kts, 10000 nm (8 kts), complement 60, 120 m; 4 – 533 TT (bow, 8); radar, sonar.

Differed from the 1st series only in a slightly lengthened hull. 24 submarines were ordered, but only 15 were laid down before September 1943. 12 submarines of the 3rd series were ordered in 1943, but not a single submarine was laid down.

All 15 laid down submarines 9.9.1943 passed into the hands of the Germans. Seven boats that were in a low degree of readiness (*Alluminio, Antimonio, Fosforo, Manganese, Silicio, Zolfo* and *Cromo*) were broken up on the stocks. The remaining 8 boats decided to complete.

Pietro Calvi 1961

Bario, Litio, Sodio, Potassio, Rame, Ferro, Piombo and *Zinco* were renamed *UIT7-14* respectively. The first three were launched, but all of them were damaged during an Allied air raid 16.3.1945 and 1.5.1945 scuttled by the Germans. The rest of the submarines that day were blown up on the stocks. In 1945, the Italians salvaged *Bario* and, after reconstruction, completed her as *Pietro Calvi*.

The following submarines were ordered but never laid down: *Amianto, Magnesio, Mercurio* (Tosi, Taranto), *Cadmio, Iridio, Oro, Ottone, Rutenio, Vanadio* (CRDA, Monfalcone). Another 12 submarines of the 3rd series were ordered: 6 from CRDA, 3 from Tosi and 3 from OTO. They possibly were named *Attinio, Azoto, Bromo, Carbonio, Elio, Molibdeno, Osmio, Ossigeno, Plutonio, Radio, Selenio* and *Tungsteno*.

CA class Type I midget submarines

Caproni, Milano: CA1, 2 (1938)
Lost: CA1, 2 (1943)
13.3 / 16.1 t, 10.0 x 2.0 x 1.6 m, 1 MAN diesel / 1 Marelli electric motor, 60 / 25 hp, 6.3 / 5 kts, 700 nm (4 kts) / 57 nm (3 kts), complement 2, 55 m; 2 – 450 TC (ext cradles, 2)

The first midget submersibles of the Italian Navy, created after the First World War. They were designed on their own initiative by Caproni, then the Navy became interested in them and issued an order for the construction of two midgets. Initially, they were supposed to be used as anti-submarine craft. Trials were unsuccessful: the boats turned out to be very unstable at periscope depth with the slightest sea waves.

In 1941, they were transferred to the 10th MAS

CA1 1941
1:625 scale

Flotilla for use as underwater transports. Diesels, torpedoes and periscope were removed. Boats were arranged to carry eight 100-kg explosive charges and three frogmen. They were supposed to be used to attack the harbors on the west coast of the United States, where they were supposed to delivered on the decks of large submarines.

Their technical data became as follows: 11.8 / 13.8 t, 10.0 x 2.0 x 1.6 m, 1 Marelli electric motor, 25 hp, 7 / 6 kts, 70 nm (2 kts), complement 3, 55 m; 8 x 100-kg explosive charges.

Both were lost 9.9.1943.

CB class midget submarines

Caproni, Milano: CB1 – 6 (1941), CB7 – 12 (1943), CB13 – 16, CB6 (*ex-CB17*), CB18 – 21 (1943 / 1943), CB1 – 4, 6 (1941 / 1944, 2nd time), CB22 – 25 (captured incomplete 1943)

CB1 1941
1:625 scale

Transferred: Romania – CB1 – 4, 6 (1943)
Lost: CB5 (1942), CB7 (1943), CB1 – 4, 6, 16 (1944), CB13 – 15, CB6 (ex-CB17), CB18, 20, 21 (1945)
Discarded: CB8 – 12 (1948)
35 / 44 t, 15.0 x 3.0 x 2.1 m, 1 Isotta-Fraschini diesel / 1 BBC electric motor, 80 / 50 hp, 7.5 / 7 kts, 1400 nm (5 kts) / 50 nm (3 kts), complement 4, 55 m; 2 – 450 TC (ext cradles, 2) or 2 mines.

An enlarged version of the CA 1st series (before reconstruction), intended to protect the coast and harbors. Until September 1943, 22 boats were laid down, of which only CB1 - 12 were completed. The remaining 10 incomplete boats were captured by the Germans. 50 more CB boats of so-called 2nd series were ordered from Caproni, but only CB23-25 were launched and remained incomplete.

Five boats, CB1-4 and 6, in September 1943 were captured by German troops and soon transferred to Romania. In January 1944 they were again returned to the Italians, this time to the puppet "Social Republic". All of them were scuttled at Constanta 25.8.1944. In addition to 5 boats in the Black Sea, in September 1943 the Germans captured damaged CB7, which was never repaired and used to complete CB13. CB13, as well as 8 more boats captured during the outfitting (CB14 - 21), were transferred to the control of the 10th MAS Flotilla of the "Social Republic". Another craft, CB22, was cancelled.

CA class Type II midget submarines

CA3 1943
1:625 scale

Caproni, Milano: CA3, 4 (1943)
Lost: CA3, 4 (1943)

12.6 / 13.8 t, 10.5 x 1.9 x 1.8 m, 1 Marelli electric motor, 25 hp, 7 / 6 kts, 70 nm (2 kts), complement 3, 55 m; (8 x 100-kg + 20 x 2-kg) explosive charges.

A slightly enlarged version of the modified boats of the 1st CA series. They were built for the 10th MAS Flotilla. Both were lost 9.9.1943.

ESCORT AND PATROL SHIPS

GM194 floating battery

GM194 (ex-Faà di Bruno, ex-GA43)	R. Arsenale di Venezia	1915	30.1.1916	(23.7.1917) / 1940	captured by Germany 9.9.1943 (Biber)

Faà di Bruno 1918

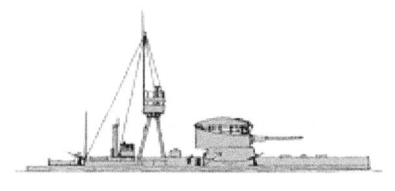

2809 / 2854 t, 55.6 x 27.0 x 2.2 m, 2 Thornycroft VTE, 2 Thornycroft boilers, 465 hp, 2.5 kts, complement 743; belt 2900 concrete, deck 40, turret 110; 1 x 2 – 381/40 Schneider 1914, 4 x 1 – 76/40 Armstrong 1916, 2 x 1 – 40/39 Vickers-Terni 1915.

The ship was designed by Rear Admiral G. Rota specifically to support ground forces near Trieste. She was a rectangular pontoon with a sloping deck. Along the perimeter, instead of an armored belt, the hull was protected with by a 2.9-m thick layer of cofferdams filled with concrete. 381-mm guns, created for the incomplete dreadnought *Christoforo Colombo*, had a maximum elevation angle of 15° and a horizontal aiming angle of 60°. Steam engines were removed from the old torpedo boat; according to some reports, their real power did not exceed 100 hp. Compared to the British monitors, *Faà di Bruno* was significantly slower but had a shallower draught, which reduced the risk of mining. *Faà di Bruno* was stricken in 1924 but survived the inter-war period and was used as a floating battery *GM194* at Genoa in 1940-1943.

The ship had a 40-mm very sloping armored deck, the turret had 110-mm face armor consisted of 3 layers (70+20+20-mm) and was installed on the barbette with 60-mm armor.

ITALY

ERITREA colonial sloop

| Eritrea | Cantieri di Castellamare di Stabia | 7.1935 | 28.9.1936 | 2.1937 | to France 2.1948 (Francis Garnier) |

2165 / 3068 t, 96.9 x 13.3 x 3.5 m, 2 Fiat diesels + 2 diesel-generators, 2 Marelli electric motors (2 shafts), 7800 + 1300 = 9100 hp, 20 kts, 320 t diesel oil, 6950 nm (11.8 kts), complement 234; 2 x 2 – 120/45 Schneider-Canet-Armstrong 1918-19, 2 x 1 – 40/39 Vickers-Terni 1917, 4 x 1 – 13.2 MG.

Designed in 1934 for service in the colonies, she was distinguished by her original machinery, which included, in addition to the main diesels, an auxiliary diesel-electric plant. The electric motors were mounted on the main shafts, it was possible to simultaneously operate both the main diesels and the electric motors. The longest cruising range was provided under electric motors, under the main diesels it was 5000 nm at 15.3 kts, under both diesels and electric motors 6120 nm at 13.3 kts. The maximum speed under diesels was 18 kts, and under electric motors 12 kts. It was planned to build a second ship of this class; she was supposed to be named *Etiopia*.

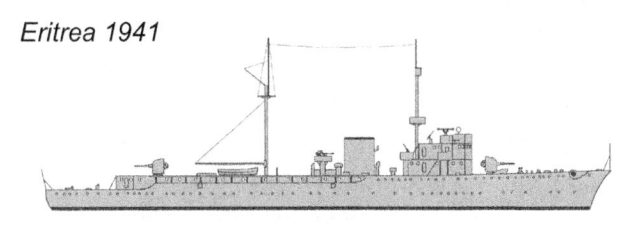

Eritrea 1941

Eritrea 1943

1940 - 1941: - 2 x 1 - 40/39; + 2 x 2 - 37/54 Breda 1938, mines.

DIANA sloop

| Diana | CNQ, Fiume | 5.1939 | 20.5.1940 | 11.1940 | sunk 29.6.1942 |

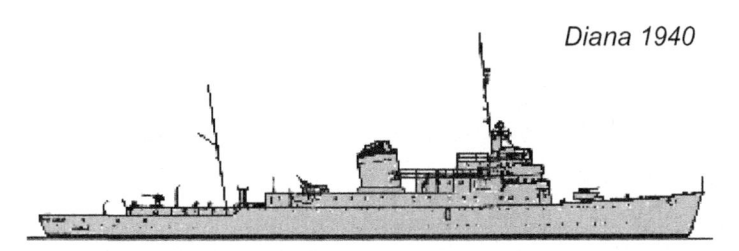

Diana 1940

1735 / 2550 t, 113.9 x 11.7 x 2.9 m, 2 sets Tosi-Beluzzo geared steam turbines, 4 Tosi boilers, 30000 hp, 32 kts, 560 t oil, complement 192; 1 x 2 – 102/35 Terni 1914, 2 x 2 – 20/65 Breda 1935, 2 x 1 – 20/65 Breda 1939, 2 DCT (38 – 42), mines.

Designed as a yacht / dispatch vessel. During the war, *Diana* served as a fast transport. In July 1941 she served as a suicide boat carrier with 9 MT, 1 MTSM and 1 MTL onboard for the attack on Malta.

Diana

Diana was sunk by British submarine *Thrasher* 29.6.1942 N of Tobruk.

GABBIANO class corvettes

Alce	OTO, Livorno	5.1942	5.12.1942	-	captured incomplete by Germany 9.9.1943 (UJ6084)
Antilope	OTO, Livorno	1.1942	9.5.1942	11.1942	captured by Germany 9.9.1943 (UJ6082)
Ape	Navalmeccanica, Castellamare di Stabia	5.1942	22.11.1942	5.1943	auxiliary 1965

Name	Builder	Laid down	Launched	Completed	Fate
Ardea	Ansaldo, Genoa	3.1943	-	-	captured incomplete by Germany 9.9.1943 (UJ2225)
Artemide	CRDA, Monfalcone	3.1942	10.8.1942	10.1942	captured by Germany 9.9.1943 (UJ2226)
Baionetta (ex-*Partigiana*)	Breda, Porto Marghera	2.1942	5.10.1942	5.1943	discarded 10.1971
Berenice	CRDA, Monfalcone	10.1942	20.5.1943	9.1943	sunk 9.9.1943
Bombarda	Breda, Porto Marghera	8.1942	10.2.1944	4.1951	discarded 11.1978
Calabrone	Navalmeccanica, Castellamare di Stabia	10.1942	27.6.1943	-	scuttled incomplete 9.1943
Camoscio	OTO, Livorno	1.1942	9.5.1942	4.1943	captured by Germany 9.9.1943 (UJ6081)
Capriolo	OTO, Livorno	6.1942	5.12.1942	(9.1943)	captured incomplete by Germany 9.9.1943 (UJ6083)
Carabina	Breda, Porto Marghera	9.1942	31.8.1943	-	captured incomplete by Germany 11.9.1943 (UJ207)
Cavalletta	Navalmeccanica, Castellamare di Stabia	12.1942	-	-	demolished on the stocks 9.1943
Cervo	OTO, Livorno	2.1943	-	-	captured incomplete by Germany 9.9.1943 (UJ6086)
Chimera	CRDA, Trieste	6.1942	30.1.1943	5.1943	discarded 5.1977
Cicala	Navalmeccanica, Castellamare di Stabia	9.1942	27.6.1943	-	scuttled incomplete 9.1943
Cicogna	Ansaldo, Genoa	6.1942	12.10.1942	1.1943	wrecked 24.7.1943
Clava	Breda, Porto Marghera	10.1943	-	-	BU 1944
Cocciniglia	Navalmeccanica, Castellamare di Stabia	1943	-	-	suspended 9.1943
Colubrina	Breda, Porto Marghera	3.1942	7.12.1942	(1.1944)	captured incomplete by Germany 11.9.1943 (UJ205)
Cormorano	Cerusa, Voltri	1.1942	20.9.1942	3.1943	discarded 7.1971
Crisalide	Navalmeccanica, Castellamare di Stabia	4.1943	8.12.1947	9.1952	discarded 12.1972
Daino	OTO, Livorno	3.1943	-	-	captured incomplete by Germany 9.9.1943 (UJ6087)
Danaide	CRDA, Trieste	5.1942	21.10.1942	2.1943	discarded 1.1968
Driade	CRDA, Trieste	5.1942	7.10.1942	1.1943	discarded 8.1966
Egeria	CRDA, Monfalcone	2.1943	3.7.1943	(1.1944)	scuttled 9.9.1943, completed as German UJ201
Euridice	CRDA, Monfalcone	7.1943	12.3.1944	-	captured incomplete by Germany 11.9.1943 (UJ204)
Euterpe	CRDA, Monfalcone	4.1942	22.10.1942	1.1943	scuttled 9.9.1943
Farfalla	Navalmeccanica, Castellamare di Stabia	4.1943	4.1.1948	2.1953	discarded 12.1971
Fenice	CRDA, Trieste	6.1942	1.3.1943	6.1943	discarded 7.1965
Flora	CRDA, Trieste	5.1942	1.12.1942	4.1943	discarded 1.1970
Folaga	Ansaldo, Genoa	6.1942	14.11.1942	2.1943	discarded 8.1965
Gabbiano	Cerusa, Voltri	1.1942	23.6.1942	10.1942	discarded 11.1971
Gazzella	OTO, Livorno	1.1942	9.5.1942	2.1943	sunk 5.8.1943
Grillo	Navalmeccanica, Castellamare di Stabia	6.1942	21.3.1943	-	scuttled incomplete 9.1943
Gru	Ansaldo, Genoa	7.1942	23.12.1942	4.1943	discarded 8.1971
Ibis	Ansaldo, Genoa	6.1942	12.12.1942	4.1943	discarded 7.1971

ITALY

Libellula	Navalmeccanica, Castellamare di Stabia	12.1942	-	-	demolished on the stocks 9.1943
Lucciola	Navalmeccanica, Castellamare di Stabia	6.1942	21.3.1943	-	scuttled incomplete 13.9.1943
Maggiolino	Navalmeccanica, Castellamare di Stabia	1943	-	-	suspended 9.1943
Marangone	Ansaldo, Genoa	3.1943	16.9.1943	(8.1944)	captured incomplete by Germany 9.9.1943 (UJ2223)
Melpomene	CRDA, Monfalcone	3.1943	29.8.1943	(4.1944)	captured incomplete by Germany 11.9.1943 (UJ202)
Minerva	CRDA, Monfalcone	4.1942	5.11.1942	2.1943	discarded 7.1969
Pellicano	Cerusa, Voltri	1.1942	12.2.1943	3.1943	discarded 7.1969
Persefone	CRDA, Monfalcone	3.1942	21.9.1942	11.1942	scuttled 9.9.1943
Pomona	CRDA, Trieste	5.1942	18.11.1942	4.1943	discarded 6.1965
Procellaria	Cerusa, Voltri	1.1942	4.9.1942	11.1942	sunk 31.1.1943
Renna	OTO, Livorno	5.1942	5.12.1942	(9.1944)	captured incomplete by Germany 9.9.1943 (UJ6085)
Scimitarra	Breda, Porto Marghera	2.1942	16.9.1942	5.1943	discarded 6.1971
Scure	Breda, Porto Marghera	10.1943	-	-	laid down as German UJ209
Sfinge	CRDA, Trieste	6.1942	9.1.1943	5.1943	discarded 6.1977
Sibilla	CRDA, Trieste	6.1942	10.3.1943	6.1943	discarded 2.1973
Spingarda	Breda, Porto Marghera	3.1942	22.3.1943	(4.1944)	captured incomplete by Germany 11.9.1943 (UJ208)
Stambecco	OTO, Livorno	3.1943	-	-	captured incomplete by Germany 9.9.1943 (UJ6088)
Strolaga	Ansaldo, Genoa	3.1943	19.9.1943	(4.1944)	captured incomplete by Germany 9.9.1943 (UJ2224)
Tersicore	CRDA, Monfalcone	4.1943	16.10.1943	-	captured incomplete by Germany 11.9.1943 (UJ203)
Tuffetto	Ansaldo, Genoa	3.1943	25.8.1943	(3.1944)	captured incomplete by Germany 9.9.1943 (UJ2222)
Urania	CRDA, Monfalcone	10.1942	21.4.1943	8.1943	discarded 8.1971
Vespa	Navalmeccanica, Castellamare di Stabia	5.1942	22.11.1942	9.1943	captured by Germany 11.9.1943 (UJ2221)
Zagaglia	Breda, Porto Marghera	2.1944	-	-	suspended 1944

660 / 728 t, 64.4 x 8.7 x 2.5 m, 2 Fiat diesels / 2 electric motors for silent search or 2 Fiat diesels (*Bombarda, Carabina*), 3500 / 300 or 3500 (*Bombarda, Carabina*) hp, 18 kts, 64 t diesel oil, 3000 nm (15 kts), complement 110; 1 x 1 – 100/47 OTO 1937, 2 x 2 – 20/65 Breda 1935, 3 x 1 – 20/70 Scotti-Isotta Fraschini 1939 or 3 x 1 – 20/65 Breda 1940 (*Urania*), 2 x 1 – 450 TT (*not on all*), 8 DCT, 2 DCR (76), 2 Ginocchio towed AS torpedoes; S-Gerät sonar, hydrophone.

Postwar completed ships were armed with 1 x 1 – 100/47 OTO 1937, 1 x 2 – 40/56 Bofors, 2 x 1 – 20/70 Oerlikon, 2 x 1 – 450 TT, 4 DCT, SO-13 radar, QCU-2 sonar.

The experience of the first year of the war in the Mediterranean showed the need for purpose-built escort ASW ships, and the need for them increased every month as the losses among the light fleet forces increased. Initially, it was supposed to create a fairly fast ship, similar in her elements to the torpedo boats of

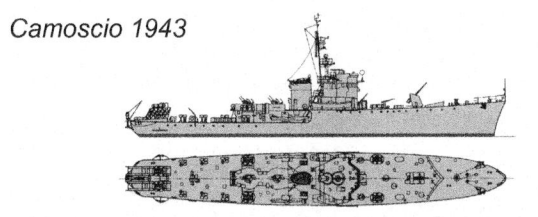

Camoscio 1943

Baionetta 1943

Minerva 1943

the *Spica* or *Pegaso* classes, but they were not so suitable for this purpose, since they were originally designed for other tasks and did not carry sufficient anti-submarine armament. In addition, torpedo boats were too large and expensive to build, which became unacceptable for a ship, the construction of which was planned in large numbers, by shipbuilders who did not have much experience in naval shipbuilding. In the summer of 1941, a 'clean' escort was chosen from several preliminary options, with moderate dimensions and speed, but with extremely strong anti-submarine armament, including even torpedoes for attacking surfaced submarines.

An interesting feature of the new ships classified as "anti-submarine corvettes" was the installation, in addition to the main diesels, of two 150-hp electric motors intended for the 6-kt silent running during attack of submarine. The battery capacity was enough for 16 nm under electric motors. Such a combined machinery was installed on all corvettes, except completed by the Germans *Bombarda* and *Carabina*.

In total, 60 corvettes were ordered, and until September 1943 28 were commissioned by the Italian Navy.

Procellaria was mined 31.1.1943 W of Sicily. *Cicogna* was damaged by British aircraft at Messina 24.7.1943 and ran aground. *Gazzella* 5.8.1943 was mined N of Sardinia. *Berenice* was sunk 9.9.1943 by German field artillery while trying to leave the harbor of Trieste.

In September 1943, many ships of this class feel into the hands of the Germans, both completed but scuttled by crews and incomplete ships at shipyards.

Artemide, *Antelope*, *Camoscio* and *Vespa* were commissioned by the Kriegsmarine as *UJ2226*, *UJ6082*, *UJ6081* and *UJ2221* respectively. The Germans completed also *Capriolo*, *Alee*, *Renna*, *Melpomene*, *Colubrina*, *Bombarda*, *Carabina*, *Spingarda*, *Tuffetto* and *Marangone*, commissioned as *UJ6083*, *UJ6084*, *UJ6085*, *UJ202*, *UJ205*, *UJ206*, *UJ207*, *UJ208*, *UJ2222* and *UJ2223*, respectively.

Carabina (*UJ207*) in February 1944 was sunk at Venice by Allied aircraft. *Colubrina* (*UJ205*) was sunk by Allied aircraft 27.3.1944 at Venice. *Marangone* (*UJ2223*) was sunk by Allied aircraft 16.8.1944 at Genoa. *Antelope* (*UJ6082*) was sunk 16.8.1944 W of Toulon by US destroyer *Endicott*. *Camoscio* (*UJ6081*) was sunk 17.8.1944 SE of Toulon by US destroyer *Somers*. *Renna* (*UJ6085*) was sunk by Allied aircraft 4.9.1944 at Genoa. *Spingarda* (*UJ208*) and *Melpomene* (*UJ202*) were sunk 1.11.1944 off Zadar by British escort destroyers *Avon Vale* and *Wheatland*. *Capriolo* (*UJ6083*), *Alee* (*UJ6084*), *Tuffetto* (*UJ2222*), *Vespa* (*UJ2221*), *Artemide* (*UJ2226*) were scuttled 24.4.1945 at Genoa. *Bombarda* (*UJ206*) was badly damaged at Venice by Allied aircraft 4.4.1944 and scuttled 25.4.1945.

Ex-French FR51 class corvettes

FR51 (ex-*La Batalleuse*)	A C de Provence, Port-de-Bouc, France	12.1937	22.8.1939	(3.1940) / 1.1943	scuttled 9.9.1943
FR52 (ex-*Commandant Rivière*)	A C de Provence, Port-de-Bouc, France	11.1936	16.2.1939	(9.1939) / 1.1943	sunk 28.5.1943
FR54 (ex-*L'Impétueuse*)	A C de France, Dunkerque, France	4.1938	17.8.1939	(5.1940)	captured incomplete by Germany 9.9.1943
FR55 (ex-*La Curieuse*)	Arsenal de Lorient, France	8.1938	11.11.1939	(1940)	captured incomplete by Germany 9.9.1943

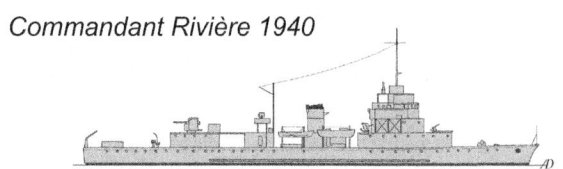

Commandant Rivière 1940

630 / 895 t, 78.3 x 8.7 x 3.3 m, 2 Sulzer diesels, 4000 hp, 20 kts, 100 t diesel oil, 10000 nm (9 kts), complement 106; 1 x 1 – 100/45 M1892 or M1932 or 1 x 2 – 90/50 M1926, (1 x 4 + 2 x 2) – 13.2 MG, 2 DCT, 1 DCR (40).

Two former 630-t French avisos *La Batailleuse* and *Commandant Rivere*, were captured at Bizerte by German troops and transferred to the Italian Navy in December 1942. They were named *FR51* and *FR52* respectively. 4 more ships, *Chamois*, *L'Impetueuse*, *La Curieuse* and *Degaigneuse*, renamed *FR53-56*, were scuttled at Toulon in November 1942, salvaged by the Italians in 1943 and put in for repairs, but by September none of them was commissioned.

FR52 was sunk during an air raid on Livorno 28.5.1943 by Allied bombers but later salvaged by the Germans and commissioned them as *SG22*. *FR51* was scuttled at La Spezia 9.9.1943, salvaged by the Germans, renamed *SG23* but scuttled again by the Germans 25.4.1945.

ITALY

Ex-French FR53 class corvette

FR53 (ex-Chamois)	Arsenal de Lorient, France	11.1936	29.4.1938	(1939)	captured incomplete by Germany 9.9.1943 (SG21)

647 / 900 t, 78.3 x 8.7 x 3.3 m, 2 Sulzer diesels, 4000 hp, 20 kts, 105 t diesel oil, 10000 nm (9 kts), complement 106; 1 x 1 – 100/45 M1892 or M1932 or 1 x 2 – 90/50 M1926, (1 x 4 + 2 x 2) – 13.2 MG, 2 DCT, 1 DCR (40).

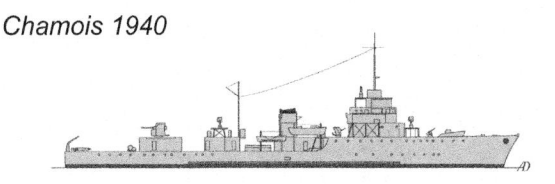

French aviso *Chamois* was scuttled at Toulon in November 1942, salvaged by the Italians in 1943, renamed *FR53* and put in for repairs, but the repairs were incomplete by September. Later she was again captured by the Germans but did not enter service and sunk by Allied bombers 15.8.1944.

Chamois 1940

Ex-French FR56 class corvette

FR56 (ex-Dédaigneuse)	F C de la Gironde, Bordeaux, France	1916	(1917)	captured incomplete by Germany 9.9.1943

310 / 410 t, 60.2 x 7.2 x 2.9 m, 2 VTE, 2 Du Temple or Normand boilers, 2200 hp, 17 kts, 85 t coal, 2000 nm (10 kts), complement 107; 2 x 1 – 100/45 M1897, 2 DCT, sweeps.

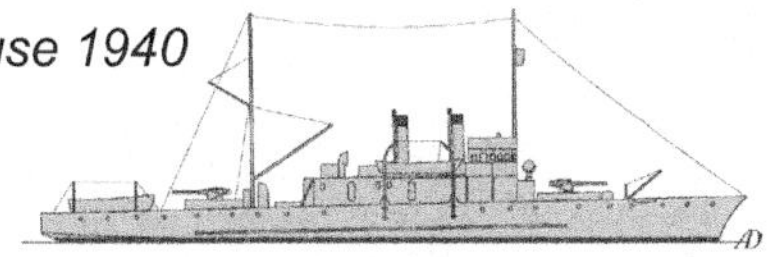

Former French aviso (ASW gunboat) scuttled at Toulon and salvaged in 1943. She was never commissioned by the Italians and recaptured by the Germans 9.9.1943.

Dédaigneuse 1940

ANDREA BAFILE class escort gunboats

Andrea Bafile	Pattison, Napoli	1920	8.12.1921	1922	stricken 1939
Carlo del Greco	Pattison, Napoli	1920	9.9.1922	1922	stricken 1939
Tolosetto Farinati	Pattison, Napoli	1920	16.5.1922	1922	stricken 1939
Ernesto Giovannini	Pattison, Napoli	3.1920	11.3.1922	1922	stricken 12.1950
Alessandro Vitturi	Pattison, Napoli	1920	27.6.1922	1922	stricken 1939

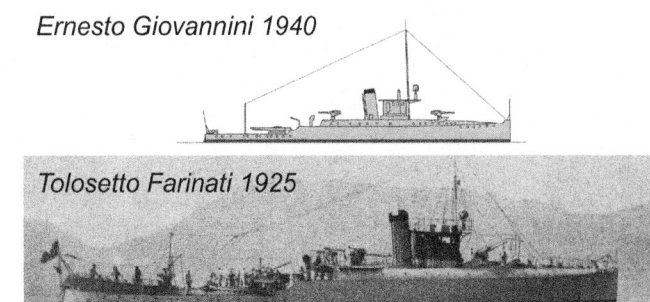

260 / 284 t, 52.0-52.1 (pp) x 5.7 x 1.8 m, 2 VTE, 2 Thornycroft boilers, 2400 hp, 24 kts, 40 t oil, 1100 nm (11 kts), complement 53; 2 x 1 – 102/35 Schneider-Armstrong 1914-15, 2 x 1 – 6.5 MG, 1 x 2 – 450 TT, 12 mines.

The design was based on the Pattison-built small torpedo boats.
1939 - 1940, *Ernesto Giovannini*: - 2 x 1 - 6.5 MG, 12 mines; + 1 x 1 - 13.2 MG, 2 DCR.

Ernesto Giovannini 1940

Tolosetto Farinati 1925

SEBASTIANO CABOTO gunboat

Sebastiano Caboto	CNR, Palermo	3.1911	20.7.1912	11.1912	scuttled 9.9.1943

877 / 1050 t, 63.4 x 9.7 x 3.0 m, 2 VTE, 2 boilers, 1200 hp, 13.2 kts, 100 t coal, complement 107; 6 x 1 – 76/40 Armstrong 1897, 4 x 1 – 6.5 MG.
A large "colonial" gunboat, served as a dispatch vessel.
Sebastiano Caboto was scuttled 9.9.1943 in shallow

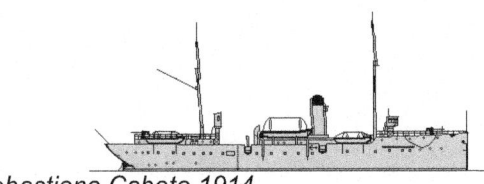

Sebastiano Caboto 1914
drawing is based on the shupbucket.com

water off Rhodes by her own crew to avoid capture, captured by the Germans 12.9.1943 and sunk in the same place by British bombers the same month under repairs.

Ex-Yugoslav ALBA gunboat

| **Alba** (ex-Beli Orao), 9.1943-**Zagabria** | CRDA, Trieste | 3.6.1939 | (1940) / 4.1941 | to Yugoslavia 12.1943 (Beli Orao) |

Zagabria 1943

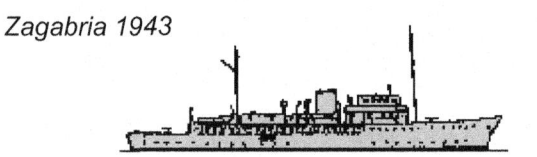

567 / 660 t, 65.0 x 8.1 x 2.8 m, 2 Sulzer diesels, 1900 hp, 18 kts; 2 x 1 - 40/67 Škoda, 2 x 1 - 13.2 MG.
Ex-Yugoslav gunboat / Royal yacht, captured and commissioned by the Italians.
After the armistice, the ship was returned to Yugoslavia.

Ex-Yugoslav CATTARO gunboat

| **Cattaro** (ex-*Dalmacija*, ex-*Niobe*) | A G Weser, Bremen, Germany | 30.8.1898 | 18.7.1899 | (25.6.1900) / 17.4.1941 | captured by Germany 11.9.1943 (Niobe) |

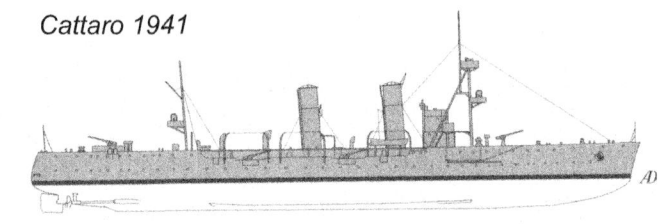

Cattaro 1941

2360 / 2953 t, 105.0 x 12.2 x 5.3 m, 2 VTE, 8 Thornycroft boilers, 8000 hp, 16 kts, 625 t coal, 4000 nm (11 kts), complement 329; steel / Krupp steel, deck 25-20, slopes 50, CT 80; 6 x 1 - 83/53 Škoda M.27, 6 x 1 - 20/70 Scotti-Isotta Fraschini 1939.
German *Gazelle*-class small cruiser was bought by Yugoslavia 24.6.1925 and rebuilt on the Deutsche Werke in Kiel in 1925-1926: the bow was rebuilt with a new stem, the forecastle deck received a new shape, superstructures and masts were also rebuilt; the ship was commissioned again 3.9.1926. When Yugoslavia surrendered, the ship was captured at Kotor and commissioned by the Regia Marina as a gunboat.
A 25-mm protective deck with 50-mm slopes protected the machinery, outside the machinery spaces the 20-mm deck had the turtleback shape. The engines had 80-mm glacises. The CT had 80-mm sides and 20-mm roof.
Cattaro 11.9.1943 was captured at Pola by German troops, renamed *Niobe* 6.12.1943, wrecked off Silba 19.12.1943, finally sunk there by British / Yugoslav *MTB276* and *MTB298*.

Auxiliary gunboats

Palmaiola 1925

More than 500 grt capacity
Aurora (1904 / 1938, 1220 t, 2 x 1 – 57/40 – sunk 9.9.1943)
Cirene (1912 / 1940, 500 grt, 2 x 1 – 76/40 – discarded 1943)
Illiria (/ 1938, 670 grt – BU 1958)
Palmaiola (1916 / 1940, 562 grt, 1 x 1 – 76/30 – discarded 1943)

100-500 grt capacity
Requisitioned: 16 (1940)
Lost: unknown, almost all lost in 1943
Former merchant vessels converted to gunboats.
Aurora was sunk by German MTB 9.9.1943 off Ancona.

Auxiliary patrol vessels and submarine chasers

100-500 grt capacity
Requisitioned: ~200 (1940)
Lost: unknown

Former merchant vessels converted to patrols and rated as escort avisos.

ITALY

COASTAL FORCES

ERMANO CARLOTTO river gunboat

Ermanno Carlotto	Shanghai Dock, China	19.6.1918	3.1921	scuttled 9.9.1943

218 t, 48.8 x 7.5 x 0.9 m, 2 VTE, 2 Yarrow boilers, 1100 hp, 14 kts, 56 t oil, complement 44; 2 x 1 – 6/40 Armstrong 1916, 4 x 1 – 6.5 MG.
"Colonial" gunboat for service on Chinese rivers.
Ermanno Carlotto was scuttled by her own crew in Shanghai 9.9.1943, salvaged by the Japanese in November 1943 and commissioned by them as *Narumi*.

Ermano Carlotto 1943

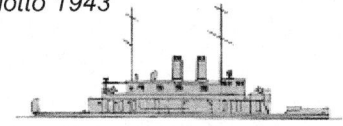

'SVAN 12-ton modified' type ('A' group) motor gunboats (MAS158 class)

Piaggio, Sestri Ponente: MAS188 (1918)
Discarded: MAS188 (1938)
11.2 / 12.1 t, 16.0 x 2.6 x 1.1 m, 2 Fiat petrol engines, 480 hp, 25 kts, 200 nm (22 kts), complement 8; 1 x 1 – 57/43 Nordenfelt 1887, 1 x 1 – 6.5 MG, 6 DC.
So-called *"12-ton"* boats designed by A. Bisio (SVAN) and built by various builders in 1916-1918.

Type 'A' MGB 1919

'Baglietto 12-ton' type ('A' group, 6th series) motor torpedo boats (MAS204 class)

Baglietto, Varazze: MAS204, 206, 210, 212, 213, 216 (1918)
Discarded: MAS212 (1939)
Lost: MAS204, 206, 210, 213, 216 (1941)
12 / 13.9 t, 16.0 x 2.6 x 1.1 m, 2 Isotta Fraschini petrol engines, 700 hp, 27 kts, 230 nm (10 kts), complement 7; 1 x 1 – 6.5 MG, 2 – 450 TT, 10 DC.
During the Second World War, the surviving MTBs reached no more than 10-15 kts within no more than 1 hour.

MAS204 class MTB 1919

'Orlando 12-ton' type ('A' group, 2nd series) motor torpedo boats (MAS218 class)

Orlando, Livorno: MAS222, 228, 230 (1918)
Discarded: MAS222, 228, 230 (1937)
12 / 12.9 t, 16.4 x 2.9 x 1.4 m, 2 Isotta Fraschini petrol engines / 2 Rognini electric motors or 2 Isotta Fraschini petrol engines (*MAS230*), 500 / 10 or 500 (*MAS230*) hp, 26 kts, 200 nm (26 kts), complement 8; 2 or 3 x 1 – 6.5 MG, 2 – 450 TT, 4 DC.
MAS222 and *228* had electric motors for silent running. The batteries allowed to maintain a 4-kt speed for 4 hours.

MAS551 experimental motor torpedo boat

OTO, Livorno: MAS551 (1919)
Discarded: MAS551 (1941)
19 t.

This boat was built for trials, entered service only in 1939, 20 years after completion, and discarded in 1941.

'SVAN Velocissimo' type ('D' group, 2nd series) motor torpedo boats (MAS415 class)

SVAN, La Spezia / Venezia: MAS418 (1922), MAS422 (1923)
Discarded: MAS422 (1937), MAS418 (1938)

18 / 21 t, 18.0 x 3.6 x 1.2 m, 3 Isotta Fraschini petrol engines / 2 Rognini electric motors (3 shafts), 1200 / 16 hp, 25.5-28 / 5 kts, 176 nm (27 kts), complement 10; 3 x

1 – 6.5 MG, 2 – 450 TT, 6 DC.
Improved and lightened version of the *MAS401* class with three shafts. The batteries allowed to maintain a 5-kt silent speed for 5 hours.

'SVAN Velocissimo 13-ton' type motor torpedo boats (MAS423 class)

SVAN, Venezia: MAS423, 425 (1929), MAS426 (1930)
Lost: MAS425 (1937), MAS423 (1943)
Discarded: MAS426 (1943)
12.6 (std) t, 16.0 x 3.0 x 1.0 m, 2 Isotta Fraschini petrol engines, 1500 hp, 40 kts, 127 nm (36 kts), complement 9; 2 x 1 – 6.5 MG, 2 – 450 TT.
Further development of the *"12-ton"* SVAN boat of WWI-era. Through the use of much more powerful engines, the speed was greatly increased.

'SVAN' type motor torpedo boats (MAS427 class)

MAS428 1937

SVAN, Venezia: MAS428 (1926), MAS429 (1927)
Discarded: MAS428 (1937), MAS429 (1938)
31 (std) (*MAS428*) or 30 (std) (*MAS429*) t, 24.0 (*MAS428*) or 22.0 (*MAS429*) x 4.0 x 1.3 m, 3 Isotta Fraschini petrol engines, 1200 hp, 26 (*MAS428*) or 28 (*MAS429*) kts, 300 nm (26 kts), complement 11; 1 x 1 – 76/30 Armstrong 1914, 2 x 1 – 6.5 MG, 2 – 450 TT, 10 DC.
Large MTBs, ordered in 1923.

'SVAN 13-ton velocissimo' type motor torpedo boats (MAS430 class)

MAS432 1940
1:625 scale

MAS430 1935

SVAN, Venezia: MAS430 (1929), MAS432 – 434 (1930), MAS437 (1934)
Lost: MAS430, 437 (1943)
Discarded: MAS432 (1943), MAS433, 434 (1949)
13.8 (std) (*MAS430*) or 14.1 (std) or 18.5 (std) (*MAS437*) t, 16.0 or 17.5 (*MAS437*) x 3.3 or 3.6 (*MAS437*) x 1.0 (*MAS430*) or 1.1 or 1.3 (*MAS437*) m, 2 Isotta Fraschini petrol engines or 2 Fiat diesels (*MAS437*), 1500 hp, 40 kts, 125 nm (36 kts) or 100 nm (40 kts) (*MAS437*), complement 9 (*MAS430*) or 13; 2 x 1 – 6.5 MG, 2 – 450 TT, 5 DC; hydrophone.
MAS430 was a further development of the *"12-ton"* SVAN boat of WWI-era. Due to the installation of much more powerful engines, the speed was significantly increased. Anti-submarine armament was represented by five small 50-kg DCs and a hydrophone.
MAS432-436 belonged to a slightly modified version of the *"SVAN 13-ton fast"* class, named *"SVAN 14-ton fast"*.
MAS437 belonged to the *"SVAN high-speed diesel"* class and was a diesel-engined version of the *"SVAN 14-ton fast"* class. Due to the installation of heavier diesels, she became somewhat larger than petrol-engined boats, but had almost the same maximum speed.
1940, *MAS432 - 434, 437*: - 2 x 1 - 6.5 MG; + 1 x 1 - 13.2 MG, 2 x 1 – 8 MG.

'Baglietto velocissimo' type motor torpedo boat (MAS431)

Baglietto, Varazze: MAS431 (1932)
Lost: MAS431 (1943)
12.3 / 15.5 t, 16.0 x 4.0 x 1.3 m, 2 Fiat petrol engines, 1500 hp, 41 kts, 100 nm (40 kts), complement 7; 2 x 1 – 8 MG, 2 – 450 TT, 6 DC; hydrophone.
Close to the *"SVAN 13-ton fast"*, but with some improvements made to the design by Baglietto. On trials, the boat reached a speed of about 45 kts and was recognized as more successful than the SVAN boats. The anti-submarine armament was represented by six small 50-kg DCs and a hydrophone.

ITALY

STEFANO TÜRR experimental motor torpedo boat

CMA, Marina di Pisa: Stefano Türr (1937)
Discarded: Stefano Türr (1941)
59 / 64 t, 32.0 x 6.0 x 0.9 m, 4 Fiat diesels, 3000 hp, 30 kts, 750 nm (25 kts), complement 16; 3 x 1 – 13.2 MG, 1 x 1 – 6.5 MG, 4 – 450 TT, 12 DC; presumably hydrophone.

Experimental MTB with increased displacement compared to all previous Italian boats. The design was developed by Baglietto. Aluminum alloys were widely used in the hull structure to reduce weight. The boat was unsuccessful and never reached the design 34 kts.

Stefano Türr 1940
1:625 scale

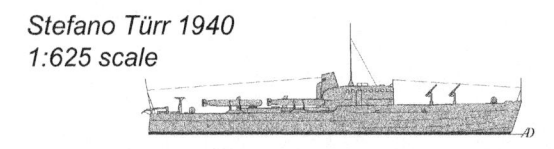

Stefano Türr 1940

'Baglietto velocissimo' type motor torpedo boat (MAS424)

Baglietto, Varazze: MAS424 (1937)
Lost: MAS424 (1943)
19 / 21 t, 16.5 x 4.3 x 1.2 m, 2 Isotta Fraschini petrol engines, 2000 hp, 45 kts, 350 nm (39 kts), complement 8; 1 x 1 – 6.5 MG, 2 – 450 TT, 6 DC; presumably hydrophone.

"Baglietto experimental class 500", a development of the *"Baglietto 1931"* class. The increase in size made it possible to increase the cruising range by three times, and the speed decreased slightly. On this boat, the design and techniques were tested, later used on the boats of the *"500"* series. The MTB received number *424* from a *"SVAN 13-ton fast"* class boat lost in 1937.
1940: - 1 x 1 - 6.5 MG; + 1 x 1 - 13.2 MG.

'Baglietto velocissimo' type motor torpedo boats (MAS451 class)

Baglietto, Varazze: MAS451, 452 (1941)
Lost: MAS451, 452 (1941)
20 / 24 t, 18.0 x 4.8 x 1.6 m, 2 Isotta Fraschini petrol engines / 2 Alfa Romeo cruising petrol engines (2 shafts), 2200 / 160 hp, 42 / 8 kts, 330 nm (42 kts), complement 11; 1 x 1 – 13.2 MG, 2 – 450 TT, 6 DC; presumably hydrophone.

"Baglietto fast" design, a development of *MAS424*. In addition to the main Isotta-Fraschini engines, they had two more 80-hp Alpha-Romeo petrol engines for cruising; the cruising range under these engines was 836 nm at 8 kts.

'Baglietto 500' type motor torpedo boats, 1st series (MAS501 class)

Picchiotti, Limite sull'Arno: MAS501, 515 - 518 (1937)
Baglietto, Varazze: MAS502 – 509, 511, 512 (1937)
CRDA, Monfalcone: MAS510, 513, 514, 525 (1937)
Celli, Venezia: MAS519 – 522 (1937)
SACIN, Venezia: MAS523 (1944- MAS MT523), MAS524 (1937)
Transferred: Sweden – MAS506, 508, 511, 524 (1940), USSR – MAS516, 519 (1949)
Lost: MAS512, 513 (1942), MAS501 – 504, 518, 522 (1943), MAS505, 507, 509 (1944)
Discarded: MAS517 (1944), MAS515 (1945), MAS MT523 (1949), MAS519, 514, 520, 521, 525 (1950)
20.7 (std) (*MAS501*) or 21 (std) (*MAS502-509, 511, 512*) or 24 (std) (*MAS510, 513-525*) t, 17.0 x 4.3 (*MAS501*) or 4.7 (*MAS502-509, 511, 512*) or 4.4 (*MAS510, 513-525*) x 1.3 m, 2 Isotta Fraschini petrol engines, 2000 hp, 42 or 41 (*MAS502-512*) kts, 1.25 t petrol, 350 nm (39 kts), complement 9; 2 (*MAS501*) or 1 (*MAS502-525*) x 1 – 13.2 MG, 2 – 450 TT, 6 DC; presumably hydrophone.

'Baglietto class 500, 1st series', development of the *MAS424*, which became the prototype of the 1st series of the *"500"* class. According to some reports, several boats of this series, in addition to the main Isotta-Fraschini engines, were equipped by 2 80-hp Alpha-Romeo petrol engines for cruising. The last boat of the series, *MAS525,* had a steel hull instead of the wooden-hulled sister-boats.
1944, *MAS MT523*: - 1 x 1 - 13.2 MG, 2 - 450 TT, 6 DC; + 3 x 1 - 20/65 Breda 1940.

MAS505

'Baglietto 500' type motor torpedo boats, 2nd series (MAS526 class)

MAS526 1940
1:625 scale

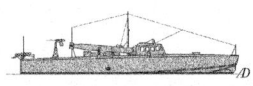

MAS528 1942

Baglietto, Varazze: MAS526 – 535 (1939)
Picchiotti, Limite sull'Arno: MAS536 – 539, MAS545 (1944- MAS MT545) (1939)
Celli, Venezia: MAS540 (1944- MAS MT540), MAS541 – 544 (1939)
CRDA, Monfalcone: MAS546 – 550 (1939), MAS551 (1941)
Transferred: Finland – MAS526 – 529 (1943), France – MAS543 (1949)
Lost: MAS534 (1939), MAS537 (1940), MAS530, 532, 533, 535, 536, 539, 542, 544, 548 – 551 (1943), MAS531, 541, 546 (1944)
Discarded: MAS MT540 (1949), MAS538, 545, 547 (1950)
26 or 21 (*MAS550*) (std) t, 18.7 x 4,7 or 4.5 (*MAS550*) x 1.5 or 1.3 (*MAS550*) m, 2 Isotta Fraschini petrol engines / 2 Alfa Romeo or Carraro cruising petrol engines (2 shafts), 2000 / 140 or 100 hp, 41.8 (*MAS526-535*) or 42 (*MAS536-549, 551*) or 45 (*MAS550*) kts, 1.25 t petrol, 360 nm (42 kts), complement 10; 1 x 1 – 13.2 MG, 2 – 450 TT, 6 DC; presumably hydrophone.
"*Baglietto class 500, 2nd series*", the lengthened version of the 1st series. In addition to the main Isotta-Fraschini engines, they had 2 70-hp Alpfa-Romeo or 50-hp Carraro petrol engines for cruising. Cruising range under these engines was 1100 nm at 6-kt speed. One boat of the series, *MAS550*, had a metal hull instead of wooden-hulled sister-boats and was somewhat smaller, due to which she had a higher speed.
1940 - 1941, many boats: - 1 x 1 - 13.2 MG; + 1 x 1 - 20/65 Breda 1939.
1944, *MAS MT540, 545*: - 1 x 1 - 13.2 MG, 2 - 450 TT, 6 DC; + 3 x 1 - 20/65 Breda 1940.
MAS531 was captured by the Germans 9.9.1943 and transferred to the RSI.

'Baglietto 500' type motor torpedo boats, 3rd series (MAS552 class)

MAS552 1941
1:625 scale

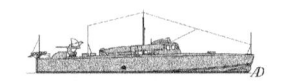

CRDA, Monfalcone: MAS552 – 554 (1941)
Lost: MAS552 – 554 (1943)
23 / 28 t, 18.7 x 4.7 x 1.4 m, 2 Isotta Fraschini petrol engines / 2 Alfa Romeo cruising petrol engines (2 shafts), 2000 / 140 hp, 43 kts, 1.25 t petrol, 395 nm (43 kts), complement 13; 1 x 1 – 13.2 MG, 2 – 450 TT, 10 DC; presumably hydrophone.
"*Baglietto class 500, 3rd series*", steel-hulled variant of the 2nd series. They had 2 70-hp petrol engines for 6-kt cruising speed.
1941-1942, some: - 1 x 1 - 13.2 MG; + 1 x 1 - 20/65 Breda 1940.

'Baglietto 500' type motor torpedo boats, 4th series (MAS555 class)

MAS558

Picchiotti, Limite sull'Arno: MAS555 – 557, 571 – 573 (1941)
Celli, Venezia: MAS558 – 560, 574 – 576 (1941)
Baglietto, Varazze: MAS561 – 570 (1941)
Lost: MAS571, 573 (1942), MAS555, 557 – 561, 563, 564, 572, 576 (1943), MAS556 (1945)
Discarded: MAS565 (1945), MAS562 (1950)
Transferred: Germany - MAS566 – 570, 574, 575 (1943)
28 t, 18.7 x 4.7 x 1.5 m, 2 Isotta Fraschini petrol engines / 2 Alfa Romeo or Carraro cruising petrol engines (2 shafts), 2000 or 2300 / 140 or 100 hp, 43 kts, 1.25 t petrol, 350 nm (42 kts), complement 13; 1 x 1 – 13.2 MG or 1 x 1 – 20/65 Breda 1940, 2 – 450 TT, 6 – 10 DC; presumably hydrophone.
"*Baglietto class 500, 4th series*" boats were identical to boats of 3rd series, but again wooden-hulled; according to some reports, *MAS555-565* had steel or composite hulls. All boats could make 6 kts under cruising engines.
MAS562 was captured by the Germans 9.9.1943, transferred to the RSI, later 29.4.1944 captured by the Americans and transferred to the Regia Marina. *MAS556* served from 9.9.1943 with the RSI fleet.

ITALY

Ex-Yugoslav MAS1D class motor torpedo boats

Thornycroft, Woolston, UK: MAS1D (*ex-Uskok*), MAS2D (*ex-Četnik*) (1942- MS47) (1928 / 1941)
Lost: MAS1D (1942)
Discarded: MS47 (1943)
15 (std) t, 16.8 x 3.4 x 1.3 m, 2 Thornycroft petrol engines, 750 hp, 37 kts, 1.6 t petrol, 220 nm (32 kts), complement 5; 2 x 1 – 7.7 MG, 2 – 450 TT, 4 DC.
Former Yugoslav MTBs built by Thornycroft. They were captured by the Italians in April 1941 and commissioned by the Regia Marina as *MAS1D* and *2D*. TTs were replaced by Italian-made ones.

Ex-Yugoslav MAS3D class motor torpedo boats

Lürssen, Vegesack, Germany: MAS3D (*ex-Orjen*) (1942- MS41) (1936 / 1941), MAS7D (*ex-Suvobor*) (1942- MS45) (1937 / 1941), MAS4D (*ex-Velebit*) (1942- MS42) (1938 / 1941), MAS5D (*ex-Dinara*) (1942- MS43), MAS6D (*ex-Triglav*) (1942- MS44), MAS8D (*ex-Rudnik*) (1942- MS46) (1939 / 1941)
Lost: MS41 – 46 (1943)
62 / 63 t, 28.0 x 4.3 x 1.5 m, 3 Daimler-Benz petrol engines, 3300 hp, 31 kts, 5.5 t petrol, 265 nm (31 kts), complement 20-21; 1 x 1 – 40/56 Bofors (*MAS7D, 8D*), 2 x 1 – 20/65 Breda 1940 (*MAS3D – 6D*), 1 x 1 – 15 MG (*MAS7D, 8D*), 1 x 1 – 6.5 MG (*MAS3D – 6D*), 2 – 550 TT, 12 – 20 DC.
Former Yugoslav MTBs built in Germany. They were captured by the Italians in April 1941 and commissioned by them as *MAS3D-8D*. Original 40-mm MGs were partly replaced by the Italian 20-mm MGs.
All boats were captured by the Germans in September 1943.

MAS3D 1942

MS Type 1 motor torpedo boats (MS11 class)

CRDA, Monfalcone: MS11 – 16, 21 – 26, 31 – 36 (1942)
Lost: MS14 (1942), MS12, 13, 15, 16, 21 – 23, 25, 26, 32 – 34, 36 (1943)
Transferred: Ftance – MS35 (1948)
Discarded: MS11 (1965), MS24 (1974), MS31 (1975)
63 (*MS11-16, 21-23*) or 64 (*MS24-26, 31-36*) t, 28.0 x 4.3 x 1.6 m, 3 Isotta Fraschini petrol engines, 3450 hp, 32 kts, 9 t petrol, 250 nm (32 kts), complement 19; 1 or 2 x 1 – 20/65 Breda 1940, 2 x 1 – 6.5 MG, 2 – 533 TT (4), 6 – 8 DC; presumably hydrophone.
Larger than MAS-boats built in the 1930s. German-built boats of the Yugoslav Navy, captured by the Italians in 1941, served as the prototype for them. After trials of these boats, which turned out to be noticeably more seaworthy than the MAS boats of the *'500'* class, in June 1941 almost exact copies were ordered. To emphasize the increased combat qualities of the new boats, their indexing was changed from MAS to MS. Composite hulls. The DCs used on the MS boats were heavier than those used on the MAS boats: 100 kg versus 50.

MS24 1943
1:625 scale

MS36 1942

MS Type 2 motor torpedo boats (MS51 class)

CRDA, Monfalcone: MS51 – 56, 61 – 66, 71 – 75 (1943), MS76 (lost incomplete 1943)
Lost: MS51, 62, 63, 66, 71 (1943)
Transferred: USSR – MS52, 53, 61, 65, 75 (1949)
Discarded: MS64 (1947), MS72 (1962), MS56, 73 (1963), MS74 (1965), MS54, 55 (1979)
66 t, 28.0 x 4.3 x 1.6 m, 3 Isotta Fraschini petrol engines, 3450 hp, 31 kts, 9 t petrol, 330 nm (31 kts), complement 19; 1 or 2 x 2 – 20/65 Breda 1935 (*except MS61*), 2 x 1 – 13.2 MG (*MS61*), 2 x 1 – 8 MG, 2 – 533 TT (4), 2 – 450

MS72 1942

TT, 8 DC (*MS51 – 56, 61 – 66, 71 - 73*), 2 SLC human torpedoes or 1 MTSM midget MTB or 1 MTM or 1 MTR explosive boat (*MS74, 75*); presumably hydrophone. Development of the 1st type with strengthened armament due to the installation of two additional 450-mm torpedo racks. The increase in displacement led to some decrease in speed. To eliminate this shortcoming, more powerful 4500-hp engines were installed on the *MS76*, the last boat of the series, providing a speed of 35 kts.

Two boats, *MS74* and *75,* were arranged as human torpedo and suicide boat carriers each with 2 SLCs or 1 MTR or 1 MTM or 1 MTSM.

Plans for the construction of another 44 boats of the types III and IV in connection with the armistice signed in September 1943 were not implemented.

MS74 and *MS75* were captured by the Germans 12 and 10.9.1943 respectively, transferred to the RSI and returned to the Regia Marina in 1945.

'Baglietto' type motor anti-submarine boats (MAS438 class)

MAS438 1937

Baglietto, Varazze: MAS438, 439 (ME38, 39) (1940-AS25, 26) (1934), MAS440, 441 (ME40, 41) (1940-AS27, 28) (1935)
Lost: AS26 (1946)
Transferred: USSR – AS27 (1949)
Discarded: AS25, 28 (1950)
41 (std) t, 22.5 x 4.3 x 1.4 m, 2 Isotta Fraschini petrol engines, 2000 hp, 32 kts, 215 nm (16 kts), complement 19; 1 x 1 – 76/40 Ansaldo 1917, 2 x 1 – 6.5 MG, DCs; hydrophone.
Purpose-built anti-submarine boats without torpedoes. According to some sources, they had 460-hp engines and made 16 kts only.
Late 1930s, all: - 1 x 1 - 76/40; + 1 x 1 - 13.2 MG, 1 x 1 – 8 MG.

'VAS type 1 motor anti-submarine boats (VAS201 class)

VAS205

Baglietto, Varazze: VAS201 – 208 (1942)
Picchiotti, Limite sull'Arno: VAS209 – 214 (1942)
Navalmeccanica, Castellamare di Stabia: VAS215 – 220 (1942)
Celli, Venezia: VAS221 – 230 (1942)
Lost: VAS202, 203, 207 – 210, 212 – 217, 219 – 221, 223, 225 – 230 (1943), VAS206 (1944)

Discarded: VAS201, 205, 222, 224 (1953), VAS204, 211, 218 (1957)
63 / 68-69 t, 28.0 x 4.3 x 1.4 m, 2 Fiat petrol engines + 1 Carraro petrol engine (3 shafts), 1500 + 300 = 1800 hp, 20 kts, 11.5 t petrol, complement 26; 2 x 1 – 20/65 Breda 1940, 2 x 2 – 8 MG, 2 – 450 TT, 30 DC; hydrophone.
Anti-submarine boats in the hulls of 'MS I type' MTBs. The 3-shaft scheme was retained, the side shafts were driven by 750-hp Fiat engines, a Carraro cruising engine with a power of 300 hp was installed on the central shaft. The boats could reach 19 knots with side engines only and 12 knots using the central engine only. TTs were intended to attack surfaced submarines. The first 14 boats had wooden hulls; the rest had composite hulls.
By 1943: many boats had 2 x 1 - 6.5 MG instead of 1 x 1 - 20/65.

'VAS type 2 motor anti-submarine boats (VAS231 class)

Baglietto, Varazze: VAS231 – 233 (1942), VAS234 – 236 (1943)
Picchiotti, Limite sull'Arno: VAS237, 238 (1942)
Navalmeccanica, Castellamare di Stabia: VAS239 – 241, 244, 245 (1943) VAS242, 243 (lost incomplete)
Celli, Venezia: VAS246 – 248 (1943)
Lost: VAS231, 232, 234, 236, 238, 239, 244, 246, 247 (1943)
Transferred: USSR – VAS245, 248 (1949)

Discarded: VAS233, 235, 240 (1953), VAS237, 241 (1957)
69 t, 28.0 x 4.7 x 1.3 m, 1 Isotta Fraschini petrol engine + 2 Carraro petrol engines (3 shafts), 1150 + 600 = 1750 hp, 21.5 kts, 11.5 t petrol, complement 26; 2 x 1 – 20/65 Breda 1940, 2 x 2 – 8 MG, 2 – 450 TT (*VAS237-248*), 30 DC (*VAS237-248*), sweeps (*VAS231-236*); hydrophone (*VAS237-248*)
An almost exact repetition of I type anti-submarine

ITALY

boats, but with a different machinery. A 1150-hp Isotta-Fraschini engine was mounted on the central shaft, the side shafts were driven by 300-hp Carraro engines. The boats reached 16 kts using the central shaft only, 14 kts using the side shafts only and 21.5 kts when all engines running. Composite hull. *VAS231-236* were arranged for minesweeping.

VAS236 1943
1:625 scale

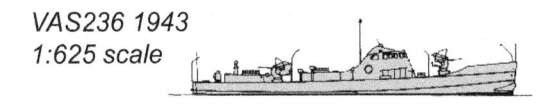

VAS240 and *241* were captured by the Germans in September 1943 as *RA265* and *RA266* respectively and returned in 1945.

'VAS type 3 motor anti-submarine boats (VAS301 class)

Cerusa, Voltri: VAS301 – 303 (1942), VAS304 – 306 (1943), VAS307 – 312 (lost incomplete)
Lost: VAS301 – 306 (1943)
75 / 90 t, 34.1 x 5.0 x 2.1 m, 3 Fiat diesels (*VAS301-304*) or 1 Isotta Fraschini petrol engine + 2 Carraro petrol engines (3 shafts) (*VAS305-312*), 1050 (*VAS301-304*) or 1150 + 600 = 1750 (*VAS305-312*) hp, 18 (*VAS301-304*) or 19 (*VAS305-312*) kts, complement 26; 2 x 1 – 20/65 Breda 1940, 2 x 2 – 8 MG, 2 – 450 TT or 1 x 1 – 37/54 Breda 1939, 30 DC; hydrophone.
Ansaldo design; steel-hulled. The first four boats had 3 350-hp Fiat diesels. The rest were supposed to be equipped with Ansaldo diesels, which, however, turned out to be unsuccessful and a machinery similar to that used on the Type 2 boats was used. These boats reached 15 knots using the central engine only, 13 knots using the side engines only and 19 knots using three engines. Some boats had 37-mm MG instead of TTs.

VAS301 1943
1:625 scale

VAS301

An order for another 24 similar boats was cancelled in September 1943.

MTS type midget motor torpedo boats

Baglietto, Varazze: MTS1 - 3 (1940)
Discarded: MTS1 - 3 (1941, presumably)
1.7 (std) t, 7.2 x 2.1 x 0.5 m, 1 Alfa Romeo petrol engine, 90 hp, 28 kts, 90 nm (28 kts), complement 2; 2 – 450 TT.
In 1939, studies began on the design of a small MTB based on a pleasure boat. The first launches of the 'MTS' type (MTS = Motoscafi di turismo, siluranti (tourist boat carrying torpedoes)) became the development of the suicide boats of the 'MTM' type. Baglietto design. Dimensions were increased to accommodate two torpedoes and two crew members. The 'MTS' launches were successfully tested in 1940, however, due to their short cruising range and low speed, reduced with torpedoes onboard to 23 kts, they did not participate in hostilities.

MTSM type midget motor torpedo boats

Baglietto, Varazze; CABI-Cattaneo, Milano: MTSM201 - 234 (1941 – 1943)
Lost: unknown; at least MTSM204, 206, 208, 210, 216, 228 (1942)
3 / 4 t, 8.4 x 2.2 x 0.6 m, 2 Alfa Romeo petrol engines, 190 hp, 32 kts, 200 nm (32 kts), complement 2; 1 – 450 TT, 2 DC.
In 1941, Baglietto designed an improved small MTB of the 'MTSM' type (the last M means 'modified'), in which they tried to eliminate the main shortcomings of the previous design: short cruising range, low seaworthiness and low speed. The number of torpedoes carried was reduced to one. Some launches could carry up to three frogmen instead of a torpedo.

MTSM type boat

MTL type midget motor torpedo boats

Baglietto, Varazze; CABI-Cattaneo, Milano: few units (1941)
Lost: unknown
7 (std) t, 9.5 m, 1 petrol engine / 1 electric motor, 22 / 8 hp, 5 kts, 120 nm (5 kts); 2 SLC human torpedoes.

A version of the MTSM boat intended to carry SLC human torpedoes. The launches could make 4 kts using the battery and electric motor.

MTSMA type midget motor torpedo boats

Baglietto, Varazze; CABI-Cattaneo, Milano: ~70 units (incomplete)
3.7 / 4.5 t, 8.8 x 2.3 x 0.7 m, 2 Alfa Romeo petrol engines, 190 hp, 29 kts, 120 nm (29 kts), complement 2; 1 x 1 – 8 MG, 1 – 450 TT, 2 DC.

The launches of the 'MTSMA' type were slightly increased compared to the 'MTSM' type. 100 units were ordered in 1943, some of the incomplete units were captured by the Germans in September 1943.

MINE WARFARE SHIPS

PANIGAGLIA class minelayers

Panigaglia	Ansaldo-San Giorgio, Muggiano	10.7.1923	12.1924	captured by Germany 8.9.1943
Buffoluto	Ansaldo-San Giorgio, Muggiano	1924	1924	discarded 1973
Vallelunga	Ansaldo-San Giorgio, Muggiano	28.5.1924	12.1924	sunk 9.9.1943

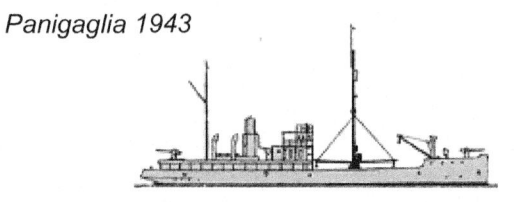

Panigaglia 1943

1071 t, 56.3 x 9.0 x 3.0 m, 2 VTE, 2 Thornycroft boilers, 1400 hp, 11 kts, 960 nm (11 kts); 2 x 1 – 100/47 OTO 1924, 1 x 1 – 6.5 MG, 50 mines.

They were classified as 'Navi Transporte Munizioni'. Could be used for minelaying.

Panigaglia was captured by the Germans 8.9.1943 at La Spezia. *Vallelunga* was scuttled at La Spezia 9.9.1943, later salvaged and recommissioned by the Germans as a minelayer but 28.5.1944 sunk by Allied aircraft.

FASANA class minelayers

Buccari	Arsenale di Castellamare di Stabia	1926	1927	scuttled 9.9.1943
Durazzo	Arsenale di Castellamare di Stabia	1.4.1926	1926	sunk 22.7.1943
Fasana	Arsenale di Castellamare di Stabia	29.9.1924	3.1925	captured by Germany 10.9.1943 (Fasana), returned 5.1945, discarded 9.1950
Pelagosa	Arsenale di Castellamare di Stabia	1926	1927	scuttled 9.9.1943

Buccari 1928

531 / 590 t, 66.3 x 9.8 x 1.7 m, 2 diesels, 700 hp, 10 kts, 20 t diesel oil, 700 nm (10 kts), complement 66; 1 x 1 – 76/40 Ansaldo 1917, 54 mines, sweeps.
Could be used as minesweepers.
Durazzo was sunk by British submarine *Safari* 22.7.1943 E of Corsica. *Fasana* was captured by German forces at Trieste 10.9.1943, scuttled by them 2.5.1945 off

ITALY

Tagliamento, salvaged in July 1945 and recommissioned in the end of 1945. *Buccari* and *Pelagosa* were scuttled by their own crews in September 1943 at La Spezia and Genoa respectively.

OSTIA class minelayers

Azio	CNR, Ancona	4.5.1927	1928	discarded 1.1957
Dardanelli	CNT, Monfalcone	29.9.1925	9.1926	to Venezuela 1938 (General Soublette)
Legnano	CNR, Ancona	5.1926	1927	sunk 5.10.1943
Lepanto	CNR, Ancona	22.5.1927	1928	scuttled 9.1943
Milazzo	CNT, Monfalcone	18.11.1925	10.1926	to Venezuela 1938 (General Urdaneta)
Ostia	CNT, Monfalcone	3.12.1925	11.1926	scuttled 8.4.1941

615 / 850 t, 62.2 x 8.7 x 2.6 m, 2 VTE, 2 water-tube boilers, 1500 hp, 15 kts, 75 t oil (*Azio, Legnano, Lepanto*) or 85 t coal (*Dardanelli, Milazzo, Ostia*), 3500 nm (10 kts), complement 66; 2 x 1 – 102/35 Terni 1914, 1 x 1 – 76/40 Ansaldo 1917, 80 mines, sweeps (fitted for).
Ordered in 1924 for service in the colonies. Could be used as minesweepers.
Late 1940s, *Azio*: + radar.
Ostia was scuttled by her crew 8.4.1941 off Massawa. *Lepanto* was scuttled by her own crew 9.9.1943 in Shanghai, but salvaged by the Japanese and commissioned them as gunboat *Okitsu*. *Legnano* was sunk by German aircraft 5.10.1943.

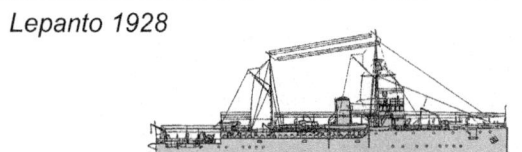

Lepanto 1928

LLegniano 1937

Auxiliary minelayer

FR60 (ex-*Castor*, ex-*Koz'ma Minin*)	1916 / 1942	3150	75.2 x 17.3 x 6.4	14	4 x 1 - 100/45, 2 x 1 – 37/54, 268 mines	scuttled 6.5.1943

FR60 was a former Russian icebreaker requisitioned by France and converted to a minelayer.

FR60 was scuttled by her own crew at Tunisia 6.5.1943.

RD1 class minesweepers

RD4	Arsenale di Castellamare di Stabia	2.1916	27.8.1916	1.1917	sunk 29.1.1943
RD6	Arsenale di Castellamare di Stabia	3.1916	26.10.1916	2.1917	to Yugoslavia 8.1947 (ML301)
RD13	Poli, Chioggia	8.1916	2.7.1917	4.1918	scuttled 9.9.1943

196 t, 35.3 x 5.8 x 2.1 m, 1 VTE, 1 boiler, 800 hp, 13 kts, 630 nm (12 kts) (*RD4, 6*) or 760 nm (12.5 kts) (*RD13*), complement 22; 1 x 1 – 76/40 Armstrong 1916 or Armstrong 1917 or Ansaldo 1916 or Ansaldo 1917, 2 x 1 – 6.5 MG, sweeps.

Minesweeper tugs. Suffered from low stability and poor seaworthiness. Wooden hulls.
RD4 was bombed by Allied aircraft in the Sicily Channel 29.1.1943. *RD13* was scuttled 9.9.1943 at Viareggio.

RD7 class minesweepers

RD7	Tosi, Taranto	5.1916	28.9.1916	3.1917	sunk 15.6.1942
RD9	Tosi, Taranto	9.1916	2.2.1917	7.1917	captured by Germany 9.9.1943 (M1226)
RD12	Tosi, Taranto	12.1916	2.7.1917	10.1917	sunk 2.5.1943

216 t, 35.5 x 5.8 x 2.1 m, 1 VTE, 1 boiler, 1000 hp, 14 kts, 750 nm (14 kts), complement 22; 1 x 1 – 76/50

Vickers 1909 (*RD7*) or 1 x 1 – 76/40 Armstrong 1916 or Armstrong 1917 or Ansaldo 1916 or Ansaldo 1917, 2 x 1 – 6.5 MG, sweeps.
RD7 was sunk 15.6.1942 in the Saronic Gulf by a mine or submarine torpedo. *RD9* was abandoned 9.9.1943 at Piraeus and captured by the Germans. *RD12* was sunk by Allied aircraft 2.5.1943 off Cape Bon.

RD15 class minesweepers

RD16	Arsenale di Castellamare di Stabia	8.1916	29.3.1917	4.1917	abandoned 23.7.1943, to Yugoslavia 8.1948 (ML302]
RD17	Arsenale di Castellamare di Stabia	9.1916	22.4.1917	5.1917	captured by Germany 9.9.1943 (M1227)
RD18	Arsenale di Castellamare di Stabia	11.1916	17.5.1917	5.1917	sunk 5.5.1943
RD20	Arsenale di Castellamare di Stabia	2.1917	14.7.1917	8.1917	sunk 11.4.1943
RD21	Arsenale di Castellamare di Stabia	7.1917	26.11.1917	1.1918	to Yugoslavia 8.1948 (ML303)
RD22	Arsenale di Castellamare di Stabia	8.1917	31.12.1917	2.1918	sunk 25.10.1943
RD23	Arsenale di Castellamare di Stabia	10.1917	21.1.1918	2.1918	sunk 5.5.1943
RD24	Arsenale di Castellamare di Stabia	11.1917	4.3.1918	3.1918	capsized 18.2.1943
RD25	Arsenale di Castellamare di Stabia	12.1917	4.4.1918	5.1918	abandoned 16.8.1943, to Yugoslavia 8.1948 (ML304)
RD26	Arsenale di Castellamare di Stabia	12.1917	15.5.1918	6.1918	captured by Germany 9.9.1943 (M1228)

RD18 1940

201 t, 35.3 (*RD16-18, 20*) or 36.5 (*RD21 - 26*) x 5.8 x 2.1 m, 1 VTE, 1 boiler, 800 (*RD16-18, 20*) or 880 (*RD21-26*) hp, 14 (*RD16-18, 20*) or 13 (*RD21-26*) kts, 600 nm (12 kts) (*RD16-18, 20*) or 650 nm (11 kts) (*RD21-26*), complement 22; 1 x 1 – 76/40 Armstrong 1916 or Armstrong 1917 or Ansaldo 1916 or Ansaldo 1917, 2 x 1 – 6.5 MG, sweeps.

RD16 was abandoned 23.7.1943 at Trapani in a damaged condition, later repaired and transferred to Yugoslavia in August 1948 as *ML302*. *RD17* and *RD26* were abandoned 9.9.1943 at Piraeus and captured by the Germans. *RD18* and *RD23* were sunk 5.5.1943 at La Goulette (Tunisia) by Allied bombs. *RD20* was sunk 11.4.1943 by Allied aircraft at Trapani. *RD22* was mined off Brindisi 25.10.1943. *RD24* capsized 18.2.1943 W of Sicily. *RD25* was abandoned 26.8.2943 near Messina, salvaged in 1945 and transferred to Yugoslavia as *ML304*.

RD27 class minesweepers

RD27	Tosi, Taranto	10.1917	16.9.1918	10.1918	to Yugoslavia 8.1948 (ML305)
RD28	Tosi, Taranto	12.1917	18.7.1918	12.1918	to Yugoslavia 9.1948 (ML306)
RD29	Tosi, Taranto	2.1918	28.8.1918	1.1919	to Yugoslavia 9.1948 (ML307)
RD30	Tosi, Taranto	3.1918	22.10.1918	2.1919	sunk 26.12.1942

200 t, 36.5 x 5.8 x 2.0 m, 1 VTE, 1 boiler, 970 hp, 14 kts, 760 nm (13 kts), complement 22; 1 x 1 – 76/40 Armstrong 1916 or Armstrong 1917 or Ansaldo 1916 or Ansaldo 1917, 2 x 1 – 6.5 MG, sweeps.
RD30 was bombed 26.12.1942 at Bizerte by Allied aircraft.

ITALY

RD31 class minesweepers

RD31	Arsenale di Castellamare di Stabia	4.1918	30.12.1918	1.1919	sunk 20.1.1943
RD32	Arsenale di Castellamare di Stabia	4.1918	8.2.1919	2.1919	discarded 6.1956
RD33	Arsenale di Castellamare di Stabia	6.1918	20.3.1919	4.1919	capsized 22.1.1943
RD34	Arsenale di Castellamare di Stabia	12.1918	12.5.1919	7.1919	discarded 6.1956
RD35	Arsenale di Castellamare di Stabia	2.1919	17.7.1919	8.1919	captured by Germany 13.9.1943 (M1229)
RD36	Arsenale di Castellamare di Stabia	3.1919	11.8.1919	11.1919	sunk 20.1.1943
RD37	Arsenale di Castellamare di Stabia	5.1919	2.10.1919	2.1920	sunk 20.1.1943

207 t, 36.5 x 5.8 x 2.2 m, 1 VTE, 1 boiler, 860 hp, 13 kts, 660 nm (10.5 kts), complement 22; 1 x 1 – 76/40 Armstrong 1916 or Armstrong 1917 or Ansaldo 1916 or Ansaldo 1917, 2 x 1 – 6.5 MG, sweeps.
RD31, *RD36* and *RD37* were sunk 20.1.1943 off Zuara by British destroyers *Kelvin* and *Javelin*. *RD33* capsized 22.1.1943 in the Gulf of Tunis. *RD35* was captured by Germans 13.9.1943 at Syra, Aegean.

R31 1928

RD38 minesweeper

RD38	Arsenale di Napoli	5.1919	28.8.1919	7.1921	sunk 18.5.1943

200 t, 36.0 x 5.8 x 2.1 m, 1 VTE, 1 boiler, 820 hp, 12 kts, 700 nm (11 kts), complement 22; 1 x 1 – 76/40 Armstrong 1916 or Armstrong 1917 or Ansaldo 1916 or Ansaldo 1917, 2 x 1 – 6.5 MG, sweeps.
RD38 was sunk 18.5.1943 at Trapani by Allied aircraft.

RD39 class minesweepers

RD39	Tosi, Taranto	1.1918	27.7.1919	11.1919	sunk 20.1.1943
RD40	Tosi, Taranto	11.1918	16.10.1919	3.1920	discarded 4.1955
RD41	Tosi, Taranto	1.1919	12.12.1919	3.1920	discarded 1.1953
RD42	Tosi, Taranto	3.1919	5.2.1920	5.1920	sunk 5.5.1943
RD43	Tosi, Taranto	6.1919	12.4.1920	7.1920	capsized 22.1.1943
RD44	Tosi, Taranto	10.1919	6.6.1920	10.1920	sunk 5.5.1943

203 t, 36.5 x 5.8 x 2.2 m, 1 VTE, 1 boiler, 750 hp, 14 kts, 700 nm (12.5 kts), complement 22; 1 x 1 – 76/40 Armstrong 1916 or Armstrong 1917 or Ansaldo 1916 or Ansaldo 1917, 2 x 1 – 6.5 MG, sweeps.
RD39 was sunk 20.1.1943 off Zuara by British destroyers *Kelvin* and *Javelin*. *RD42* was sunk 5.5.1943 at La Goulette, Tunisia by Allied bombs. *RD43* capsized 22.1.1943 in the Gulf of Tunis. *RD44* was sunk 5.5.1943 by Allied aircraft off Bizerte.

RD45 class minesweeper

RD49	Pattison, Napoli	6.1919	24.11.1921	3.1922	captured by Germany 9.9.1943 (TR106)

212 t, 38.0 x 6.0 x 1.9 m, 1 VTE, 1 boiler, 1150 hp, 12.5 kts, 740 nm (12 kts), complement 22; 1 x 1 – 76/40

RD49 1943

Armstrong 1916 or Armstrong 1917 or Ansaldo 1916 or Ansaldo 1917, 2 x 1 – 6.5 MG, sweeps.

RD49 was captured by the Germans 9.9.1943 at La Spezia and scuttled in 1945.

RD55 class minesweepers

RD55	Migliardi, Savona	11.1918	16.2.1923	7.1925	sunk 25.5.1943
RD56	Migliardi, Savona	11.1918	14.3.1923	10.1925	sunk 9.1.1943
RD57	Migliardi, Savona	1.1919	6.3.1923	11.1926	sunk 5.5.1943

RD55

212 t, 35.5 x 5.8 x 2.2 m, 1 VTE, 1 boiler, 870 hp, 12.5 kts, 700 nm (11 kts), complement 22; 1 x 1 – 76/40 Armstrong 1916 or Armstrong 1917 or Ansaldo 1916 or Ansaldo 1917, 2 x 1 – 6.5 MG, sweeps.

RD55 was sunk 25.5.1943 off Messina by Allied aircraft. *RD56* was sunk 9.1.1943 at Bizerte by Allied aircraft, salvaged and sunk again by Allied aircraft 24.3.1943 in the same place. *RD57* was bombed 5.5.1943 at La Goulette, Tunisia by Allied aircraft.

ALBONA class minesweepers

Albona (ex-RD58, ex-MT130)	Danubius, Porto Ré, Austria-Hungary	10.1917	20.7.1918	1.1920	captured by Germany 10.9.1943 (Albona)
Laurana (ex-RD59, ex-MT131)	Danubius, Porto Ré, Austria-Hungary	10.1917	24.8.1918	2.1920	captured by Germany 11.9.1943 (Laurana)
Rovigno (ex-RD60, ex-MT132)	Danubius, Porto Ré, Austria-Hungary	11.1917	28.9.1918	7.1920	captured by Germany 10.9.1943 (Rovigno)

128 / 145 t, 31.8 x 6.5 x 1.7 m, 2 VC, 1 Yarrow boiler, 280 hp, 11 kts, 4 t oil, complement 27; 1 x 1 – 76/40 Armstrong 1917, sweeps.
Former Austro-Hungarian mine transports. At the time of the Armistice, they were incomplete and were completed for the Italian Navy in 1920.

1941 - 1942, all: + 6 x 1 - 20/70 Scotti-Isotta Fraschini 1939.
Albona and *Rovigno* were captured by the Germans 10.9.1943 at Syros, *Laurana* was captured by the Germans 11.9.1943 at Venezia.

PELLEGRINO MATTEUCCI class minesweeping trawlers

Pellegrino Matteucci (ex-Merluzzo)	Deutsche Werk, Kiel, Germany	1924	1934	sunk 21.5.1941
Mario Sonzini (ex-Acciuga), 9.1943- **Tramaglio**	Deutsche Werk, Kiel, Germany	1924	1934	captured by Germany 9.9.1943
Giovanni Berta (ex-Triglia)	Unterweser, Bremen, Germany	1924	1934	sunk 12.6.1940
Giuseppe Biglieri (ex-Dentice)	Deutsche Werk, Kiel, Germany	1924	1934	scuttled 8.4.1941

Giovanni Berta 1936

620 (std) t, 42.3 x 7.4 x 3.7 m, 1 VTE, 1 boiler, 450 hp, 9 kts, complement 28; 2 x 1 – 76/40 Ansaldo 1917, 2 x 1 – 6.5 MG, sweeps.
Former trawlers purchased by the Navy in 1931 and converted to minesweepers in 1934. *Pellegrino Matteucci* was officially rated as a transport.
Pellegrino Matteucci was sunk 21.5.1941 by a mine laid by British minelayer *Abdiel* off Cape Ducato. *Tramaglio* was captured by the Germans 9.9.1943 at Piraeus and commissioned by them as a submarine chaser *UJ2111*.

ITALY

Giovanni Berta ran ashore at Tobruk 12.6.1940 after being attacked by British ships. *Giuseppe Biglieri* was scuttled by her crew at Massawa 8.4.1941, later salvaged by the British and served as HMS *Biglieri* until 1946.

Ex-German VIESTE class minesweepers

Vieste *(ex-Meteo, ex-M119)*	Neptun, Rostock, Germany	1917	22.6.1918	(8.1918) / 12.1921	captured by Germany 11.9.1943
Crotone *(ex-Cotrone, ex-Abastro, ex-M120)*	Neptun, Rostock, Germany	1917	24.7.1918	(9.1918) / 12.1921	captured by Germany 9.9.1943 (Kehrwieder)

525 / 560 t, 59.6 x 7.3 x 2.2 m, 2 VTE, 2 Marine boilers, 1850 hp, 16 kts, 115 t coal, 2400 nm (10 kts), complement 40; 2 x 1 – 105/42 Ubts C/16, 30 mines, sweeps.
Former German minesweepers of the *M97* class, transferred under reparations.
Vieste was captured by the Germans at Naples 11.9.1943. *Crotone* was captured by the Germans at La Spezia 9.9.1943 and commissioned by them

Meteo 1921

as *Kehrwieder*.

Ex-German LURANNA class minesweepers

Luranna *(ex-Fiumana II, ex-FM38)*, 1945- **Fiumana II**	Unterweser, Lehe, Germany	1919		(1923) / 1938	stricken ~1945
Arco Azurro *(ex-Fiumana I, ex-FM37)*	Unterweser, Lehe, Germany	1919		(1923) / 1939	sunk 23.10.1942

185 / 205 t, 45.5 x 6.0 x 1.4 m, 2 VTE, 1 Marine boiler, 750 hp, 14.3 kts, 35 t coal, 600 nm (14 kts), complement 35; 1 x 1 – 76/40 Armstrong 1916 or Armstrong 1917 or Ansaldo 1916 or Ansaldo 1917, sweeps.
Shallow-draught flat-bottomed minesweepers intended to work on rivers and in bays with a depth up to 2.3 m of the German *FM37* class. According to modern classification, they were coastal minesweepers, according to German classification they were large motorboats. *FM37* and *FM38* were completed

Luranna 1938

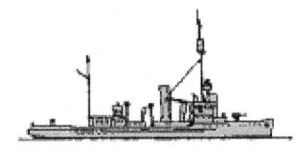

in 1923 for a merchant owner, but in 1938-1939 requisitioned by the Italian Navy and commissioned as minesweepers.
Arco Azurro was sunk 23.10.1942 at Genoa by Allied aircraft.

D1 minesweeper

D1	CNR, Ancona	1937	1938	lost 9.1943

188 t, 33.4 x 6.6 x 2.2 m, 1 diesel, 450 hp, 10 kts, complement 18; 1 x 1 – 86/40 Ansaldo 1917, sweeps.
First Italian attempt to create a purpose-built minesweeper. The design was based on the hull of a trawler.

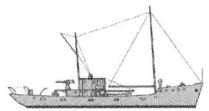

D1 1940

D1 was lost for unknown cause in September 1943.

Ex-Yugoslav SELVE class minesweepers

Eso *(ex-Sokol, ex-M144)*	Neptun, Rostock, Germany	1918	19.3.1919	(6.1919) / 4.1941	sunk 19.1.1943
Selve *(ex-Galeb, ex-M100)*	Tecklenborg, Geestemünde, Germany	1917	23.5.1918	(6.1918) / 4.1941	sunk 6.11.1942
Vergada *(ex-Orao, ex-M97)*	Tecklenborg, Geestemünde, Germany	1917	28.3.1918	(4.1918) / 4.1941	to Yugoslavia 12.1943 (Orao)

Unie *(ex-Kobac, ex-M121)*	Neptun, Rostock, Germany	1917	10.9.1918	(10.1918) / 4.1941	sunk 30.1.1943
Zirona *(ex-Jastreb, ex-M112)*	Tecklenborg, Geestemünde, Germany	1917	12.11.1918	(10.1919) / 4.1941	wrecked 25.11.1941
Zuri *(ex-Labud, ex-Gavran, ex-M106),* 6.1942- **Oriole**	Reiherstieg, Hamburg, Germany	1917	8.7.1918	(3.1919) / 4.1941	scuttled 10.7.1943

Selve 1941

515 / 690 t, 59.6 x 7.3 x 2.2 m, 2 VTE, 2 Marine boilers, 1850 (*Eso, Unie, Zuri*) or 1840 hp, 16 kts, 115 t coal, 2000 nm (14 kts), complement 51; 2 x 1 – 90/45 M1926, 2 x 1 – 7.9 MG, 30 mines, sweeps.

Former Yugoslav minesweepers, purchased by them in Germany in 1921 without armament. Belonged to the *M57* class. Used by the Italian Navy mainly as patrols.
Eso and *Selve* were sunk by British aircraft off Djerba 19.1.1943 and at Benghazi 6.11.1942 respectively. *Unie* was sunk by US aircraft 30.1.1943 at Bizerte. *Zirona* was damaged by British aircraft at Benghazi and ran ashore 25.11.1941. *Oriole* was scuttled by her crew 10.7.1943 at Augusta.

Ex-Yugoslav ARBE class small minesweeper - minelayers

Arbe *(ex-Malinska, ex-MT135)*	Danubius, Kraljevica, Yugoslavia	12.1917	1931	(1931) / 4.1941	captured by Germany 9.9.1943
Meleda *(ex-Mljet, ex-MT137)*	Danubius, Kraljevica, Yugoslavia	2.1918	1931	(1931) / 4.1941	to Yugoslavia 12.1943 (M3)
Pasman *(ex-Mosor, ex-MT134)*	Danubius, Kraljevica, Yugoslavia	12.1917	1931	(1931) / 4.1941	captured by Germany 9.9.1943 (Pasman)
Solta *(ex-Meljine, ex-MT136)*	Danubius, Kraljevica, Yugoslavia	12.1917	1931	(1931) / 4.1941	to Yugoslavia 12.1943 (M1)
Ugliano *(ex-Marjan, ex-MT133)*	Danubius, Kraljevica, Yugoslavia	11.1917	1931	(1931) / 4.1941	to Yugoslavia 2.1944 (M2)

Ugliano 1941

115 (as minesweeper) or 128 (as minelayer) t, 29.4-30.1 x 6.7 x 1.7 m, 2 VTE, 1 boiler, 280 hp, 11.6 kts, complement 27; 1 x 1 - 47/40 Škoda, 1 x 1 - 7.9 MG, 20 - 34 mines or sweeps.

Austro-Hungarian mine transports, laid down during World War I, completed for Yugoslavia in 1931. They were captured by the Italians in 1941 and commissioned by the Regia Marina as minesweepers.
Arbe and *Pasman* were captured by the Germans 9.9.1943 at Šibenik.

Auxiliary minesweepers

Requisitioned: 983 (1940-1942)
Lost: unknown
Discarded: unknown.
983 small fishing and merchant vessels of less than 500 gross tons were requisitioned by the Regia Marina during the war for use as minesweepers. 490 were in service 10.6.1940, 678 01.01.1942 and 587 01.08.1943.

VEDETTA class minesweeping boats

Vigilante 1940

CRDA, Trieste: Vedetta, Vigilante (1937)
Discarded: Vedetta, Vigilante (1951)
70 t, 26.1 x 4.3 x 1.3 m, 2 diesels, 400 hp, 12 kts, complement 21; 1 x 1 – 76/40 Ansaldo 1917, 3 x 1 – 13.2 MG, sweeps.
Small inshore minesweepers.

ITALY

Ex-Yugoslav D10 small minesweeper

Marinearsenal Pola, Austria-Hungary: D10 (ex-D2, ex-Tb36, ex-Uhu) (1888/1941)
Lost: D10 (1943)
77 / 88 t, 39.9 x 4.8 x 1.9 m, 1 VC, 1 boiler, 900 hp, 18 kts, 19 t coal, complement 18; 2 x 1 – 7.9 MG, sweeps.
Former Yugoslav TS, former Austro-Hungarian torpedo boat. Captured by the Italians and was used as a minesweeper.
D10 was captured by the Germans 11.9.1943 at Kumbor.

Tb36 1890

Ex-French FR74 small minesweeper

Matthews Boat, Port Clinton, USA: FR74 (ex-Ch81, ex-C81, ex-SC386) (1918/1942)
Lost: FR74 (1943)
75 / 85 t, 33.5 x 4.5 x 1.7 m, 3 Standard petrol engines, 660 hp, 18 kts, 1000 nm (12 kts), complement 27; 1 x 1 – 75/35 M1897, 1 DCT, sweeps.

Ch81 1940

Former French submarine chaser, captured 8.12.1942 by the Germans at Bizerte and transferred to the Italians.
FR74 was scuttled 6.5.1943 by Italian crew.

RDV101 class minesweeping boats

RDV101	Baglietto, Varazze	(11.1944)	captured incomplete by Germany 9.1943 (RD101)
RDV102	Baglietto, Varazze	1949	discarded 6.1958
RDV103	Baglietto, Varazze	1949	discarded 7.1958
RDV104	Baglietto, Varazze	1949	survey vessel 6.1959
RDV105	Baglietto, Varazze	1949	discarded 9.1954
RDV106	Baglietto, Varazze	1949	discarded 1.1959
RDV107	Baglietto, Varazze	1949	discarded 9.1959
RDV108	Baglietto, Varazze	1949	discarded 1959
RDV109	Baglietto, Varazze	(3.1944)	captured incomplete by Germany 9.1943 (RD109)
RDV110	Baglietto, Varazze	(5.1944)	captured incomplete by Germany 9.1943 (RD110)
RDV111	Baglietto, Varazze	(9.1944)	captured incomplete by Germany 9.1943 (RD111)
RDV112	Baglietto, Varazze	(1.1945)	captured incomplete by Germany 9.1943 (RD112)
RDV113	Baglietto, Varazze	9.1945	discarded 9.1965
RDV114	Baglietto, Varazze	-	captured incomplete by Germany 9.1943 (RD114)
RDV115	CRDA, Monfalcone	(3.1945)	captured incomplete by Germany 9.1943 (RD115)
RDV116	CRDA, Monfalcone	(1944)	captured incomplete by Germany 9.1943 (RD116)
RDV117	CRDA, Monfalcone	-	captured incomplete by Germany 9.1943 (RD117)
RDV118	CRDA, Monfalcone	-	captured incomplete by Germany 9.1943 (RD118)
RDV119	CRDA, Monfalcone	-	captured incomplete by Germany 9.1943 (RD119)
RDV120	CRDA, Monfalcone	-	captured incomplete by Germany 9.1943 (RD120)
RDV121	CRDA, Monfalcone	-	captured incomplete by Germany 9.1943 (RD121)
RDV122	CRDA, Monfalcone	-	captured incomplete by Germany 9.1943 (RD122)
RDV127	Celli, Venice	(4.1945)	captured incomplete by Germany 9.1943 (RD127)
RDV128	Celli, Venice	-	captured incomplete by Germany 9.1943 (RD128)
RDV129	Celli, Venice	-	captured incomplete by Germany 9.1943 (RD129)
RDV130	Celli, Venice	-	captured incomplete by Germany 9.1943 (RD130)
RDV131	Celli, Venice	6.1949	discarded 1.1959
RDV132	Celli, Venice	6.1949	discarded 9.1959
RDV133	Celli, Venice	6.1949	discarded 1959
RDV134	Celli, Venice	6.1949	discarded 9.1959
RDV135	OTO, Livorno	-	captured incomplete by Germany 9.1943 (RD135)
RDV136	Picchiotti, Limite sul Arno	1949	discarded 1959
RDV140	Picchiotti, Limite sul Arno	1949	discarded 1959

RDV141	Soriente, Salerno	-	captured incomplete by Germany 9.1943 (RD141)
RDV146	Soriente, Salerno	-	captured incomplete by Germany 9.1943 (RD146)
RDV147	Costaguta, Genoa-Voltri	-	captured incomplete by Germany 9.1943 (RD147)
RDV148	Costaguta, Genoa-Voltri	1946	discarded 7.1958
RDV149	Costaguta, Genoa-Voltri	1945	survey vessel 1960

RDV124 (ex-RDV134) 1951

101 / 110 t, 34.0 x 5.8 x 1.4 m, 2 Isotta-Frascini petrol engines or 4 Fiat diesels (2 shafts) (*RDV113, 149*), 2300 or 2000 (*RDV113, 149*) hp, 17 kts, 10 t petrol or diesel oil, complement 24; 1 x 1 – 20/65 Breda 1940, sweeps. Fast coastal minesweepers, the Italian analogue of the German R-boats.

AMPHIBIOUS WARFARE SHIPS

ADIGE water tanker with landing ability

Adige	Arsenale di Castellammare de Stabia	1927	31.10.1928	4.1929	captured by Germany 8.9.1943

Adige 1930

810 t, 47.0 x 9.6 x 2.3 m, 2 diesels, 280 hp, 8 kts, complement 33; 4 x 1 – 8 MG, 48 mines as a minelayer, infantry battalion as a landing ship.
Water tanker with landing capability. She had a small bow ramp.
8.9.1943, *Adige* was captured by German troops at Patras and commissioned by the Kriegsmarine.

SESIA class water tankers with landing ability

Sesia	CNT, Riva Trigoso	1933	1934	1934	water tanker 1943, stricken 6.1972
Garigliano	CNT, Riva Trigoso	1933	1934	1934	captured by Germany 13.9.1943 (Dwarsläufer)
Tirso	CNT, Riva Trigoso	1935	1937	8.1937	to France 12.1948
Scrivia	CNT, Riva Trigoso	1935	1937	10.1937	scuttled 9.9.1943

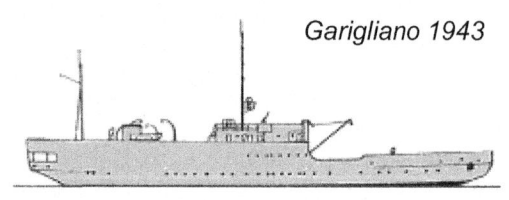

Garigliano 1943

Garigliano 1937

1055 / 1141 t, 66.1 x 10.1 x 4.2 m, 2 FIAT diesels, 600 hp, 10.5 kts, 5000 nm (6 kts), complement 36; 4 x 1 – 13.2 MG, 118 mines as a minelayer; 1000 troops, light tanks, vehicles as a landing ship.
Water tankers with landing capability, with small bow ramps.
1939-1940, all: - 4 x 1 - 13.2 MG; + 2 x 1 - 20/65 Breda 1939/40, 3 x 1 – 8 MG.
Garigliano was captured by German troops 13.9.1943 at La Maddalena, commissioned by the Kriegsmarine as minelayer *Dwarsläufer* (later *Oldenburg*). 25.4.1945 she was scuttled by her own crew. *Scrivia* was scuttled by her own crew at La Spezia 9.9.1943.

ITALY

MZ-A type landing barges

MZ701	CRDA, Monfalcone	5.1942	discarded 1943/47
MZ702	CRDA, Monfalcone	5.1942	discarded 1943/47
MZ703	CRDA, Monfalcone	5.1942	discarded 1943/47
MZ704	CRDA, Monfalcone	5.1942	captured by Germany 9.1943 (F2704)
MZ705	CRDA, Monfalcone	6.1942	discarded 1943/47
MZ706	CRDA, Monfalcone	5.1942	captured by Germany 9.1943 (F2706)
MZ707	CRDA, Monfalcone	6.1942	discarded 1943/47
MZ708	CRDA, Monfalcone	5.1942	captured by Germany 9.1943 (F2708)
MZ709	CRDA, Monfalcone	5.1942	captured by Germany 9.1943 (F2709)
MZ710	CRDA, Monfalcone	6.1942	discarded 1943/47
MZ711	CRDA, Monfalcone	6.1942	captured by Germany 9.1943 (F4711)
MZ712	CRDA, Monfalcone	6.1942	discarded 1943/47
MZ713	CRDA, Monfalcone	6.1942	to Yugoslavia 12.1943 (D206)
MZ714	CRDA, Monfalcone	6.1942	discarded 1943/47
MZ715	CRDA, Monfalcone	6.1942	discarded 1943/47
MZ716	CRDA, Monfalcone	6.1942	discarded 1943/47
MZ717	CRDA, Monfalcone	6.1942	to Yugoslavia 12.1943 (D219)
MZ718	CRDA, Monfalcone	6.1942	discarded 1943/47
MZ719	CRDA, Monfalcone	6.1942	discarded 1943/47
MZ720	CRDA, Monfalcone	6.1942	discarded 1943/47
MZ721	CRDA, Monfalcone	6.1942	discarded 1943/47
MZ722	CRDA, Monfalcone	6.1942	discarded 3.1995
MZ723	CRDA, Monfalcone	6.1942	discarded 1943/47
MZ724	CRDA, Monfalcone	6.1942	captured by Germany 9.1943 (F2724)
MZ725	CRDA, Monfalcone	6.1942	discarded 1943/47
MZ726	CRDA, Monfalcone	6.1942	discarded 3.1963
MZ727	CRDA, Monfalcone	7.1942	discarded 1943/47
MZ728	CRDA, Monfalcone	7.1942	discarded 3.1984
MZ729	CRDA, Monfalcone	7.1942	discarded 4.1988
MZ730	CRDA, Monfalcone	7.1942	discarded 1943/47
MZ731	CRDA, Monfalcone	7.1942	discarded 1943/47
MZ732	CRDA, Monfalcone	1942	discarded 1943/47
MZ733	CRDA, Monfalcone	1942	discarded 1943/47
MZ734	CRDA, Monfalcone	1942	discarded 1943/47
MZ735	CRDA, Monfalcone	1942	discarded 1943/47
MZ736	CRDA, Monfalcone	1942	discarded 1943/47
MZ737	CRDA, Monfalcone	1942	discarded 1987
MZ738	CRDA, Monfalcone	1942	discarded 1943/47
MZ739	CRDA, Monfalcone	1942	discarded 1943/47
MZ740	CRDA, Monfalcone	1942	discarded 1943/47
MZ741	CRDA, Monfalcone	1942	discarded 1943/47
MZ742	CRDA, Monfalcone	1942	discarded 1943/47
MZ743	CRDA, Monfalcone	1942	discarded 1943/47
MZ744	Ansaldo, Genoa	6.1942	captured by Germany 10.1943 (F4744)
MZ745	Ansaldo, Genoa	6.1942	discarded 1943/47
MZ746	Ansaldo, Genoa	6.1942	discarded 1943/47
MZ747	Ansaldo, Genoa	6.1942	discarded 1943/47
MZ748	Ansaldo, Genoa	6.1942	discarded 1943/47
MZ749	Ansaldo, Genoa	6.1942	captured by Germany 9.1943 (F4749)
MZ750	Ansaldo, Genoa	1942	discarded 1943/47

MZ751	CT, Riva Trigoso	6.1942	captured by Germany 9.1943 (F2751)
MZ752	CT, Riva Trigoso	1942	discarded 1943/47
MZ753	CT, Riva Trigoso	1942	discarded 1943/47
MZ754	CT, Riva Trigoso	2.1942	captured by Germany 9.1943 (F2754)
MZ755	CT, Riva Trigoso	1942	discarded 1943/47
MZ756	CT, Riva Trigoso	1942	discarded 1943/47
MZ757	CT, Riva Trigoso	1942	discarded 1943/47
MZ758	CT, Riva Trigoso	1942	discarded 1992
MZ759	CT, Riva Trigoso	1942	discarded 1943/47
MZ760, 1943- MZ703	CM, Pietra Ligure	6.1942	captured by Germany 11.1943 (F2703)
MZ761	CM, Pietra Ligure	1942	discarded 1943/47
MZ762	CM, Pietra Ligure	1942	discarded 1943/47
MZ763	CM, Pietra Ligure	1942	discarded 1943/47
MZ764, 1943- MZ759	CM, Pietra Ligure	8.1942	captured by Germany 9.1943 (F2759)
MZ765, 1943- MZ760	CNR, Palermo	8.1942	captured by Germany 9.1943 (F2760)

MZ709 1943

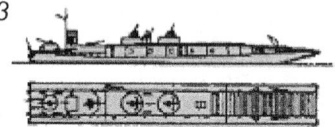

140 / 239 t, 47.0 x 6.5 x 1.0 m, 3 Ferrovie diesels, 450 hp, 11 kts, 4.1 t diesel oil, 1450 nm (8 kts), complement 13; 1 x 1 – 76/40 Ansaldo 1917, 2 x 1 – 20/65 Breda 1940; 65 t of cargo or 200 troops.

German MFP-A type design with Italian diesels and armament. Many of them were captured by German troops in September 1943.

MZ-B type landing barges

MZ766	CNR, Palermo	8.1943	discarded 1943/47
MZ767	CNR, Palermo	(late 1943)	captured incomplete by Germany 9.1943 (F0767)
MZ768	CNR, Palermo	(10.1943)	captured incomplete by Germany 9.1943 (F2768)
MZ769	CNR, Palermo	(9.1943)	captured incomplete by Germany 9.1943 (F0769)
MZ770	CNR, Palermo	(10.1943)	captured incomplete by Germany 9.1943 (F0770)
MZ771	CRDA, Monfalcone	2.1943	discarded 1943/47
MZ772	CRDA, Monfalcone	1.1943	discarded 1943/47
MZ773	CRDA, Monfalcone	1.1943	discarded 1943/47
MZ774	CRDA, Monfalcone	1.1943	discarded 1943/47
MZ775	CRDA, Monfalcone	2.1943	discarded 1943/47
MZ776	CRDA, Monfalcone	2.1943	discarded 7.1981
MZ777	CRDA, Monfalcone	3.1943	captured by Germany 9.1943 (F4777)
MZ778	CRDA, Monfalcone	3.1943	to the USSR 1949 (BDB-69)
MZ779	CRDA, Monfalcone	3.1943	discarded 1943/47
MZ780	CRDA, Monfalcone	3.1943	to the USSR 1949 (BDB-70)
MZ781	CRDA, Monfalcone	3.1943	to the USSR 1949 (BDB-71)
MZ782	CRDA, Monfalcone	3.1943	discarded 1943/47
MZ783	CRDA, Monfalcone	3.1943	captured by Germany 9.1943 (F2783)
MZ784	CRDA, Monfalcone	3.1943	discarded 12.1979
MZ785	CRDA, Monfalcone	3.1943	captured by Germany 9.1943 (F4785)
MZ786	CRDA, Monfalcone	3.1943	discarded 1943/47
MZ787	CRDA, Monfalcone	3.1943	discarded 1943/47
MZ788	CRDA, Monfalcone	3.1943	discarded 1943/47
MZ789	CRDA, Monfalcone	3.1943	discarded 1943/47
MZ790	CRDA, Monfalcone	3.1943	discarded 1943/47
MZ791	CRDA, Monfalcone	3.1943	discarded 1943/47
MZ792	CRDA, Monfalcone	3.1943	discarded 1943/47

ITALY

MZ793	CRDA, Monfalcone	3.1943	discarded 1943/47
MZ794	CRDA, Monfalcone	3.1943	discarded 1943/47
MZ795	CRDA, Monfalcone	3.1943	captured by Germany 9.1943 (F4795)
MZ796	CRDA, Monfalcone	3.1943	discarded 1943/47
MZ797	CRDA, Monfalcone	3.1943	discarded 1943/47
MZ798	CRDA, Monfalcone	3.1943	discarded 1943/47
MZ799	CRDA, Monfalcone	3.1943	captured by Germany 9.1943 (F4799)
MZ800	CRDA, Monfalcone	3.1943	discarded 1984

174 / 279 t, 46.5 x 6.5 x 1.0 m, 3 Ferrovie diesels, 450 hp, 11 kts, 4.1 t diesel oil, 1450 nm (8 kts), complement 13; 1 x 1 – 76/40 Ansaldo 1917, 2 x 1 – 20/65 Breda 1940; 65 t cargo or 200 troops.
MZ-A with modified superstructure and redesigned bow.

MZ769 1943

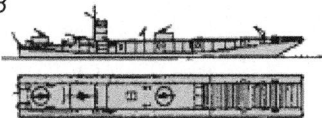

LCT(2) type tank landing craft

MZ34 *(ex-NSC(L)34, ex-LCT(R)167)*	Tees-Side Bridge, Middlesborough, UK	17.11.1941	(1.1942) / 5.1945	discarded 10.2008

296 / 460 t, 48.8 x 9.5 x 1.6 m, 3 Paxman diesels, 1380 hp, 11 kts, 41 t diesel oil, 1350 nm (11 kts), complement 12; 2 x 1 – 20/70 Oerlikon; 3 40-t or 7 20-t tanks or 250 t of cargo.
Former RN LCT(2) craft, transferred in May 1945.

AUXILIARY VESSELS INTENDED FOR COMBAT SUPPORT

Submarine tenders

Città di Siracusa	Odero, Terni	1910	1910	distilling ship 1938

3593 t, 110.9 x 13.0 x 5.0 m, 1 VTE, 10 boilers, 12000 hp, 20 kts, 2 x 1 – 76/40.

Alessandro Volta *(ex-Caprera)*	Cantieri di Castellamare di Stabia	1921	1924	sunk 8.10.1943
Antonio Pacinotti *(ex-Città di Sassari)*	Cantieri di Castellamare di Stabia	1922	1925	BU 1952

2727 t, 88.1 x 11.0 x 4.6 m, 2 sets geared steam turbines, 4 (*Alessandro Volta*) or 2 (*Antonio Pacinotti*) boilers, 7500 hp, 19 kts; 4 x 1 – 76/40.
Alessandro Volta was mistakenly sunk by British MTBs in the Aegean Sea 8.10.1943.

Alessandro Volta 1932

Repair ship

Quarnaro	Scoglio Ulivi, Pola	30.7.1924	1.1927	captured by Germany 9.9.1943

7185 t, 114.8 x 14.8 x 6.1 m, 1 VTE, 3 boilers, 2300 hp, 11 kts; 3 x 1 – 102/45, 2 x 1 – 13.2 MG.

Quarnaro was captured by the Germans 9.9.1943 at Gaeta and scuttled by them as a blockship 20.9.1943.

Oilers

Bronte	Orlando, Livorno	1904	1904	captured by the UK 21.8.1941

9500 t, 119.2 x 14.4 x 7.6m, 2 VTE, 4000 hp, 14.5 kts, complement 72; 4 x 1 – 76/40.

Could carry coal and oil. *Bronte* was captured by British troops at Bandar-Shalpur 21.8.1941.

Nettuno	CNR, Palermo	22.2.1916	1916	BU 1954
Giove	CNR, Palermo	1916	1916	lost 1941

10310 t, 127.0 x 15.6 x 7.3 m, 2 VTE, 4230 hp, 14.8 kts, complement 76; 2 (*Giove*) or 3 (*Nettuno*) x 1 – 120/45, 2 x 1 – 76/40.
Giove was lost at Massawa in 1941.

Brennero	Bacini, Riva Trigoso	1921	1922	confiscated 30.3.1941

9790 t, 104.7 x 18.0 x 7.5 m, 1 VTE, 2 boilers, 2600 hp, 10.9 kts; 4 x 1 – 120/45, 2 x 1 – 76/40.
Brennero was confiscated by the US Government in New York 30.3.1941, returned to Italy in 1948 and stricken in 1954.

Urano	Deutsche Werke, Kiel, Germany		1922	1922	stricken 1954

11200 t, 126.3 x 16.5 x 7.0 m, 2 diesels, 2000 hp, 11 kts, complement 84; 2 x 1 – 120/45, 2 x 1 – 76/40.

Tarvisio	CN di Castellamare di Stabia	1927	1928	to France 1948

11600 t, 113.5 x 18.0 x 6.9 m, 2 sets geared steam turbines, 3 boilers, 2600 hp, 10 kts, complement 108; 4 x 1 – 120/45, 2 x 1 – 76/40.

Sterope	CNQ, Fiume	17.7.1940	9.1940	captured by Germany 9.9.1943

10600 t, 1 diesel, 14 kts.
Sterope was captured by the Germans 9.9.1943 at Genoa and scuttled

CUSTOMS

D'AMATO MARONGIU boat

Cantieri Marvi, Venezia: D'Amato Marongiu (1930)
Discarded: D'Amato Marongiu (1950s)

42 t, 24.0 m, 11 kts; 1 x 1 – 76/40 Ansaldo 1917, 1 x 1 – 6.5 MG.

CARON class boats

CNQ, Fiume: Caron, Cotugno (1934)
Discarded: Caron, Cotugno (1950s)

60 t, 23.1 m, 13 kts; 1 x 1 – 76/40 Ansaldo 1917, 3 x 1 – 7.5 MG.

SPANEDDA boat

CNQ, Fiume: Spanedda (1938)
Discarded: Spanedda (1950s)

63 t, 25.3 m, 13 kts; 1 x 1 – 76/40 Ansaldo 1917, 3 x 1 – 7.5 MG.

ITALY

SHIP-BASED AIRCRAFT

Fighters

Reggiane Re.2000 (10, 1941—1943)

Re.2000-III catapultabile: 11.00 x 7.99 x 3.20 m, 20.4 m², 2070 / 2880 kg, 1 Piaggio P.XI RC40, 985 hp, 530 km/h, 1300 (450) km, 12.5 m/s, 11500 m, 1 seat; 2 x 12.7 Breda-SAFAT.
Re.2000-III catapultabile (catapult fighter, 10 built in 1941, serv 1941-1943, catapult take-off, shore landing).

Re.2000-III catapultabile:

Seaplanes and flying boats

Macchi M.7 (129, 1923-1940)

M.7ter: 9.95 x 8.10 x 2.95 m, 26.4 m², 800 / 1100 kg, 1 Lorraine-Dietrich, 400 hp, 200 km/h, 700 (167) km, 6500 m, 1 seat; 2 x 7.7 Vickers.
M.7ter (fighter flying boat, 100 built 1923-1927, serv. 1923-1940, unfolding wings); **M.7ter AR** (fighter flying boat, 29 built 1923-1927, serv. 1923-1940, folding wings).

M.7ter

Piaggio P.6 (15, 1928-1937)

P.6ter: 13.50 x 9.80 m, 2360 kg, 1 Fiat A.20, 410 hp, 195 km/h, 480 (162) km, 2 seats; 1 x 7.7 Vickers.
P.6ter (reconnaissance seaplane, 15 built in 1928, serv. 1928-1937).

P.6ter

FIAT CR.20 (46, 1928-1938)

CR.20: 9.80 x 6.71 x 2.79 m, 25.5 m², 970 / 1390 kg, 1 Fiat A.20, 410 hp, 276 km/h, 750 (251) km, 8500 m, 1 seat; 2 x 7.7 Vickers.
CR.20idro (fighter seaplane, 46 built 1928-1929, serv. 1928-1938).

CR.20idro

Macchi M.41 (35, 1929-1939)

M.41bis: 11.12 x 8.66 x 3.12 m, 31.9 m², 1107 / 1537 kg, 1 Fiat A.20, 420 hp, 262 km/h, 700 (227) km, 6.7 m/s, 7500 m, 1 seat; 2 x 7.7 Vickers.
M.41bis (fighter flying boat, 25 built in 1929, serv. 1929-1939); **M.71** (fighter flying boats, 10 built in 1931, serv. 1931-1939, catapult gear).

M.41bis

CANT 25AR

Ro.43

Ca.316

CANT 25 (34, 1931-1943)

CANT 25: 11.20 x 8.60 x 3.00 m, 27.5 m², 1000 / 1400 kg, 1 Fiat A.20, 440 hp, 265 km/h, 900 (235) km, 5500 m, 1 seat; 2 x 7.7 Vickers.
CANT 25M (fighter flying boat, 14 built in 1931-1933, serv. 1931-1943, folding wings); **CANT25AR** (fighter flying boat, 20 built in 1931-1933, serv. 1931-1943, catapult gear)

IMAM (Meridionali) Ro.43/Ro.44 (180, 1937-1943)

Ro.43: 11.58 x 9.72 x 3.50 m, 33.4 m², 1440 / 1880 kg, 1 Piaggio P.XR, 700 hp, 300 km/h, 1500 (245) km, 6600 m, 1-2 seats; 2 x 7.7 Breda-SAFAT
Ro.44: 11.57 x 9.71 x 3.55 m, 33.4 m², 1770 / 2200 kg, 1 Piaggio P.XR, 700 hp, 330 km/h, 1200 (316) km, 7200 m, 1 seat; 2 x 12.7 Breda-SAFAT.
Ro.43 (reconnaissance seaplane, 130 built 1937-1940, serv. 1937-1943, 2 seats, long range, 2 x 7.7 MG); **R0.44** (fighter seaplane, 50 built 1937-1938, serv. 1937-1943, 1 seat, short range, 2 x 12.7 MG).

Caproni Ca.316 (14, 1941)

Ca.316: 15.87 x 12.89 x 5.11 m, 38.0 m², 4000 / 4804 kg, 2 x Piaggio P,VII C.16, 2 x 430 hp, 328 km/h, 2110 (300) km, 6000 m, 3 seats; 1 x 12.7 Breda-SAFAT, 1 x 7.7 Breda-SAFAT, 400 kg bombs
Ca.316 (reconnaissance seaplane, 14 built in 1941, serv. 1941)

NAVAL WEAPONS

Guns

Machine guns

Caliber, mm	Bore length, cal	No of bores	Type of mount	Guns used	Year	Ships used on	Maximum elevation angle, °	Shell mass, kg	Initial velocity, m/s	Rate of fire of one bore, rpm	Fire range / AA ceiling, km
6.5		1	Colt M1915	6.5mm FM Colt M1915	1915	many	90				
6.5	80.0	1	Breda M1930	6.5mm FM Breda M1930	1930	many	90		629	450 - 500	
7.9	79.0	1	MG15	7.9mm MG15	1941	some	90	0.010	760	450 - 500	

ITALY

Caliber, mm	Bore Length, cal	No of bores	Type of mount	Guns used	Year	Ships used on	Maximum elevation angle, °	Shell mass, kg	Initial velocity, m/s	Rate of fire of one bore, rpm	Fire range / AA ceiling, km
7.9	79.0	1	MG34	7.9mm MG34	1941	some	90	0.010	760	800 - 900	
8.0		1	Fiat M1914	8mm FM Fiat M1914	1914	many	90				
8.0		1	Fiat M1914/35	8mm FM Fiat M1914/35	1935	many	90				
8.00	80.0	1	Hotchkiss MG	8mm Hotchkiss Mil	1942	ex-French	90				
8.00	80.0	2	Hotchkiss MG	8mm Hotchkiss Mil	1942	ex-French	90				
8.00	80.0	4	Hotchkiss MG	8mm Hotchkiss Mil	1942	ex-French	90				
8.0	92.5	1	Breda M1937	8mm FM Breda M1937	1937	many	90		790	450 - 500	
12.7	62.2	1	Mk VI	0.5`` Vickers Mk III No. 3 MG	1926	some	~90	0.038	768	150 - 200	0.7 / 0.3
12.7	62.2	2	Mk IV, V, VC	0.5`` Vickers Mk III No. 2 MG	1945	some	~90	0.038	768	150 - 200	0.7 / 0.3
13.2	75.7	1	Breda M1931	13.2mm FM Breda M1931	1931	many	80	0.051	790	500	6.0 / 4.0
13.2	75.7	2	Breda M1931	13.2mm FM Breda M1931	1931	many	90	0.051	790	500	6.0 / 4.0
13.2	76.0	2	M1929	13.2mm Hotchkiss M1929 Mil	1942	some	90	0.052	800	200	7.2 / 4.2
13.2	76.0	4	M1929	13.2mm Hotchkiss M1929 Mil	1942	some	90	0.052	800	200	7.2 / 4.2
13.2	90.0	1	Browning	13.2mm Browning Mil	1942	some	80	0.052	893	150 - 200	2.4 / 2.4
15.0	83.6	1	MG151	15mm MG151	1943	few	90	0.057	960	700	

Automatic guns

Caliber, mm	Bore Length, cal	No of bores	Type of mount	Guns used	Year	Ships used on	Maximum elevation angle, °	Shell mass, kg	Initial velocity, m/s	Rate of fire of one bore, rpm	Fire range / AA ceiling, km
20.0	65.0	1	Breda M1939	20mm/65 Breda 1939	1940	few	90	0.134	840	240	5.5 / 2.9
20.0	65.0	1	Breda M1940	20mm/65 Breda 1940	1941	many	90	0.134	840	240	5.5 / 2.9
20.0	65.0	1	MPLC/30	2cm FlaK 38	1943	SS	85	0.120	875	450 - 500	4.8 / 3.7
20.0	65.0	2	RM 1935	20mm/65 Breda 1935	1936	many	100	0.134	840	240	5.5 / 2.9
20	65	2	LM44U	2cm FlaK 38	1943	SS	78	0.120	875	450 - 500	4.8 / 3.7
20.0	65.0	4	Vierling L/38	2cm FlaK 38	1943	m. b. some DE	90	0.120	875	450 - 500	4.8 / 3.7
20.0	70.0	1	1S	20mm/70 Oerlikon M1941	1941	few	90	0.123	844	250 - 320	4.7 / 3.0

20.0	70.0	1	3S	20mm/70 Oerlikon M1941	1942	few	87	0.123	844	250 - 320	4.7 / 3.0
20.0	70.0	1	Mk I, IA, II, IIA, IIIA, VIIA	20 mm/70 Mk II	1945	many	85	0.123	844	250 - 320	4.7 / 3.0
20.0	70.0	1	Mk VIIIA	20 mm/70 Mk II	1945	PS, YP, PT	20	0.123	844	250 - 320	3.9
20.0	70.0	2	Mk V, VC, IX, XIA, XIIA	20 mm/70 Mk II	1945	many	85	0.123	844	250 - 320	4.7 / 3.0
20.0	77.0	1	Scotti M1939	20mm/70 Scotti-Isotta Fraschini M1939	1940	many	85	0.125	830	250	4.7 / 3.0
20.0	77.0	1	Scotti M1941	20mm/70 Scotti-OM M1941	1942	SS	85	0.125	830	250	4.7 / 3.0
20.0	77.0	2	RM 1935	20mm/70 Scotti-Isotta Fraschini M1939	1940	many	85	0.125	830	250	4.7 / 3.0
37.0	42.5	1	Maxim-Nordenfelt M1897	1-pdr Maxim-Nordenfelt M1897	1914	some	65	0.480	610	75	3.2
37.0	43.0	1	Vickers M1914	1.5-pdr Vickers Mk 1	1914	few	80	0.700	640	30	1.8 / 1.5
37.0	50.0	1	CA/SMCA M1925	37mm M1925	1942	CL, DD, TB, SL	80	0.725	850	30 - 42	7.2 / 5.5
37.0	50.0	2	CAD M1933	37mm M1933	1942	CL, DD, TB, SL	80	0.725	850	30 - 42	7.2 / 5.5
37.0	50.0	2	CAIL M1933	37mm M1933	1942	CL, DD, TB, SL	80	0.725	850	30 - 42	7.2 / 5.5
37.0	54.0	1	Breda M1939	37mm/54 Breda 1939	1940	BB	90	0.823	800	120	7.8 / 5.0
37.0	54.0	1	RM 1939	37mm/54 Breda 1939	1933	many	90	0.823	800	120	7.8 / 5.0
37.0	54.0	2	Breda M1932	37mm/54 Breda 1932	1933	many	80	0.823	800	120	7.8 / 5.0
37.0	54.0	2	Breda M1938	37mm/54 Breda 1938	1939	many	80	0.823	800	120	7.8 / 5.0
37.0	69.2	1	FlaK LM42	3.7cm FlaK M/42	1944	SS	90	0.644	845	180	6.6 / 4.9
40.0	39.4	1	Vickers-Terni M1915	40mm/39 Vickers-Terni 1915	1915	many	80	0.900	610	50 - 75	4.5 / 2.0
40.0	39.4	1	Vickers-Terni M1917	40mm/39 Vickers-Terni 1917	1917	many	80	0.900	610	50 - 75	4.5 / 2.0
40.0	39.4	1	Vickers-Terni M1930 mod.	40mm/39 Vickers-Terni 1917	1931	many	80	0.900	610	50 - 75	4.5 / 2.0

ITALY

Caliber, mm	Bore Length, cal	No of bores	Type of mount	Guns used	Year	Ships used on	Maximum elevation angle, °	Shell mass, kg	Initial velocity, m/s	Rate of fire of one bore, rpm	Fire range / AA ceiling, km
40.0	56.3	2	Mk 1	40 mm/56 Bofors Mk 1,2	1944	many	90	0.900	881	120	10.1 / 7.0
40.0	56.3	4	Mk 2	40 mm/56 Bofors Mk 1, 2	1944	DE - BB	90	0.900	881	120	10.1 / 7.0
40.0	56.3	1	Mk 3	40 mm/56 Bofors Mk 1, 2, M1	1944	many	90	0.900	881	120	10.1 / 7.0

Light guns

Caliber, mm	Bore Length, cal	No of bores	Type of mount	Guns used	Year	Ships used on	Maximum elevation angle, °	Shell mass, kg	Initial velocity, m/s	Rate of fire of one bore, rpm	Fire range / AA ceiling, km
37.0	40.0	1	Hotchkiss M1902	1-pdr Hotchkiss M1902	1902	some old ships	15	0.480	610	25	3.2
47.0	40.0	1	Mk IC HA, IV HA, VI HA	Hotchkiss 3-pdr QF Mk I, II	1914	Many	60	1.50	574	20	7.2 / ~4.0
47.0	40.0	1	Mk V HA	Hotchkiss 3-pdr QF Mk I, II	1941	PS, YP	70	1.50	574	20	7.2 / ~4.0
47	44	1		Škoda	1943	captured ships					
47.0	45.0	1	Nordenfelt M1889	3-pdr. Nordenfelt M1889	1889	many	25	1.50	597	20	6.1
47.0	50.0	1	Vickers M1900	3-pdr Vickers M1900	1900	many	30	1.50	785	25	~7.5
47.0	50.0	1	Mk III HA	Vickers 3-pdr QF Mk I, II	1914	Many	80	1.50	785	25	~7.5 / 4.5
57.0	40.0	1	Hotchkiss M1884	6-pdr Hotchkiss 1884	1884	many	25	2.72	538	20	~7.0
57	43.0	1	Nordenfelt M1887	6-pdr. Nordenfelt M1887	1887	many	15	2.90	665	20	7.4
65.0	64.0	1	Ansaldo-Terni M1939	Ansaldo-Terni 1939	never	never	90	4.08	950	20	7.5
66.0	50.0	1	Škoda K16	7cm/50 Škoda K16	1920	ex-Austrian CL, DD	20	4.50	880	10 - 15	9.1
66.0	50.0	1	Škoda K16	7cm/50 Škoda K16	1920	ex-Austrian CL, DD	90	4.50	880	10 - 15	10.0 / 6.1
76.2	23.0	1	Ansaldo M1918	76.2mm/23 Ansaldo M1918	1918	few	65	4.28	420	6 - 8	7.5 / 4.5
76.2	30.0	1	Armstrong M1914	76.2mm/30 Armstrong M1914	1914	small ships	65	4.28	550	6 - 8	9.0 / 5.5

76.2	40.0	1	P Mk I, I*	12-pdr / 12cwt Elswick Pattern "N"	1894	many	30	5.87	681	15	7.5
76.2	40.0	1	P Mk I, I*	12-pdr / 12cwt Vickers Mk "Z"	1894	many	30	5.87	681	15	7.5
76.2	50.0	1	Vickers M1909	76.2mm/50 Vickers 1909	1909	many	20	5.67	792	15	8.5
76.2	40.0	1	Armstrong M1916	76.2mm/40 Armstrong 1916	1916	many	42	6.50	680	15	10.0
76.2	40.0	1	RM 1916	76.2mm/40 Ansaldo 1916	1916	many	65	6.00	690	15	10.0 / 5.0
76.2	40.0	1	Armstrong M1917	76.2mm/40 Armstrong 1917	1917	many	42	6.50	680	15	10.0
76.2	40.0	1	Ansaldo M1917	76.2mm/40 Ansaldo 1917	1917	many	75	6.00	690	15	10.0 / 6.0
88.0	45.0	1	MPLC/13	8.8cm FlaK L/45 (SK C/13)	1920	CL, DD	70	10.0	650	15	11.8
90.0	50.0	1	Ansaldo M1938	90mm/50 Ansaldo 1938	1940	BB	75	10.1	860	12	16.0/10.8
90.0	50.0	1	OTO M1939	90mm/50 OTO 1939	1940	BB	75	10.1	860	12	16.0/10.8
90.0	50.0	1	M1926	90mm/50 M1926	1942	CA, CL, FS, NL	80	9.51	850	10	15.4 / 10.6
90.0	50.0	2	M1930	90mm/50 M1930	1942	CA, CL	80	9.51	850	10	15.4 / 10.6
100.0	43.0	1	OTO M1927	100mm/43 OTO 1927	1927	SS	35	13.8	800	8 - 10	11.0
100.0	45.0	1	M1892	100mm/45 M1892	1942	BC, FS	20	16.0	703	6	~14.0
100.0	45.0	1	M1897	100mm/45 M1897	1942	CA, FS, PC, ML	20	16.0	703	6	~14.0
100.0	45.0	1	M1897 Tᵉ 1917	100mm/45 M1897 Tᵉ 1917	1942	PGT, SS, SL, FS, PGR	20	16.0	703	6	~14.0
100.0	45.0	1	M1925	100mm/45 M1925	1942	SS	70	14.5	760	10	15.8 / 9.5
100.0	45.0	1	M1932	100mm/45 M1932	1942	FS	34	15.0	755	10	15.0
100.0	45.0	2	M1932	100mm/45 M1932	1942	TB, FS	34	15.0	755	10	15.0
100.0	47.0	1	Škoda K10	10 cm/50 Škoda K10	1920	ex-Austrian CL	18	13.8	880	8 - 10	11.0
100.0	47.0	1	Škoda K11	10cm/50 Škoda K11	1920	ex-Austrian DD	18	13.8	880	8 - 10	11.0

ITALY

Caliber, mm	Bore Length, cal	No of bores	Type of mount	Guns used	Year	Ships used on	Maximum elevation angle, °	Shell mass, kg	Initial velocity, m/s	Rate of fire of one bore, rpm	Fire range / AA ceiling, km
100.0	47.0	1	OTO M1931	100mm/47 OTO 1931	1931	SS	32	13.8	840	8 - 10	12.6
100.0	47.0	1	OTO M1931	100mm/47 OTO 1931	1931	TB, DE, FS	45	13.8	855	8 - 10	15.2
100.0	47.0	1	OTO M1935	100mm/47 OTO 1935	1935	SS	32	13.8	840	8 - 10	12.6
100.0	47.0	1	OTO M1935	100mm/47 OTO 1931	1935	TB, DE, FS	60	13.8	855	8 - 10	15.2
100.0	47.0	1	RM 1937	100mm/47 OTO 1931	1937	TB, DE, FS	60	13.8	855	8 - 10	15.2
100.0	47.0	1	OTO M1937	100mm/47 OTO 1937	1937	TB, DE, FS	60	13.8	855	8 - 10	15.2
100.0	47.0	1	OTO M1938	100mm/47 OTO 1938	1938	SS	32	13.8	840	8 - 10	12.6
100.0	47.0	2	OTO M1924	100mm/47 OTO 1924	1924	BB, CA, CL	85	13.8	850	8 - 10	15.2 / 8.0
100.0	47.0	2	OTO M1927	100mm/47 OTO 1927	1927	BB, CA, CL	85	13.8	850	8 - 10	15.2 / 8.0
100.0	47.0	2	OTO M1928	100mm/47 OTO 1928	1928	BB, CA, CL	85	13.8	850	8 - 10	15.2 / 8.0

Medium guns

Caliber, mm	Bore Length, cal	No of bores	Type of mount	Guns used	Year	Ships used on	Maximum elevation angle, °	Shell mass, kg	Initial velocity, m/s	Rate of fire of one bore, rpm	Fire range / AA ceiling, km
101.6	35.0	1	Terni M1914	101.6mm/35 Terni 1914	1914	DD, TB, SL, SS	45	13.7	750	10 - 15	11.7
101.6	35.0	1	Schneider-Armstrong M1914-15	101.6mm/35 Schneider-Armstrong 1914-15	1915	DD, TB, SL, SS	45	13.7	750	10	11.7
101.6	40.0	1	P Mk IX, S Mk I	4``/40 QF Mk IV	1941	SS	20	14.1	722	13	8.8
101.6	45.0	1	Schneider-Canet M1917	101.6mm/45 Schneider-Canet 1917	1917	DD	30	13.7	850	10	14.7
101.6	45.0	1	Schneider-Armstrong M1917	101.6mm/45 Schneider-Armstrong 1917	1917	DD and smaller	35	13.7	850	10 - 15	15.0
101.6	45.0	2	Schneider-Armstrong M1919	101.6mm/45 Schneider-Armstrong 1919	1919	DD	35	13.7	850	10 - 15	15.0
105.0	45.0	1	Tbts LC/16	10.5cm Tbts L/45	1920	DD	50	14.7	890	15	~14
105.0	45.0	1	Ubts LC/16	10.5cm Ubts L/45	1920	DD	50	14.7	890	15	~14
120.0	15.0	1	OTO M1933	120mm/15 OTO 1933	1933	CA, DD	50	19.8	400	5 - 6	6.4

120.0	15.0	1	OTO M1934	120mm/15 OTO 1934	1934	CA, DD	50	19.8	400	5 - 6	6.4
120.0	27.0	1	OTO M1924	120mm/27 OTO 1924	1924	SS	65	19.4	730	5 - 6	10.9 / 7.8
120.0	45.0	1	Armstrong M1918	120mm/45 Armstrong 1918	1918	AMC and auxiliary	30	23.2	750	5 - 6	14.0
120.0	45.0	1	Schneider-Canet-Armstrong M1918	120mm/45 Schneider-Canet-Armstrong 1918	1918	DD, SL	30	23.2	750	5 - 6	14.0
120.0	45.0	1	OTO M1931	120mm/45 OTO 1931	1931	SS	32	22.0	730	8	14.0
120.0	45.0	2	Schneider-Canet-Armstrong M1918/19	120mm/45 Schneider-Canet-Armstrong 1918/19	1919	DD, SL	30	23.2	750	5 - 6	14.0
120.0	45.0	2	Vickers Terni M1924	120mm/45 Vickers Terni 1924	1924	DD	33	23.2	850	7	15.5
120.0	45.0	2	OTO M1926	120mm/45 OTO 1926	1926	DD	33	23.2	850	7	15.5
120.0	46.0	1	Škoda	120mm/46 Škoda	1941	DD	35	24.0	850	7	15.5
120.0	50.0	1	Armstrong M1909	120mm/50 Armstrong 1909	1909	BB, CL	20	22.8	840	5 - 6	12.5
120.0	50.0	1	Ansaldo M1940	120mm/50 Ansaldo 1940	1940	DD	45	23.5	950	6 - 7	19.6
120.0	50.0	2	Ansaldo M1926	120mm/50 Ansaldo 1926	1926	DD	45	23.5	950	6 - 7	19.6
120.0	50.0	2	OTO M1931	120mm/50 OTO 1931	1931	DD	33	23.5	950	6 - 7	18.2
120.0	50.0	2	OTO M1933	120mm/50 OTO 1933	1933	BB	42	23.5	950	6 - 7	19.4
120.0	50.0	2	Ansaldo M1936	120mm/50 Ansaldo 1936	1936	DD	40	23.5	950	6 - 7	18.9
120.0	50.0	2	OTO M1936	120mm/50 OTO 1936	1936	DD	35	23.5	950	6 - 7	18.2
120.0	50.0	2	Ansaldo M1937	120mm/50 Ansaldo 1937	1937	DD	42	23.5	950	6 - 7	19.4
130.0	40.0	1	M1919	130mm/40 M1919	1942	DD	36	34.9	725	4 - 5	18.9
130.0	45.4	2	M1935	130mm/45 M1935	1942	DD	35	32.1	800	10	~18.0
135.0	45.0	2	OTO M1938	135mm/45 OTO 1938	1938	CL, DD	45	32.7	825	6 - 7.5	19.6
135.0	45.0	2	Ansaldo M1938	135mm/45 Ansaldo 1938	1938	CL, DD	45	32.7	825	6 - 7.5	19.6
135.0	45.0	3	OTO M1937	135mm/45 OTO 1937	1937	BB	45	32.7	825	6 - 7.5	19.6

ITALY

Caliber, mm	Bore Length, cal	No of bores	Type of mount	Guns used	Year	Ships used on	Maximum elevation angle, °	Shell mass, kg	Initial velocity, m/s	Rate of fire of one bore, rpm	Fire range / AA ceiling, km
138.6	40.0	1	M1923	138.6mm/40 M1923	1942	DD	35	40.6	700	5 - 6	18.2
140.0	56.0	1	Škoda	140mm/56 Škoda	1941	DD	45	39.8	880		23.4
149.1	42.4	1	MPLC/13	15cm SK L/45	1920	CL	19	45.3	835	5 - 7	13.5
149.1	42.2	1	MPLC/17	15cm Tbts KL/45	1920	DD	30	45.3	680	4 - 5	14.5
149.1	47.0	1	Škoda K10	15cm/50 Škoda K10	1920	CL	15	45.5	880	4 - 5	12.0

Heavy guns

Caliber, mm	Bore Length, cal	No of bores	Type of mount	Guns used	Year	Ships used on	Maximum elevation angle, °	Shell mass, kg	Initial velocity, m/s	Rate of fire of one bore, rpm	Fire range / AA ceiling, km
152.4	45.0	1	Schneider M1909	152.4mm/45 Schneider 1909	1909	CA, CL, DD	20	47.0	830	5 - 7	14.3
152.4	50.0	1	Armstrong M1909	152.4mm/50 Armstrong 1909	1909	BB	13	47.0	895	5 - 7	10.2
152.4	53.0	2	Ansaldo M1926	152.4mm/53 Ansaldo 1926	1926	CL	45	50.0	1000	5	28.4
152.4	53.0	2	OTO M1929	152.4mm/53 OTO 1929	1929	CL	45	50.0	1000	5	28.4
152.4	55.0	2	Ansaldo M1934	152.4mm/55 Ansaldo 1934	1934	CL	45	50.0	910	4 - 5	25.7
152.4	55.0	3	Ansaldo M1934	152.4mm/55 Ansaldo 1934	1934	BB, CL	45	50.0	910	4 - 5	25.7
152.4	55.0	3	OTO M1936	152.4mm/55 OTO 1936	1936	BB	45	50.0	910	4 - 5	25.7
152.4	55.1	3	M1930	152.4mm/55 M1930	1942	CL	45	54.2	870	7 - 8	26.5
190.5	45.0	2	Elswick Pattern "C"	190.5mm/45 Elswick Pattern "C"	1909	CA	25	90.9	864	2.5	22.0
190.5	45.0	2	Vickers Mk "D"	190.5mm/45 Vickers Mk "D"	1909	CA	25	90.9	864	2.5	22.0
203.2	50.0	2	Ansaldo M1924	203.2mm/50 Ansaldo 1924	1924	CA	45	125.3	905	3.3	31.3
203.2	53.0	2	Ansaldo M1927	203.2mm/53 Ansaldo 1927	1927	CA	45	110.6	940	3.8	30.5
203.2	53.0	2	Ansaldo M1929	203.2mm/53 Ansaldo 1929	1929	CA	45	110.6	940	3.8	30.5
254.0	45.0	2	Elswick Pattern "W"	10``/45 Elswick Pattern "W"	1909	CA	25	227	870	2.6	25.0
320.0	43.8	2	M1934	320mm/43.8 M1934	1934	BB	27	525	830	2	29.4
320.0	43.8	2	M1936	320mm/43.8 M1936	1936	BB	30	525	830	2	30.3

320.0	43.8	3	M1934	320mm/43.8 M1934	1934	BB	27	525	830	2	29.4
320.0	43.8	3	M1936	320mm/43.8 M1936	1936	BB	30	525	830	2	30.3
381.0	40.0	1	Elswick Pattern "A"	15``/40 Elswick Pattern "A"	1917	MON	30	884	700	0.5	34.6
381.0	40.0	1	Vickers Mk "A"	15``/40 Vickers Mk "A"	1917	MON	30	884	700	0.5	34.6
381.0	50.0	3	Ansaldo M1934	381mm/50 Ansaldo 1934	1940	BB	35	885	870	1.3	42.3

Torpedoes

Caliber, mm	Type	Year	Ships used on	Full mass, kg	Length, kg	Explosive charge	Explosive mass, kg	Fire range, km	Speed, kts
400	40cm 26V, Toulon/St-Tropez	1942	submarines	674	5.14	TNT	144	2 3	44 35
450	18`` Mk VIII	1914	submarines	1736		TNT	145	2.3 3.7	35 29
450	SI200/450 x 5.36		MTB	930	5.36	TNT	200	2	44
450	SI170/450 x 5.25		MTB	860	5.25	TNT	170	4	37
450	W110/450 x 5.5		MTB	770	5.50	TNT	110	2	43
450	W170/450 x 5.75		MTB	930	5.75	TNT	170	1 2	48 42
450	W200/450 x 5.75	1940	submarines	930	5.75	TNT	200	3 8	44 30
533	W270/533.4 x 7.2 Veloce	1940	submarines	1700	7.20	TNT	270	4 12	50 30
533	W270/533.4 x 7.2 'F'		submarines, surface ships	1550	6.84	TNT	270	4 8	48 36
533	W250/533.4 x 6.5		submarines, surface ships	~1500	6.50	TNT	250	3 10	43 28
533	W260/533.4 x 6.86		submarines, surface ships	1700	6.86	TNT	270	3 7 9.2 12	42 32 30 26
533	W260/533.4 x 7.20		submarines, surface ships	1700	7.20	TNT	270	3 7 9.2 12	42 32 30 26
533	SI270/533.4 x 7.2 'I'		submarines	~1700	7.20	TNT	270	4 8	49 38
533	SI270/533.4 x 7.2		surface ships	1700	7.20	TNT	270	4 8 12	46 35 29
533	SI250/533.4 x 7.5		surface ships	1700	7.50	TNT	250	3 12	40 26

ITALY   117

550	55cm 23D, Toulon	1942	cruisers	2068	8.28	TNT	310	6	43
								14	35
								20	29
550	55cm 23DT, Toulon	1942	destroyers	2068	8.28	TNT	310	9	39
								13	35
550	55cm 24V, Toulon	1942	submarines	1490	6.60	TNT	310	4	45
								8	35

Suicide craft

Type	Year	Number	Displacement, t	Length x breadth x draught, m	Machinery, power, h. p.	Max speed, kts	Warhead mass, kg	Complement
MAT	1936	2	1	4.7xx	Petrol engine, 95	32	330	1
MTM	1941	28	1	5.6x1.9	Petrol engine, 95	33	300	1

Depth charges

Type	Year	Mass, kg	Type and mass of explosive, kg	Maximal depth setting, m	Type of piston
B TG 50/1917	1917		50	100	hydrostatic
B TG 100/1927	1927		100	100	hydrostatic
B TG 50/1927	1927		50	100	hydrostatic
B TG 50/1936	1936	64	50		hydrostatic
B TG 100/?			100		hydrostatic

Mines

Type	Year	Type of laying	Type of fuse	Carried on	Targets	Lying depth, m	Full mass, kg	Explosive mass, kg
VE	1911	moored	contact	surface ships	surface ships		760	145
Harlé 75/M1911	1911	moored	contact	surface ships	surface ships	100		75
Harlé 70/M1916	1916	moored	contact	surface ships	surface ships	100		70
Harlé 100/M1916	1916	moored	contact	surface ships	surface ships	100		100
SG 125/1916	1916	moored	contact	submarines	surface ships			125
UC 200/1921	1921	moored	contact	submarines	surface ships			200
Elia 145/1925	1925	moored	contact	surface ships	surface ships			145
Bollo P125/1928	1928	moored	contact	surface ships	surface ships			125
Elia P145/1930	1930	moored	contact antenna	surface ships	surface ships, submarines	~300		145
P150	1930s	moored	contact	submarines	surface ships	300		150
Bollo P125/1932	1932	moored	contact antenna	surface ships	surface ships, submarines			125

Name	Year	Type	Trigger	Target	Against	Depth (m)		Charge (kg)
Bollo P125/1935	1932	moored	contact antenna	surface ships	surface ships, submarines			125
Italia M1932	1932	moored	contact	submarines	surface ships, submarines	500	1100	150
P150/1935	1935	moored	contact	submarines	surface ships	300		150
P200 (P5)	1936	moored	contact	surface ships	surface ships, submarines	100	1150	200
Coloniale P125	1930s	moored	contact	surface ships	surface ships	200		125
P4/150/1938 CR	1938	moored	contact	surface ships	surface ships	200	825	150
EMC	1938	moored	contact	surface ships	surface ships	100 - 500		300
UMA	1930s	moored	contact	surface ships	submarines	50 - 100		30
UMB	1939	moored	contact	surface ships	submarines	65 - 300		40
UMB m KA	1939	moored	contact	surface ships	submarines	65 - 300		40
EMC m KA	1939	moored	contact	surface ships	surface ships	200 - 400		250 - 285
EMC m An Z	1939	moored	antenna	surface ships	surface ships, submarines	200 - 350		285 - 300
EMD m An Z	1939	moored	antenna	surface ships	surface ships, submarines	100 - 200		150
EMF	1939	moored	magnetic	surface ships	surface ships, submarines	200 - 500		350
EMC m An Z n/A	1941	moored	antenna	surface ships	surface ships, submarines	100 - 500		285 - 300
UMA (K)	1942	moored	contact	surface ships	surface ships	50 - 100		30
EMC m Kette	1943	moored	contact	surface ships	surface ships	100 - 200		250
EMC m Kette u Reißleine	1943	moored	contact and snagline	surface ships	surface ships	100 - 200		250

Printed in Great Britain
by Amazon